New Casebooks

SHAKESPEARE IN PERFORMANCE

New Casebooks

POETRY

WILLIAM BLAKE Edited by David Punter
CHAUCER Edited by Valerie Allen and Ares Axiotis
COLERIDGE, KEATS AND SHELLEY Edited by Peter J. Kitson
JOHN DONNE Edited by Andrew Mousley
SEAMUS HEANEY Edited by Michael Allen
PHILIP LARKIN Edited by Stephen Regan
PARADISE LOST Edited by William Zunder
VICTORIAN WOMEN POETS Edited by Joseph Bristow
WORDSWORTH Edited by John Williams

NOVELS AND PROSE

AUSTEN: *Emma* Edited by David Monaghan
AUSTEN: *Mansfield Park* and *Persuasion* Edited by Judy Simons
AUSTEN: *Sense and Sensibility* and *Pride and Prejudice* Edited by Robert Clark
CHARLOTTE BRONTË: *Jane Eyre* Edited by Heather Glen
CHARLOTTE BRONTË: *Villette* Edited by Pauline Nestor
EMILY BRONTË: *Wuthering Heights* Edited by Patsy Stoneman
ANGELA CARTER Edited by Alison Easton
WILKIE COLLINS Edited by Lyn Pykett
JOSEPH CONRAD Edited by Elaine Jordan
DICKENS: *Bleak House* Edited by Jeremy Tambling
DICKENS: *David Copperfield* and *Hard Times* Edited by John Peck
DICKENS: *Great Expectations* Edited by Roger Sell
ELIOT: *Middlemarch* Edited by John Peck
E. M. FORSTER Edited by Jeremy Tambling
HARDY: *Jude the Obscure* Edited by Penny Boumelha
HARDY: *Tess of the D'Urbervilles* Edited by Peter Widdowson
JAMES: *Turn of the Screw* and *What Maisie Knew* Edited by Neil Cornwell and Maggie Malone
LAWRENCE: *Sons and Lovers* Edited by Rick Rylance
TONI MORRISON Edited by Linden Peach
GEORGE ORWELL Edited by Byran Loughrey
SHELLEY: *Frankenstein* Edited by Fred Botting
STOKER: *Dracula* Edited by Glennis Byron
STERNE: *Tristram Shandy* Edited by Melvyn New
WOOLF: *Mrs Dalloway* and *To the Lighthouse* Edited by Su Reid

DRAMA

BECKETT: *Waiting for Godot* and *Endgame* Edited by Steven Connor
APHRA BEHN Edited by Janet Todd
SHAKESPEARE: *Antony and Cleopatra* Edited by John Drakakis
SHAKESPEARE: *Hamlet* Edited by Martin Coyle
SHAKESPEARE: *King Lear* Edited by Kiernan Ryan
SHAKESPEARE: *Macbeth* Edited by Alan Sinfield
SHAKESPEARE: *The Merchant of Venice* Edited by Martin Coyle
SHAKESPEARE: *A Midsummer Night's Dream* Edited by Richard Dutton
SHAKESPEARE: *The Tempest* Edited by R. S. White
SHAKESPEARE: *Twelfth Night* Edited by R. S. White
SHAKESPEARE ON FILM Edited by Robert Shaughnessy
SHAKESPEARE IN PERFORMANCE Edited by Robert Shaughnessy
SHAKESPEARE'S HISTORY PLAYS Edited by Graham Holderness
SHAKESPEARE'S TRAGEDIES Edited by Susan Zimmerman
WEBSTER: *The Duchess of Malfi* Edited by Dympna Callaghan

GENERAL THEMES

FEMINIST THEATRE AND THEORY Edited by Helene Keyssar
POSTCOLONIAL LITERATURES Edited by Michael Parker and Roger Starkey

---

New Casebooks Series
Series Standing Order
ISBN 0-333-71702-3 hardcover
ISBN 0-333-69345-0 paperback
(***outside North America only***)

You can receive future titles in this series as they are published by placing a standing order. Please contact your bookseller or, in case of difficulty, write to us at the address below with your name and address, the title of the series and the ISBN quoted above.

Customer Services Department, Macmillan Distribution Ltd
Houndmills, Basingstoke, Hampshire RG21 6XS, England

New Casebooks

SHAKESPEARE IN PERFORMANCE

EDITED BY ROBERT SHAUGHNESSY

First published 2000 by
MACMILLAN PRESS LTD
Houndmills, Basingstoke, Hampshire RG21 6XS
and London
Companies and representatives
throughout the world

ISBN 0-333-74123–4 hardcover
ISBN 0-333-74124–2 paperback

A catalogue record for this book is available from the British Library.

This book is printed on paper suitable for recycling and made from fully managed and sustained forest sources.

10 9 8 7 6 5 4 3 2 1
09 08 07 06 05 04 03 02 01 00

Printed in Hong Kong

Published in the United States of America by
ST. MARTIN'S PRESS, INC.,
Scholarly and Reference Division
175 Fifth Avenue, New York, N.Y. 10010

ISBN 0–312–23311–6
ISBN 0–312–23312–4

Contents

Acknowledgements vii

General Editor's Preface ix

Introduction: ROBERT SHAUGHNESSY 1

1. Stage Space and the Shakespeare Experience 24
   J. L. STYAN
2. The Arrow in Nessus: Elizabethan Clues and Modern Detectives 42
   ALAN C. DESSEN
3. The Rhetoric of Performance Criticism 61
   W. B. WORTHEN
4. Bifold Authority in Shakespeare's Theatre 78
   ROBERT WEIMANN
5. 'To Represent such a Lady' 100
   KATHLEEN McCLUSKIE
6. Text and Performance: *The Taming of the Shrew* 123
   GRAHAM HOLDERNESS
7. Race and the Comedy of Abjection in *Othello* 142
   MICHAEL D. BRISTOL
8. Royal Shakespeare: Theatre and the Making of Ideology 171
   ALAN SINFIELD
9. Robert Lepage's Intercultural *Dream* Machine 194
   BARBARA HODGDON

10. Acting against Bardom: Some Utopian Thoughts on Workshops 218
SIMON SHEPHERD

Further Reading 235

Notes on Contributors 240

Index 243

Acknowledgements

The editor and publishers wish to thank the following for permission to use copyright material:

Alan C. Dessen, for material from *Elizabethan Stage Conventions and Modern Interpreters* (1984), pp. 1–18, by permission of Cambridge University Press; Barbara Hodgdon, for 'Looking for Mr Shakespeare after "The Revolution"; Robert Lepage's Intercultural *Dream* Machine', from *Shakespeare, Theory, Performance,* ed. James C. Bulman (1966), pp. 171–90, by permission of Routledge; Graham Holderness, for material from the 'Introduction' to *Shakespeare in Performance: 'The Taming of the Shrew'*, Manchester University Press (1988), pp. 1–17, by permission of the author; Kathleen McLuskie, for material from *Renaissance Dramatists,* Harvester Wheatsheaf (1989), pp. 100–21, by permission of Pearson Education Ltd; Simon Shepherd, for material from 'Acting against Bardom: some Utopian Thoughts on Workshops; from *Shakespeare in the Changing Curriculum',* ed. Lesley Aers and Nigel Wheale (1991), pp. 90–107, by permission of Routledge; Alan Sinfield, for material from 'Royal Shakespeare: Theatre and the Making of Ideology', from *Political Shakespeare: Essays in Cultural Materialism,* ed. J. Dollimore and A. Sinfield (1985), pp. 158–81, by permission of Manchester University Press; J.L. Styan, for 'Stage Space and the Shakespeare Experience', from *Shakespeare and the Sense of Performance: Essays in the Tradition of Performance Criticism in Honour of Bernard Beckerman*, ed. Marvin Thompson and Ruth Thompson, Associated University Presses (1989), pp. 195–209, by permission of the author; Robert Weimann, for material from 'Bifold Authority in Shakespeare's Theatre, *Shakespeare Quarterly*, 39:4 (1988),

401–17, by permission of *Shakespeare Quarterly*; W.B. Worthen, for 'Deeper Meanings and Theatrical Techique: The Rhetoric of Performance Criticism', *Shakespeare Quarterly*, 40:4 (1989), 441–55, by permission of *Shakespeare Quarterly*.

Every effort has been made to trace the copyright holders but if any have been inadvertently overlooked the publishers will be pleased to make the necessary arrangement at the first opportunity.

General Editors' Preface

The purpose of this series of New Casebooks is to reveal some of the ways in which contemporary criticism has changed our understanding of commonly studied texts and writers and, indeed, of the nature of criticism itself. Central to the series is a concern with modern critical theory and its effect on current approaches to the study of literature. Each New Casebook editor has been asked to select a sequence of essays which will introduce the reader to the new critical approaches to the text or texts being discussed in the volume and also illuminate the rich interchange between critical theory and critical practice that characterises so much current writing about literature.

In this focus on modern critical thinking and practice New Casebooks aim not only to inform but also to stimulate, with volumes seeking to reflect both the controversy and the excitement of current criticism. Because much of this criticism is difficult and often employs an unfamiliar critical language, editors have been asked to give the reader as much help as they feel is appropriate, but without simplifying the essays or the issues they raise. Again, editors have been asked to supply a list of further reading which will enable readers to follow up issues raised by the essays in the volume.

The project of New Casebooks, then, is to bring together in an illuminating way those critics who best illustrate the ways in which contemporary criticism has established new methods of analysing texts and who have reinvigorated the important debate about how we 'read' literature. The hope is, of course, that New Casebooks will not only open up this debate to a wider audience, but will also encourage students to extend their own ideas, and think afresh about their responses to the texts they are studying.

John Peck and Martin Coyle
University of Wales, Cardiff

in order to keep the spectators standing), every detail of the Globe underlines its claim to be an exact replica of Shakespeare's own theatre, a space in which the authentic and authoritative spirit of his plays may be recaptured; in the words of Mark Rylance, the Globe's first Artistic Director, Shakespeare 'intended meaning to be found in the imaginary space between audience and actor, hence the absolute necessity to explore the architecture that Shakespeare chose to define that space'.[1] Architectural fidelity at the Globe is matched by an equivalent archaeological concern for the historical authenticity of the other material components of performance. Actors wear hand-stitched Elizabethan costumes: for the 1997 *Henry V*, according to the theatre's own publicity, these were authentic even down to the itchy underwear (lending a new piquancy to Chorus's report that 'Now all the youth of England are on fire / And silken dalliance in the wardrobe lies' [II.0.1–2]); all-male casting (with adults rather than boys) has been repeatedly employed; and audiences are encouraged to imitate the presumed behaviour of their Elizabethan ancestors by catcalling, interjecting witty ripostes, cheering the heroes and booing the villains.

As the site of a unique convergence between academic scholarship, the theatrical profession, cultural philanthropy and the entertainment industry, Shakespeare's Globe throws into sharp relief long-standing and key questions about the nature of Shakespearean performance. Although the Globe's scholarly mentors and supporters have been more circumspect and cautious in their claims as to the 'authenticity' of the experience that it affords than some of its more bardolotrous advocates, there is general agreement that the theatre will enable actors, audiences, and the theatre historians among them, to advance their understanding of the sheer physical logistics of staging early modern plays. Andrew Gurr writes that 'the Globe offers the opportunity of making a variety of new measurements, ranging from how long it takes to walk offstage, to the acoustics of a soliloquy directed at only one section of the total surround of the audience'; and from such calibrations 'we hope will grow a new sense of what Shakespeare wanted from his performances'.[2] According to this view, the Globe is a laboratory space for experimental stagings, which will progressively reveal the true lineaments of Shakespeare's dramaturgy. However, its potential significance as a theatrical and cultural force is even more far-reaching. The rediscovery of Shakespeare is not an end in itself: it is the first step towards the recreation of a genuinely accessible and democratic popular theatre – such as the original Globe was supposed to have been. The opposing view, however, is that in both its cultural aspirations and its claims to historical accuracy, the Globe is a project which is at best touchingly misguided and at worst a manipulative and ethically questionable exercise in reactionary nostalgic fantasy.[3] At the most basic level, the emphatically persuasive materiality of the Globe is profoundly deceptive: no matter how closely its plaster, straw and timbers are made to resemble the materials from which Elizabethan theatres were constructed, the building's physical structure means something entirely different when removed from the complex network of social, cultural and ideological relationships that, historically, informed its very fabric. Moreover, the question of what kind of theatrical encounters are possible in the Globe is further complicated by doubts as to whether it is a 'theatre' at all, or merely another version of the theme park: to attend a performance at the Globe as a surrogate Elizabethan is to adopt the kind of Disneyland double consciousness simultaneously composed of amused engagement and sceptical distance; one has to register (as, it has been suggested, is also the case at the Swan Theatre at Stratford-upon-Avon) that 'the theatre is already a set'.[4]

Mired in contradictions as the Globe may be, it is nonetheless the logical culmination of a scholarly tradition which extends back to the end of the eighteenth century, and which is driven by the desire to recover the authentic identity of Shakespeare's plays through the recovery of their original conditions of performance. It is a tradition which, stemming from the work of the editor Edmund Malone, who published his ground-breaking work on the Elizabethan stage along with his edition of the complete works of Shakespeare in 1790 (whose innovation, as Gurr points out, was to render theatre history 'not only a respectable activity but a practicable one'[5]), is characterised by repeated attempts to afford scholarly hypothesis an architectural form. These began with the unrealised proposals by the German scholars Ludwig Tieck and Johan Schlegel to build a replica Elizabethan stage in Dresden in the 1830s; in England alone these have ranged from the near-universally derided efforts of William Poel and his Elizabethan Stage Society to validate his polemical scholarship through Elizabethan-style performances within Victorian theatres at the end of the nineteenth and the beginning of the twentieth centuries, to Nugent Monck's Maddermarket Theatre in Norwich in the 1920s, Terence Gray's hybrid of Greek and Elizabethan theatrical forms at the Cambridge Festival Theatre in the same period, the Mermaid Tavern in Southwark in the 1930s, the Royal Shakespeare Company's Swan in the 1980s, the mock-ups used in Laurence Olivier's 1944 film of *Henry V* and, more recently, *Shakespeare in Love* (1998), and, finally, the Bankside Globe itself. Further afield, ersatz Globes and Globe derivatives can be found at Stratford, Ontario, in the Folger Shakespeare Library in Washington, and, in the shape of the Panasonic Globe Theatre, in Tokyo.

These experiments have been conducted alongside developments in historical scholarship, commencing with Malone's discovery of the papers of the theatrical entrepreneur Philip Henslowe at Dulwich College in 1790. Throughout the Victorian period, the patient industry of organisations such as the Shakespeare Society and the New Shakspere Society, and individual scholars such as John Payne Collier, F. J. Furnivall and J. Halliwell-Phillipps, assembled a mass of data on the Elizabethan stage from sources as diverse as Henslowe's inventories, the contract for building of the Fortune Theatre in 1599, plague and court records, the documents of the Revels Office, and the minutes of the Privy Council. In 1888 the written traces of the Elizabethan stage were supplemented by the discovery in the library of the University of Utrecht of a crucial piece of visual evidence: a copy of Johannes de Witt's sketch of the interior of the Swan playhouse. Accompanying all this was the related work of the facsimile reproduction and publication of the original quarto playtexts, first by Collier, Furnivall and Halliwell-Phillipps, and subsequently by the pioneers of the 'new bibliography': A. W. Pollard, W. W. Greg, R. B. McKerrow and J. Dover Wilson.[6]

The professionalisation and institutionalisation of literary studies in the early twentieth century propelled theatre research into a new phase. In 1923 the labours of the Victorian antiquarians became available to the expanding constituency of Shakespeare scholars through the publication of E. K. Chambers's four-volume *The Elizabethan Stage*; this was followed in 1931 by Greg's *Dramatic Documents from the Elizabethan Playhouses*.[7] But this historicism was of more than archaeological significance. The detailed investigation of the physical (and, to a limited extent, economic and social) milieu of the theatres provided the ground for a further historical differentiation to be made, which revolved around the specific qualities of Elizabethan conventions of theatrical representation. The conditions of this were polemically articulated by M. C. Bradbrook in

1932; weighing in against the exponents of 'appreciative criticism', she wrote that their neglect of the historical approach made them 'liable to blunder on questions of tone; to mistake conventions for faults, to rationalise an illogical custom of the theatre, or to miss the point of a device'.[8] The specific enemy was naturalism (or even, perhaps, post-Renaissance modernity itself), for it was 'very necessary to approach the Elizabethan drama without any of the preconceptions about the nature of drama which are drawn from reading Ibsen, Shaw, Racine, Dryden'.[9] This was, as J. L. Styan points out, 'an outright attack upon the academic Shakespeare industry'; and although the avowed aim was 'to blow away ... the transcendental fog of nineteenth-century thinking about Shakespeare',[10] the move to discredit appreciative and character-based readings was also an attempt to prise Shakespeare from the grasp of the common reader, the close reader, the theatre professional and the ordinary theatregoer. By stressing the *difference* of Shakespeare's drama, situating it not only in the context of a premodern theatrical system but within what amounted to an alternative mode of cultural consciousness, Bradbrook's exposition of conventions during the 1930s had not a little in common with the historicist literary criticism developed in the following decade by fellow Cambridge scholar E. M. W. Tillyard, who influentially argued for the existence of an 'Elizabethan World Picture', structured according to principles of order and hierarchy. As 'the genuine ruling ideas of the age', these were so thoroughly imbibed by Shakespeare and his contemporaries as to be 'quite taken for granted by the ordinary educated Elizabethan', but nonetheless 'essential as basic assumptions and invaluable at moments of high passion'.[11]

If Tillyard's vision of an ordered and unified Elizabethan society in which everyone knew their place within a cosmic scheme imagined as 'a series of beings stretching from the lowest of inanimate objects up to the archangel nearest to the throne of God' and metaphorically represented in terms of 'a chain, a series of corresponding planes, and a dance to music'[12] lacked in theatrical urgency what it gained in intellectual rigour, other writers during the 1940s made concerted efforts to reconcile a stratified account of the Elizabethan mental and social world with the conventions and staging practices of the popular playhouse. In *Shakespeare's Audience* (1941), Alfred Harbage proposed that the Globe was frequented by 'a large and receptive assemblage of men and women of all ages and of all classes' willing to submerge their antagonisms in the collaborative act of theatregoing, and whose 'collective mind' could be glimpsed in Shakespeare's drama.[13] S. L. Bethell, similarly, concluded that Shakespeare's Globe was 'a truly national theatre, with the cultural stratification one of degree only'; theatrical conventions operated as 'an unconscious and organic outgrowth of playhouse psychology; a body of traditional assumptions held in common by playwright and audience'.[14] The critical and ideological affinities with Tillyard are clear: Shakespeare's playhouse is an indispensable component of the old world order.

To conceive of all this scholarly endeavour solely in terms of a potentially exclusionary antiquarian interest is, however, only to tell part of the story. Elizabethan stage revivalism has been oriented as much towards a hoped-for future as to an idealised past; for much of the twentieth century, the search for authenticity has in part been conducted in the spirit of modernism. It is very evident in the theory and practice of William Poel, whose Elizabethanism echoes that of T. S. Eliot (with whom his later work was contemporaneous); a more generally acceptable practical compromise between modernity and the non-illusionism of the Elizabethan stage was worked out on the professional stage by Harley Granville-Barker in the first two decades of the century, in the shape of 'an almost uncut text ... a simple stylised décor, with a builtout forestage, no footlights, and a breakneck speed in delivery from his cast'.[15] However, Barker's enduring critical and theatrical legacy lay in the five volumes of his *Prefaces to Shakespeare*, published between 1927 and 1937; works which retain sufficient currency for the director of the Royal National Theatre, Richard Eyre, to write in a foreword to the 1993 reprint that 'it's the only critical work on Shakespeare that's made any impact on me'.[16] Barker's *Prefaces*, written from the standpoint of the theatre professional, coincided with initial forays into the field by academics whose critical work has been associated with high modernism. In 1936 G. Wilson Knight augmented his highly impressionistic series of image-based readings of Shakespeare's plays with the volume *Principles of Shakespearean Production*, which was derived from his own rather idiosyncratic theatrical activities. He asserted that the Shakespeare play 'is primarily an aural time-sequence with rhythmic modulations, but nevertheless creates in the mind a result that may be imaged as spatial, solid, and rich in sense-suggestion', and proposed a magnificently regal and spiritual mode of production which would 'make a leap to the inward meaning and use the play's surface as expression'.[17]

But the real surge in this mode of performance criticism came in the postwar period, which saw the formation of a new alliance between pedagogy, historical scholarship and contemporary Shakespearean production, partly through the explicit repositioning of Shakespearean performance alongside the work of the major modernist and avant-garde innovators in twentieth-century theatre practice. In parallel with this there emerged a body of work preoccupied with Shakespearean metadrama, as the writings of critics such as Anne Righter and James L. Calderwood aroused interest in the self-reflexive qualities of the plays.[18] This alliance was crucial to the early work of the Royal Shakespeare Company under the direction of Peter Hall and John Barton during the 1960s, which led the reaction against the naturalistic, the pictorial and the decorous. In a succession of productions, ranging from the 1962 *King Lear* through *The Wars of the Roses* the following year to *A Midsummer Night's Dream* in 1970, the company raided the theatres of Jarry, Artaud, Brecht, Meyerhold, Beckett and Grotowski, appropriating the work of practitioners who had themselves occasionally ransacked Renaissance drama for their own ends, in order to re-invent Shakespeare as a modern.[19]

In a synergy between the professional theatre and scholarship, this recasting of Shakespeare as a non-realist dramatist found its complementary support systems within academic criticism, which increasingly saw cause for celebration in the Shakespearean theatre's progressive disavowal of the extraneous, inessential and inauthentic as it worked towards what J. L. Styan, hailing a 'revolution' in critical consciousness and production practice, called 'the half-apprehended mystery of a supremely non-illusory drama and theatre' rooted in 'the spirit of Elizabethan role-playing and ritual', wherein 'the play on the stage expanding before an audience is the source of all valid discovery'.[20] If the work of the RSC at Stratford in the 1960s and 1970s temporarily appeared to endorse Styan's conclusion (premature, as it turned out) that 'the straining towards a psychological and pictorial realism for Shakespeare is all in the past', it also seemed to herald a newly amicable relationship between practitioners and academics: 'the scholar will modify the actor's illumination, the actor will modify the scholar's, a process of infinite adjustment'.[21] This prediction coincided with the emergence in the late 1970s of a new strain within stage-centred criticism which has now become a dominant strand: the critical documentation and discussion of past and present productions.

As disparate as the varied critical and theatrical endeavours that constituted this breathless transit towards the future of Shakespearean performance might seem, the common thread running through all of this was the shared sense that their ultimate goal would be some kind of recovery of Shakespeare's theatre, although whether this was to be in matter or in spirit remained open to debate. Appropriately enough, the most eloquent formulation of the convergence between the early modern and the modernist is offered not by an academic writer but by the director whose own Shakespearean work from the 1950s onwards most fully (and most influentially) exemplifies this alliance of the classical and the avant-garde: Peter Brook. His much read book, *The Empty Space*, published in 1968, while meditating upon the essential nature of theatre (organised into a four-part taxonomy of Deadly, Rough, Holy and Immediate), is profoundly preoccupied with Shakespeare. Asserting that 'our need ... is to find a way forwards, back to Shakespeare', Brook invokes an Elizabethan stage which 'enabled the dramatist effortlessly to whip the spectator through an unlimited succession of illusions', the physical structure of which 'was a diagram of the universe as seen by the sixteenth-century audience and playwright – the gods, the court and the people – three levels, separate and yet often intermingling – a stage that was a perfect philosopher's machine'.[22] For Brook, however, the object is not to attempt to reconstruct that stage in a material form but to recover its fundamental principles, and hence the metaphysical essence of Shakespeare, through practice: 'in this respect, our work on Shakespeare production is always to make the plays "modern", because it is only when the audience comes into direct contact with the plays' themes that time and conventions vanish'.[23] Such is the Shakespeare that the Shakespeare revolutionaries might dream of: at its heart is a conception of his stage as a space of timeless, universal and essential truths. *The Empty Space* begins, famously, with a statement that is also a challenge: 'I can take any empty space and call it a bare stage. A man walks across this empty space whilst someone else is watching him, and this is all that is needed for an act of theatre to be engaged.'[24] Behind this rhetorical attempt to reduce theatre to its essentials, that is, to a raw and unmediated encounter between performer and spectator, stand the stark exigencies of workshop and rehearsal practice as well as a century of anti-naturalistic avant-garde and experimental performance; but also a compellingly seductive vision of their ultimate progenitor, the Elizabethan stage, envisaged as a bare platform, alien to naturalistic introspection and meretricious deception, denuded of elaborate scenery and lighting effects, and without the cumbersome and alienating apparatus of the proscenium arch; a stage which nonetheless forged a uniquely intimate bond between actors and audience. If this is the utopian fantasy that is enacted under the summer skies on the stage of Shakespeare's Globe at Bankside, it is one with a long-established and not undistinguished pedigree.

II

Thirty years of theoretical reflection and critical performance practice have put us in a position to interrogate practically every term of Brook's imperiously territorial assertion: far from being empty, the space of performance bears the traces of power, memory and desire; the universal male subject who strides so confidently across it is no mere given but an agent of and within ideology; the gaze of the spectator who looks on is directed here rather than there by the determinants of gender, race and class.[25] Moreover, lodging a script in the performer's hand, or memory, multiplies the interpretative frameworks within which the encounter between the watcher and the watched takes place; make that script the text of a play by Shakespeare, and it takes on almost unimaginably tortuous and endlessly decipherable cultural and theatrical ramifications.

To recognise the ideological dimensions of performance, however (which, to put it another way, is to acknowledge the true discursive richness of any theatrical event), is to part company with the established body of performance criticism which has been briefly anatomised above. The highpoint of the so-called Shakespeare revolution in the mid-1970s also marked the emergence of a theoretically inflected and explicitly politicised critical practice geared towards a radically different revolutionary agenda. The performance criticism, which, after a century of struggle for dominance, finally seemed to offer a future for Shakespeare studies through a resolution of some of its more intractable disciplinary contradictions, was rudely upstaged by forces that might have wished it consigned it to history along with the humanist criticism within which it orginated. If, by 1984, an editorial in a special issue of *Shakespeare Quarterly* devoted to pedagogy recognised that the revolution had been so complete that the interdependence of performance, pedagogy and criticism was now an orthodoxy, it also darkly added that there was 'more than a hint of another revolution in the new "-isms" that are now finding their way into academic discourse on Shakespeare and his stage'.[26] In the first instance, however, the criticisms assembled under the rubrics of New Historicism and cultural materialism (with a few notable exceptions) took a while to get round to a serious consideration of theatre and performance. Theory's initial impact on the understanding of the early modern stage was to effect a transformation upon what, by a strange proprietorial logic, continues to be called 'Shakespeare's theatre'; the almost magical zone of authorial will or desire, whose metaphysical residues are deposited in the plays themselves. Instead it became, in a picture heavily indebted to Michel Foucault's account of the specular nature of power and the spectacular nature of disciplinary coercion, a site of punishment and ideological ratification.[27] Thus in Stephen Greenblatt's highly influential formulation, 'theatrical values do not exist in a realm of privileged literariness, of textual or even institutional referentiality. Shakespeare's theatre was not isolated by its wooden walls, nor was it merely the passive reflector of social and ideological forces that lay entirely outside of it'; indeed, 'theatricality ... is not set over against power, but is one of power's essential modes'.[28] The advantage of this approach (leaving aside the fact that the walls of the Globe were not, strictly speaking, 'wooden') was that it emphatically restored Shakespeare's drama to its historical place within the complex field of forces of power and ideology that constituted the theatrical culture of early modern London; the downside was not only that it formed part of a gloomy scenario of violent coercion, containment and repression (Greenblatt's notorious 'there is subversion, no end of subversion, only not for us'[29]), but that as merely another component in the New Historicist project of reading the entirety of Elizabethan culture as one vast text, the stage could sometimes seem more abstract and intangible than ever. Jonathan Dollimore's *Radical Tragedy*, published in 1984, presented a more optimistically subversive model of Renaissance drama as preoccupied with 'a critique of ideology, the demystification of political and power relations and the decentring of "man"', and characterised by 'a radical social and political realism'.[30] Dollimore cites Genet, Artaud and Brecht as modern exponents of the scandal and disarray that he traces within Elizabethan and Jacobean drama, but offers only a notional description of the actual theatre within which it was staged, apart from the suggestion that it was one in which seventeenth-century institutions and ideologies 'were subjected to sceptical, interrogative and subversive representations'.[31] Writing in 1985, Michael Bristol complained that both Greenblatt's and Dollimore's models were 'reductionist', in that 'plays are entities that occupy centre stage and convey messages, subversive or otherwise, to an audience'.[32] Drawing in particular upon Mikhail Bakhtin's theories of the relations between popular culture and carnival, Bristol offered a more nuanced account of the drama of the public playhouses that enlarged its scope for dissidence and, dare one say it, for pleasure.

Bristol's work was followed three years later by that of Steven Mullaney who, in *The Place of the Stage*, situated the playhouses within the highly charged symbolic topography of the city, arguing that the drama 'was born of the contradiction between a Court that ... licensed and maintained it and a city that sought its prohibition', and that its significance lay in its 'embodying that contradiction, dislocating itself from the confines of the existing social order and taking up a place on the margins of society'.[33] After Mullaney, a succession of studies of the Elizabethan stage have extended the project of placing its drama within the fields of social and cultural history, with varying emphases. Douglas Bruster, for example, focuses upon the economic forces shaping theatrical culture, concluding that 'London's playhouses can best be understood in terms of commerce, as centres for the production and consumption of an aesthetic product'; Jean Howard, conversely, reads the drama in terms of 'the social struggles generated by the dual facts of massive social change and equally massive resistance to its acknowledgement'.[34] From the mid-1980s onwards, moreover, and largely as a consequence of the increasing impact of feminist theory upon Renaissance studies, the issue of gender representation on the early stage has developed as an important focus of interest, with particular attention being paid to the practice of boy players taking the parts of women in the public theatres.[35] More recently, historicist scholarship has begun to address the matter of the theatrical construction of racial difference on the Renaissance stage (as well as the implications of this for the cultural politics of the present) – a topic largely avoided by theatre historians since the publication of Eldred Jones's *Othello's Countrymen* as far back as 1965.[36] Finally, the second half of the 1990s saw an intensification of debate around the relations between original performance, the texts of Shakespeare's plays, and current editorial practice.[37]

On the face of it, then, it would appear that development of Shakespeare studies since the 1980s has fulfilled the hopes of the

Shakespeare revolution in that the theatre and performance have become fully assimilated into its field of enquiry and argument, albeit in ways that could hardly have been predicted at the outset. It also needs to be remembered that the period in which the Bankside Globe project came to fruition saw the publication of important works within a longer-established tradition of performance-based historical scholarship which might consider itself rather less sympathetic to contemporary theory, in particular the one-volume edition of Stanley Wells and Gary Taylor's Oxford edition of the complete works.[38] But the apparent centrality of performance within Shakespeare studies, especially within New Historicism, requires a significant qualification. By and large the emphasis upon the Renaissance stage means that it is always an *absent*, conjectural theatre that is the focus of critical attention, an entity to be assembled from documents and re-presented as narrative (the same is true of traditional theatre history, of course). It is a stage in theory, as it were, rather than practice. Citing Mullaney as an example, Simon Shepherd and Peter Womack criticise the processing of Renaissance drama as 'a set of symbols, capable of focusing historical, political and psychic themes all at once through a kind of allegorical layering'; the end result is that 'history is now fully fictionalised, and placed at the disposal of the critic-fantasist to fashion into whatever pattern he can render rhetorically coherent'.[39] If the attractiveness of the early modern stage lies in this amenability to critical appropriation, contemporary Shakespearean performance may be less inviting on these terms, and has until relatively recently been peripheral to the concerns of theory. Such attention as was paid to modern production during the 1980s emerged from the schools of criticism associated with cultural materialism in Britain, and tended to concentrate upon the reactionary aspects of the main institutions of the professional Shakespearean theatre.

As a number of essays in this collection demonstrate, the problem with modern performance is that it is unquestioningly implicated within the liberal humanist ideology of the dominant critical tradition (which in part explains its appeal to previous generations of stage-centred critics); as Alan Sinfield puts it, the basic assumption is that 'because human nature is always the same the plays can be presented as direct sources of wisdom'.[40] If cultural materialism has good reason to be wary of the claims of theatre professionals and their academic supporters, a more radical path could be to treat Shakespeare 'as a historical phenomenon, implicated in values which are not ours, but which can in production be made to reveal themselves, can become contestable'.[41] This is the method advocated by Brecht, who urged that 'what really matters is to play the old works historically, which means setting them in powerful contrast to our own time',[42] and whose own dialectical theatre practice provides a practical model of political intervention in Shakespeare. The question remains, however, as to how the critical insights of theory can be used to inform and transform our practical negotiations with Shakespeare (in connection with this, it must be said that cultural materialism has generally proved more adept at scrutinising the documents generated around and by Shakespearean performance than at reading performance itself). One kind of answer is proposed by Simon Shepherd in the final essay in this book, but whatever Shakespearean theatrical practice results, it is likely to be of a very different order to that currently on offer on the stages of the RSC or the Bankside Globe.

III

The essays in this collection have been selected to provide an initial mapping of a diverse and heterogeneous field of enquiry, firstly to give a sense of the development of Shakespearean performance studies over the past two decades, and secondly in order to indicate some of the possibilities of dialogue between contemporary theory and Shakespearean theatre. J. L. Styan's investigation of the spatial dynamics of Shakespearean performance and their relations with the spoken text, stage directions and the geography of the Elizabethan playhouse (essay 1), provides a concise instance of the mode of performance criticism within which he has been a key player. Styan focuses upon space as a dramaturgical dimension which is in excess of the words on the page but discernible both within its notations and through reference to their original conditions of staging, citing a range of examples where an awareness of spatial orientation (and of the particular meanings that attached to the topography of the Elizabethan stage) enlarges and enriches the interpretative possibilities of the verbal text. One of the key features of this stage is its capacity to foster the interplay between different theatrical styles, modes of address and planes of reality, so that space can both join and divide dramatis personae, actors and audience.

Styan proposes that a contemporary corollary for the Elizabethan 'Shakespeare experience' might be found either in a replica of the Globe (the Bankside Globe was unfinished when the essay was written) or in the adoption of Brook's empty space 'both as an acting area and a region of the mind'.[43] In this respect he is relatively unperturbed by the distance between modern and early modern staging practices. Alan Dessen (essay 2) considers the relationship between the two to be rather more problematic, and starts by challenging 'common-sense' assumptions about reading, interpretation and acting which, he argues, shape in potentially misleading ways our response to Elizabethan texts. Establishing that the dominant initial framework of interpretation is governed and administered by the regime of realist representation, Dessen draws upon Raymond Williams's account of dramatic conventions as 'the terms upon which author, performers and audience agree to meet'[44] to demonstrate that the protocols of engagement of the Renaissance theatre were radically different, perhaps unrecognisable, to the naturalism-dominated theatres of the modern period.

If Dessen's approach inclines towards a more historically differentiated approach to the theatrical text, W. B. Worthen (essay 3) takes his implied critique several stages further in his scrutiny of the rhetorical claims of performance criticism, and of the unexamined assumptions about the performance potentialities of Shakespeare's text that underpin them. Worthen identifies a persistent tendency within stage-centred criticism to assume a Stanislavskian conception of character both as a universal norm and as a given in relation to the Shakespearean text, and traces the strategies of legitimation employed by performers and performance critics to naturalise certain forms of production practice as authorially sanctioned (or determined). Worthen's point that particular styles of Shakespearean performance are inextricably linked to shifting, and conflicting, ideologies of character and self forms part of Robert Weimann's discussion (essay 4) of the relations between the actor's varied modes of address, competing forms of theatrical and political authority, and the newly evolving concept of authorship in the Elizabethan theatre. In his earlier work, *Shakespeare and the Popular Tradition in the Theater* (first published in German in 1967, English translation 1978), Weimann elaborated an influential model of the Renaissance stage in terms of its transitional status between medieval and the modern modes of representation.[45] The legacy of the medieval dramaturgy lay in the complex negotiations between the formal, relatively illusionistic space of the *locus* and the unlocalised, audience-aware, non-illusionistic *platea* (the areas, respectively, of kings and clowns), and their associated styles of performance; in addition, the Renaissance saw the beginnings of a more fully developed vocabulary of realism. In this essay, Weimann incorporates the historicist scholarship that had followed his earlier study, accentuating the connections between the dialectical structure and movement of the drama and the stresses and contradictions of post-Reformation, late Tudor England.

The Elizabethan theatre's capacity to articulate the social and political tensions of its time was particularly noticeable in what proved to be one of its most controversial (but also, for the modern theatre historian, most ambiguous) staging conventions: the habit of employing cross-dressed boy players in the female roles. As I indicated in the previous section, this practice has been the subject of eager academic scrutiny and lively debate in recent years, in that it is a crucial element in the construction of gender and sexuality on the Renaissance stage. Kathleen McLuskie's view (essay 5) is that the significance of the boy player's occupation of the lady's place cannot be easily fixed or defined because the entire ensemble of social and ideological practices that constitute the formation of gender and sexuality in the period were themselves undergoing drastic change; gender representation on the stage was almost always provisional, specific and localised in its implications and effects, and constrained by the determinants of context and genre. McLuskie also emphasises the theatrical self-consciousness of Elizabethan drama as another key factor in its constructions of gender, and in this respect her argument echoes that of Graham Holderness in his examination of *The Taming of the Shrew* (essay 6). Proceeding from an analysis of the relations between the 1594 Quarto *The Taming of a Shrew*, the Folio version, modern productions of the play and its conjectured original conditions of staging, Holderness argues that the Christopher Sly framework (which is incomplete in the Folio text) not only requires us to rethink our responses to the comedy but is also only one manifestation of a self-critical, interrogative theatricality that is characteristic of Shakespeare's work as a whole, and that necessarily complicates any easy suppositions about its politics, sexual or otherwise.

As its stage history has made clear, the association of *The Taming of the Shrew* with the fantasies of male supremacism has rendered it an increasingly controversial (and, to some commentators, thoroughly offensive) text in this regard; one of the more telling aspects of performance (and of some varieties of performance criticism) is that it can highlight issues which more deskbound modes of interpretation might prefer to evade, ignore or disguise. If the representation of gender is one such area of contention, *Othello* supplies an equally troubling history of the staging of racial difference. Critics and theatre practitioners have evolved strategies to compensate for the perceived gap between the beliefs of Shakespeare and his contemporaries about race and later liberal sensibilities: in the case of the *Shrew* by construing progressive or even feminist sympathies beneath the play's misogynist facade, and in *Othello* by reading Shakespeare's portrayal of the Moor as, at least, sympathetic and, at best, positive, noble and heroic. Drawing upon the sociological theory of Emile Durkheim and Mikhail Bakhtin's account of the carnivalesque, Michael D. Bristol (essay 7) provocatively queries such strategies, proposing that Othello is a racial caricature bereft of depth and complexity, introduced as a comic stooge whose chief function is to destabilise the institution of marriage itself. Far from feeling sympathy with Othello, Shakespeare's audiences would have viewed him as a comic buffoon in a grotesque farce (modelled upon the ritual pattern of charivari) of transgression, exposure and punishment, engineered by Iago, whose actions and sentiments they would have enthusiastically endorsed. Not surprisingly, Bristol contends, the unmitigatedly racist dimension of the play, inscribed by its originating cultural context, has been suppressed (with varying degrees of success) in its subsequent traditions of performance – not least because its admission would make the play's complicity with the historical development of racial oppression, injustice and violence, particularly in Europe and the United States, all too painfully evident. Surveying its performance history in this light, Bristol finds evidence in audience reactions to the play of a recurrent guilt and anxiety that seems to bear out this point.

IV

Bristol's reading of *Othello*, which might well make many Shakespeareans uneasy, poses with particular acuteness the general problem of the relationship between the text then and now, a theatrical dialectic that has been defined by Robert Weimann as that of 'past significance and present meaning'.[46] The final three essays in this volume address this question directly by examining the politics of Shakespeare's contemporary theatrical reproduction. As was pointed out earlier, the output of the Royal Shakespeare Company, and of its formative figures Peter Brook, Peter Hall and John Barton, has been central to the developing dialogue between theatre and the academy, in the sense that it has both absorbed and reflected scholarship and exercised an influence upon it. Alan Sinfield (essay 8) exposes the ideological infrastructure of the RSC's Shakespeare work in terms of its connections with the cultural policies of postwar welfare capitalism, and foregrounds the contradictory nature of the company's prevailing ethos of 'Shakespeare-plus-relevance'. Concentrating mainly upon directorial pronouncements about the RSC's landmark events, Sinfield identifies a reactionary drift in the work, propelled by a residual attachment to the traditional authenticating presence of Shakespeare, that belies its claims to radicalism, and speculates upon the possibilities of a mode of production that would seek not to participate in but to dispute that authority.

By directing attention towards the cultural history that much performance analysis tends to exclude from the record, Sinfield raises key questions about the ways in which Shakespearean production can, and should, be documented; but he stops short of detailed examination of particular production strategies and effects. Theatre history is, generally, a positivist discipline, which, with due acknowledgement of its limits and partiality, customarily takes the theatre review as crucial primary evidence in the task of reconstructing the performance event. But what if the theatre review were to be re-read less as an eye-witness account and more as a cultural document, shaped and inhabited by the contradictions, anxieties and misrecognitions of the discourse it inhabits? This perspective is adopted by Barbara Hodgdon (essay 9), in a discussion which wields the tools of psychoanalytic and postcolonial theory to delve into the rich loam of critical discourse occasioned by Robert Lepage's production of *A Midsummer Night's Dream* at the Royal National Theatre in June 1992, unearthing its not-so-secret fantasies of sex and empire, and mapping their cultural logic. These responses were provoked by a staging of the *Dream* which, by revelling in the play of differences between and within performers, text, theatrical context and *mise-en-scène*, not only provided a postmodern response to Brook's canonically modernist reading but also pointed (albeit problematically) to one of the future directions of Shakespearean performance. Simon Shepherd (essay 10) presents a different, although related, avenue of possibility, generated by the experience of theoretically informed practical work in the context of the workshop rather than the finished performance. Furnishing precise and usable examples of workshop techniques which draw (most visibly) upon the radical praxis of Brecht and Augusto Boal in order to engage in critical, politically aware and pleasurable ways with texts that are viewed as material for interrogation rather than dutiful reproduction, Shepherd proposes an avowedly 'utopian' alternative mode of theatrical exploration of Shakespeare, against the dominant forms of professional (and non-professional) practice.

Shepherd's essay raises a crucial final issue, in that it highlights the point that much of the work of performance-centred Shakespeare criticism has (rather like theory itself) emerged from university departments of English Literature rather than of drama or theatre studies. Inevitably, therefore, the initial perspective of theoretically inclined performance criticism has been that of the spectator rather than the theatre maker. Since the loudest and most persuasive voices upon the business of staging Shakespeare today have also tended to be those of professional practitioners institutionally and temperamentally implicated within a status quo endorsed by a tradition of performance criticism largely hostile to theory, this may be regrettable but it is hardly surprising. But if the study (and practice) of Shakespeare in performance entails not only the reading of theatrical culture but also making interventions into it, a new critical and theatrical vocabulary, with changed accents, will need to find spaces in, and from which, to speak. What could emerge is a different kind of Shakespearean performer: no longer the complacent protagonist in an all-too-familiar drama mouthing the platitudinous received wisdom of a cultural icon, but a critical agent willing to interrogate the text and to engage with the different orders of subjectivity that it affords, who does not automatically subordinate the practical and ethical contingencies of the here and now to the alleged universality of Shakespeare. Moreover, if one of the most adventurous elements within performance criticism has been its willingness to establish points of contact between Renaissance texts and the theatrical avant-garde, a theorised, reinvigorated approach to Shakespeare in production might also wish to engage with the new modes of contemporary experimental performance (represented by companies such as the Wooster Group in the United States and Forced Entertainment in the UK) which are rooted as much in live art and performance art as in drama and theatre. As raw material, Shakespeare's texts might then take their place within a body of work in which the representational space of the stage is fractured and divided, often by the presence of media technology, where speech and action are characterised by game-playing, parody and quotation from a wide range of high and low cultural sources, and where narrative and character are problematised, placed in flux, or held in abeyance; in the words of Forced Entertainment's Tim Etchells, the 'prevalent idea is that both the character/performer and the stage are zones of possibility in which a number, or any number of contradictory things may lie, awaiting discovery'.[47] Such a theatre is 'deeply and always political', but forgoes 'the suspect certainties of what other people called political theatre', occupying 'the territory between the real and the phantasmagoric, between the actual landscape and the media one, between the body and imagination'.[48] This is work which is not only well aware of postmodern theory but also willing to investigate its efficacy in practical terms; if the major effort has been to put Shakespearean performance to the test of theory in order to reveal its contradictions, evasions and shortcomings and also (occasionally) its potential for change, the challenge now is for performance to return the interrogation on its own terms. Without resorting to what W. B. Worthen identifies (in traditional performance criticism's more polemical guises) as the tactic of disallowing any interpretation not manifestly achievable in performance, Shakespearean production could at least begin to investigate what it can do and theory can't (and vice versa).

Towards the end of the third section of *The Empty Space*, Peter Brook seems to propose a manifesto for a Shakespeare without illusions when he announces that 'we must open our empty hands and show that really there is nothing up our sleeves. Only then can we begin.'[49] But the disarming candour of the showman's gesture is, of course, a ruse, calculated to divert attention from the real trickery that is going on elsewhere. Theory supplies one way of seeing through the pretence, theatrical performance itself another. If crossing the threshold of the stage puts us in better position to understand the existing mechanisms through which Shakespeare's texts are conjured into all kinds of dubious life, it also affords us the opportunity to dismantle them, and to put something better in their place. Then, perhaps, we can really begin.

NOTES

1. Mark Rylance, 'Playing the Globe: Artistic Policy and Practice', in *Shakespeare's Globe Rebuilt*, ed. J. R. Mulryne and Margaret Shewring (Cambridge, 1997), p. 175.
2. Andrew Gurr, 'Staging at the Globe', in *Shakespeare's Globe Rebuilt*, pp. 159, 168.
3. For a range of views on the matter of 'authentic' reconstructions and their relation to theatre archaeology, see John Drakakis, 'Theatre, ideology, and institution: Shakespeare and the roadsweepers', in *The Shakespeare Myth*, ed. Graham Holderness (Manchester, 1988); Graham Holderness, 'Shakespeare and heritage', *Textual Practice*, 6 (1992), 247–63; Peggy Phelan, 'Playing Dead in Stone: or, When is a Rose not a Rose?', in *Performance and Cultural Politics*, ed. Elin Diamond (Routledge, 1996); Alan C. Dessen, 'Globe Matters', *Shakespeare Quarterly*, 49 (1998), 195–8; Lois Potter, 'A Stage Where Every Man Must Play a Part?', *Shakespeare Quarterly*, 50 (1999), 74–86.
4. Peter Womack, 'The Sign of the Light Heart: Jonson's *The New Inn*, 1629 and 1987', *New Theatre Quarterly*, 18 (1989), 164.
5. Gurr, 'Shakespeare's Globe: A History of Reconstructions and Some Reasons for Trying', in *Shakespeare's Globe Rebuilt*, p. 27.
6. See Gary Taylor, *Reinventing Shakespeare: A Cultural History from the Restoration to the Present* (London, 1990), pp. 162–230; Hugh Grady, *The Modernist Shakespeare: Critical Texts in Material World* (Oxford, 1991), pp. 28–73.
7. E. K. Chambers, *The Elizabethan Stage*, 4 vols (Oxford, 1923); W. W. Greg, *Dramatic Documents from the Elizabethan Playhouses*, 2 vols (Oxford, 1931).
8. M. C. Bradbrook, *Elizabethan Stage Conditions* (Cambridge, 1932), p. 4.
9. M. C. Bradbrook, *Themes and Conventions of Elizabethan Tragedy* (Cambridge, 1935), pp. 1–2.
10. J. L. Styan, *The Shakespeare Revolution: Criticism and Performance in the Twentieth Century* (Cambridge, 1977), pp. 7, 5.
11. E. M. W. Tillyard, *The Elizabethan World Picture* (Harmondsworth, 1963), p. 7.
12. E. M. W. Tillyard, *Shakespeare's History Plays* (Harmondsworth, 1962), p. 19.
13. Alfred Harbage, *Shakespeare's Audience* (New York, 1941), pp. 158, 160.

14. S. L. Bethell, *Shakespeare and the Popular Dramatic Tradition* (London, 1944), pp. 28–9.

15. John Gielgud, 'Foreword', Harley Granville-Barker, *Prefaces to Shakespeare*, 8 vols (London, 1984). See Dennis Kennedy, *Granville-Barker and the Dream of Theatre* (Cambridge, 1985).

16. Richard Eyre, 'Foreword', *Granville Barker's Prefaces to Shakespeare* (London, 1993), p. v.

17. G. Wilson Knight, *Shakespearean Production*, revised edn (London, 1964), pp. 41–3.

18. See, for example, Anne Righter, *Shakespeare and the Idea of the Play* (London, 1962); James L. Winny, *The Player King* (London, 1968); James L. Calderwood, *Shakespearean Metadrama* (Minneapolis, MA, 1971), and *Metadrama in Shakespeare's Henriad* (Berkeley, CA, 1979).

19. See Robert Shaughnessy, *Representing Shakespeare: England, History and the RSC* (Hemel Hempstead, 1994).

20. J. L. Styan, *The Shakespeare Revolution: Criticism and Performance in the Twentieth Century* (Cambridge, 1977), pp. 235, 255.

21. Ibid., pp. 232–3, 237.

22. Peter Brook, *The Empty Space* (Harmondsworth, 1972), p. 97.

23. Ibid., p. 107.

24. Ibid., p. 11.

25. For critiques of Brook, see Graham Ley, 'The Rhetoric of Theory in Brook's "The Empty Space"', *New Theatre Quarterly*, 35 (1993), 246–54; David Moody, 'Peter Brook's Heart of Light: "Primitivism" and Intercultural Theatre', *New Theatre Quarterly*, 41 (1995), 33–9.

26. John F. Andrews, 'From the Editor', *Shakespeare Quarterly*, 35 (1984), 516.

27. See Michel Foucault, *Discipline and Punish: The Birth of the Prison*, trans. Alan Sheridan (Harmondsworth, 1977).

28. Stephen Greenblatt, 'Invisible bullets: Renaissance authority and its subversion, *Henry IV* and *Henry V*', in *Political Shakespeare: Essays in Cultural Materialism*, ed. Jonathan Dollimore and Alan Sinfield, second edn (Manchester, 1994), pp. 32–3.

29. Ibid., p. 45.

30. Jonathan Dollimore, *Radical Tragedy: Religion, Ideology and Power in the Drama of Shakespeare and his Contemporaries*, second edn (Hemel Hempstead, 1989), pp. 4–5.

31. Ibid., p. 5.

32. Michael D. Bristol, *Carnival and Theater: Plebeian Culture and the Structure of Authority in Renaissance England* (New York and London, 1985), p. 18.

33. Steven Mullaney, *The Place of the Stage: License, Play, and Power in Reniassance England* (Chicago, 1988), p. vii.

34. Douglas Bruster, *Drama and the Market in the Age of Shakespeare* (Cambridge, 1992), p. 3; Jean E. Howard, *The Stage and Social Struggle in Early Modern England* (London, 1994), p. 10.

35. See, for example, Lisa Jardine, *Still Harping on Daughters* (Brighton, 1983); Catherine Belsey, 'Disrupting sexual difference: meaning and gender in the comedies', in *Alternative Shakespeares*, ed. John Drakakis (London, 1985); Phyllis Rackin, 'Androgyny, Mimesis, and the Marriage of the Boy Heroine on the English Renaissance Stage', *PMLA*, 102 (1987), 29–41; Jean E. Howard, 'Crossdressing, the Theatre, and Gender Struggle in Early Modern England', *Shakespeare Quarterly*, 39 (1988), 418–40; Susan Zimmerman (ed.), *Erotic Politics: Desire on the Renaissance Stage* (New York and London, 1992); Michael Shapiro, *Gender in Play on the Shakespearean Stage: Boy Heroines and Female Pages* (Ann Arbor, MI, 1994); Juliet Dusinberre, 'Squeaking Cleopatras: Gender and Performance in *Antony and Cleopatra*', in *Shakespeare, Theory and Performance*, ed. James C. Bulman (London, 1996); Stephen Orgel, *Impersonations: the Performance of Gender in Shakespeare's England* (Cambridge, 1996); Tracy Sedinger, '"If sight and shape be true": The Epistemology of Crossdressing on the London Stage', *Shakespeare Quarterly*, 48 (1997), 63–79.

36. Eldred Jones, *Othello's Countrymen: The African in English Reniassance Drama* (Oxford, 1965). See also Elliot Tokson, *The Popular Image of the Black Man in English Drama 1550–1688* (Boston, 1982); Ania Loomba, *Gender, Race, Reniassance Drama* (Manchester, 1989); Dympna Callaghan, '"Othello was a white man": properties of race on Shakespeare's stage', *Alternative Shakespeares 2*, ed. Terence Hawkes (London and New York, 1996); John J. Joughlin (ed.), *Shakespeare and National Cultures* (Manchester, 1997); Ania Loomba and Martin Orkin (eds), *Post-Colonial Shakespeares* (London and New York, 1998).

37. See, for example, Margaret de Grazia, 'The essential Shakespeare and the material book', *Textual Practice*, 2 (1988), 69–86; Paul Werstine, 'Narratives About Printed Shakespeare Texts: "Foul Papers" and "Bad Quartos"', *Shakespeare Quarterly*, 41 (1990), 65–86; Graham Holderness and Bryan Loughrey, 'Text and Stage: Shakespeare, Bibliography, and Performance Studies', *New Theatre Quarterly*, 34 (1992), 179–91; Janette Dillon, 'Is There a Performance in this Text?',

Shakespeare Quarterly, 45 (1994), 74–86; Phebe Jensen, 'The Textual Politics of *Troilus and Cressida*', *Shakespeare Quarterly*, 46 (1995), 414–23; Gabriel Egan, 'Myths and Enabling Fictions of "Origin" in the Editing of Shakespeare', *New Theatre Quarterly*, 49 (1997), 41–7.

38. Stanley Wells and Gary Taylor (eds), *William Shakespeare: The Complete Works* (Oxford, 1986). The 1980s and 90s have also seen the ongoing publication of the New Cambridge Shakespeare and the third series of the Arden, both of which are critically and editorially considerably more alert to the plays' histories of performance than their predecessors.

39. Simon Shepherd and Peter Womack, *English Drama: A Cultural History* (Oxford, 1996), pp. 109–10.

40. See p. 190 below

41. Ibid.

42. Bertolt Brecht, *The Messingauf Dialogues*, trans. John Willett (London, 1965), pp. 63–4.

43. See below, p. 25.

44. Raymond Williams, *Drama from Ibsen to Brecht*, revised edn (London, 1968), p. 13.

45. Robert Weimann, *Shakespeare and the Popular Tradition in the Theater: Studies in the Social Dimension of Dramatic Form and Function*, ed. Robert Schwartz (Baltimore, MD, 1978).

46. Robert Weimann, 'Shakespeare on the modern stage: past significance and present meaning', *Shakespeare Survey*, 20 (1967), 113–20.

47. Tim Etchells, 'Diverse Assembly: Some Trends in Recent Performance', in *Contemporary British Theatre*, ed. Theodore Shank (Basingstoke, 1994), p. 108.

48. Tim Etchells, *Certain Fragments: Contemporary Performance and Forced Entertainment* (London and New York, 1999), p. 19.

49. Brook, *The Empty Space*, p. 109.

1

Stage Space and the Shakespeare Experience

J. L. STYAN

A target for performance criticism must be the recreation of the authentic qualities present in the play performed, recapturing its special spirit, its best style, its own mode of working on an audience. Such an attempt at recreation is not to pin the butterfly, but to enable it to fly. Yet whatever aspects of drama and performance we may choose – the quality of speech, its use of music and song, its symbolism of gesture and movement, properties and costume, the degree of realism in characterisation, any of a hundred and one elements of drama – at some point discussion will turn on the problem that besets all dramatic representation: what kind and degree of 'illusion' must its audience undergo if the relationship between actor and audience is to be the most appropriate, and if the manipulation of stimulus and response is to be at the maximum subtlety? In the case of Shakespeare and his contemporaries, we shall best hope to answer this sort of question when we have an authentic replica of the Elizabethan Globe Theatre in which to work and play.

For many years we have spoken of dramatic conventions as the key to understanding a play from an earlier theatre or from another culture, as if the identification of prologues and epilogues, soliloquies and asides, elements of characterisation and plotting, time and place, and other details would solve the problems of comprehension. Some part of this is true: if we knew, say, how a soliloquy was delivered by an actor to an audience in its own time, we might begin to assess what was important for its success in performance.

But conventions per se are as nothing unless we also know their place in the general aesthetic of performance – what and how far the audience accepted, assimilated, and believed at that time.

A valid starting point could well be the 'empty space' occupied by the actor, with what is done and said in it. Peter Brook's celebrated empty space[1] is both an acting area and a region of the mind, and both of these are the focus of the spectator's attention. It is as if Shakespeare exemplified some such theory of performance and response by his use of the empty stage of the Elizabethan theatre, thrust aggressively into its auditorium, demanding full attention, rich with imminent possibilities for direct communication, awaiting its spokesman, and until he came magnetising its viewer. The space was neutral until it was engaged, of course, but its very neutrality was a challenge. Coleridge insisted that the very nakedness of the stage was an advantage, since it gave the playwright his liberty to do what he wanted in the *form* that he chose, as well as liberating the imagination of the audience to accept or reject what it saw and heard.

While we think of the bare Elizabethan stage as a battleground for the action of the play, actor set against actor, it is more accurately the battleground where the playwright can pit the actor against the spectator. It is natural for us to think of the Elizabethan space in terms of the localising and temporal conventions, for it is in the modern style to fill any space with indications of place and time. So it is quick and easy for us to accept that 'this is Illyria, lady' or 'This is the forest of Arden', and for us to hasten in our minds to populate and decorate the new territory from such light and glancing references. We are as ready to adopt Shakespeare's clock upon hearing ''Tis now struck twelve, get thee to bed, Francisco' or 'Get me a taper in my study, Lucius'. Nevertheless, it is less natural and more true to remember that there are rarely any constant reminders of Shakespeare's place and time, and his stage is primarily and properly the target area for imaginative thought and emotion.

The actor in his or her space, through voice and gesture and movement, soon asserts dominance and takes charge of the region of our mind, and for most of the action of the play this is occupied by the promptings of human relationships, those between actor and spectator. The less the audience concentrates on where the actor *is*, the more it will accept what he is standing *for:* the neutrality of the platform's space implies the strongest commitment by author, actor, and audience to the particular relationships of the play.

Hamlet takes place in the castle of Elsinore, yes, but where is 'To be or not to be'? – to affect us this speech may need space, but hardly any place. 'This is Illyria, lady' – very good, but of course it is still the same old stage we know well, and the line becomes almost a private joke between Shakespeare and his audience. Occasionally a localising line is even more metatheatrical: 'When shall I come to the top of that same hill?' asks Gloucester on Dover Cliff, and in this instance Shakespeare, the audience, and the character Edgar all know there is no cliff at all. We may conclude that the convention of localising on the Elizabethan stage seems rather nebulous and, as a theory of Elizabethan dramaturgy, even a kind of nonsense. At one point there appear to be four men in Desdemona's bedroom – Iago, Roderigo, Othello, and Lodovico – who, by the arguments of localising, if not of modesty, must leave before she can undress for bed.

So it is with the convention of time. When the spectators need to check the clock or the calendar, it seems that they are so advised. In *Measure for Measure*, Act IV, scene ii, the Provost announces, 'Tomorrow morning are to die Claudio and Barnardine', and a little later he says to Claudio, ''Tis now dead midnight, and by eight tomorrow / Thou must be made immortal', while after a few moments more Angelo advances the deadly hour to 'four'. In *All's Well That Ends Well*, Act IV, scene iii, both the plot and the subplot seem to come to a head at midnight: just before this hour is set the time for Parolles to be ambushed by his friends, and at midnight also is Bertram instructed to come to Diana's bed in preparation for the substitution of Helena: a busy night for all concerned, but especially the audience. Of course we are never asked to confirm these times, only to feel their urgency. Or night passes (in *A Midsummer Night's Dream, Henry V, Antony and Cleopatra*), lovers will stray, soldiers prepare to die, and yet the stage conveniently remains its usual daylit self. As an audience we are indulgent; and without our general tolerance the story of the play could not go forward. By keeping the stage free from the clutter of place and time, we are again the sharers who enable the actors to act.

From this principle of imaginative neutrality shared by author, actor, and audience all things theatrical can follow. Shakespeare and his contemporaries could pursue extraordinary dramatic freedoms: an acrobatic development of the chronicle play that leaped from one part of the realm to another, from court to camp, from the highborn to the low; pastoral fantasies like *A Midsummer*

Night's Dream and *As You Like It* that compelled their audience to make and perceive plays within plays and roles upon roles in order to explore the human condition and its illusions; or by a series of devices of alienation those comedies that juxtaposed the realities of sex and war, sex and class, and sex and religion in the ambiguous persons of the problem girls Cressida, Helena, and Isabella. These innovations were the direct result of a fluid stage that encouraged not merely the leaps of place and time, but also the quick changes of tone and style designed to expose the areas of the mind where conflict and paradox lie.

The discussion of spatial relationships that follows is hesitantly outlined by a few examples chosen for analysis – hesitantly because no two instances in Shakespeare are finally alike. What I have to say nevertheless seems to fall into categories of a sort:

1. The space that relates the actor directly to his audience and calls for a recognisable intimacy of speech. This is the space that joins.
2. The space that distinguishes between an actor who is intimate with his audience and another who is not, so that the former appears to distance the latter. This is the space that divides.
3. The space that permits a double or triple intimacy, thereby setting up a contrast and conflict of 'simultaneous' staging. This space simultaneously joins and divides the stage and audience.
4. The space in which an actor is temporarily 'upstaged' or denied intimacy with his audience, while he may return with ironic force to urge a contradiction. This is a deceptive division of space.
5. The space that cheats and deceives those on the stage and can be seen to tell lies. This space is almost palpable and speaks to us like a character.

First, the space that joins. 'Soliloquy' is a late seventeenth- or eighteenth-century literary concept, and 'speaking to oneself' was not a device that Shakespeare or the Elizabethan stage would have recognised. However, addressing the audience was a normal and constant activity ('The soliloquy always to the pit – that's a rule', insisted Mr Puff in Sheridan's *The Critic*). It was a convention by which an actor gave himself completely to the house, putting him in direct touch with the spectators; it was the primary device to encourage sharing. Alone on the great platform, a solitary figure made a powerful statement to the spectator, one not so much about the character's state of mind (the lines would do that), but about the actor's need to reach out to his audience with intimacy and immediacy. The play that jumps to mind by its abundance of soliloquies is *Hamlet*, a tragedy in which the device perfectly exemplifies the actor's urge to step outside his play, even outside his part, alone on indeterminate space, and create a few moments of the highest excitement and attention. In such a play, the playwright and the actor take their audience point by point through the action, commenting on events, anticipating the future, compelling us to think like the Prince, and indeed shaping the structure of the play by making sure that we remain partners to the enterprise. In this sense, word and deed, what is heard and what is seen, are essentially inseparable in the spatial treatment of the Elizabethan platform.

In the case of a villain-hero in tragedy like Richard III or Macbeth, it is a matter of the greatest importance that the actor get into immediate touch with his audience lest its thought and feeling be allowed to drift and escape. Whether Gloucester declares the winter of his discontent in the shape of a catlike Emlyn Williams (Old Vic, 1937), a smooth-tongued tyrant like Donald Wolfit (Strand Theatre, 1942), a chillingly ironic intellectual like Laurence Olivier (New Theatre, 1944), a leering Alec Guinness jogging his legs as he sits on the balcony (Ontario, 1953), a giant crab like Douglass Watson (Connecticut, 1964), a wounded spider like Donald Madden (New York, 1970), or the beetle of Anthony Sher on his crutches (Royal Shakespeare Theatre, 1985), the first perverse objective of that remarkable opening soliloquy is to accommodate the monstrous 'received idea' that legend has imposed upon the audience to this play. *Richard III* opens with its actor alone on the empty stage for a lengthy period of time to ensure that his audience learn to collaborate with villainy: the playwright and not the historian is to take possession of the action, and against all reason we willingly participate in the outrageous events of the play.

One scene in *Romeo and Juliet* (II.v) seems to have been a remarkable experiment in spatial organisation because in it Juliet seems to win the audience by soliloquy and then surrenders the precious, intimate territory so gained in order to upstage the speaker. The scene has Juliet waiting for the Nurse to bring her the news of the marriage arrangements with Romeo, and immediately we are charmed by a conventional soliloquy that efficiently identifies the hour, the issue, and the character's state of mind:

> The hour struck nine when I did send the Nurse,
> In half an hour she promis'd to return.
> Perchance she cannot meet him. That's not so.
> O, she is lame. Love's heralds should be thoughts
> Which ten times faster glides than the sun's beams
> Driving back shadows over lowering hills. ...
> (II.v.1–6)

Here Juliet has given us direct information about the clock, and then, alone on the stage, she at once conveys her anxiety by a broken, kinetic line ('That's not so.') designed to animate the player. By now she is within arm's length of the audience as her amorous desires are lyricised by a poetry of another order ('Love's heralds should be thoughts'), so that we share the quality of her anticipation, as well as laugh a little at her youthful impatience. Her anger finally overwhelms her softer feelings, and Shakespeare arranges that her lines actually serve as a stage direction, telling the Nurse how to make her entrance:

> But old folks, many feign as they were dead –
> Unwieldy, slow, heavy, and pale as lead.
> (II.v.16–17)

Juliet's own movement is the very opposite, since she runs upstage on

> O God she comes. O honey Nurse, what news?,
> (II.v.18)

and we are not to forget the great depth of the platform.

Begins the farce of having this Nurse refuse to disclose the information requested of her:

> I am aweary, give me leave awhile.
> Fie, how my bones ache. What a jaunce have I!
> (II.v.25–6)

Can she be as tired as she says? No, indeed – for we are soon given hints enough that she is enjoying her moment of superiority by deliberately prolonging Juliet's agony of mind. So the Nurse works her way downstage, fixing the audience with a wicked eye:

> Jesu, what haste. Can you not stay awhile?
> Do you not see that I am out of breath?
> (II.v.29–30)

The Nurse is now on the platform where Juliet was, probably sharing her joke with a wink or a nod, and no doubt breathing unnaturally heavily the while. For the joy in this scene lies in the fact that the audience knows all that there is to know about this marriage – it was after all party to the arrangement with Romeo – so that the plot per se has no need of this scene at all. A factor of possibly greater importance is nevertheless at work here in the mixing of the lyrical and the prosaic, the humorous and the pathetic, contrary ingredients that lie at the heart of this play. Both Juliet and the Nurse must have the chance to manipulate the audience, and the critical working space nearest the centre of the playhouse must be occupied by both equally.

The space that joins has already given way to the space that divides, and given one character onstage who sufficiently shares his or her thoughts with us, there will be another who accordingly will be 'distanced'. Of many straightforward instances, Lady Macbeth's sleepwalking scene (*Macbeth*, V.i) springs to mind. The sleepwalker addresses no words to us. On the abstract, open spaces of the platform lit only by daylight, Lady Macbeth carries her taper and gropes through her nightmare in a darkness of her own. The empty space is the tortured arena for the re-enactment of her part in the murder of Duncan: her eyes are open, but their sense is shut, while we observe and witness like the Doctor of Physic and the Waiting Gentlewoman, who, like the audience, 'observe' and 'stand close'. Are they hiding? – no, no more than is the spectator. For they, not the Queen, are our surrogates on the stage, and their comments throughout are for our ears: 'What a sigh is there! The heart is sorely charg'd'; 'I would not have such a heart in my bosom for the dignity of the whole body' (V.i.51–3). They are close, secret observers, standing still on the perimeter of the stage adjacent to the audience. But not only are our eyes open; so too is our 'sense'.

The distancing space is felt on countless occasions, and it always lends a judgmental and sometimes a comic perspective to the comparison between the selected characters onstage. The scenes between Orsino and Viola in *Twelfth Night* offer familiar instances. When, for example, in Act II, scene iv the lovelorn Duke is mouthing his blustering sentiments about true love, the fact that Viola as Cesario is his audience, lovelorn herself and scarcely able to disguise her feelings as well as she can her clothes, must upstage him. He calls her to him:

Come hither, boy. If ever thou shalt love,
In the sweet pangs of it remember me:
For such as I am, all true lovers are,
Unstaid and skittish in all motions else,
Save in the constant image of the creature
That is belov'd. How dost thou like this tune?
Viola It gives a very echo to the seat
Where love is thron'd.
Duke Thou dost speak masterly.
My life upon't, young though thou art, thine eye
Hath stay'd upon some favour that it loves.
Hath it not, boy?
Viola A little, by your favour.
(II.iv.15–25)

Whether the Duke is sitting or pacing, Viola is unable to take her eyes off him and must repeatedly turn away to save her modesty and her disguise. His every remark is registered in her expression, which is altogether a better exemplar of staid and unskittish motions. If Orsino touches her (and 'My life upon't' warrants a playful slap on the boyish shoulder), Viola's reaction of amorous desire must positively convey a 'constant image'. All very amusing for us, but we are smiling at both of them in different ways, for they have been separated here, not by the depth of the platform, but by a relative space used flexibly to mark a physical relationship.

The physical relationship, conveyed on the Elizabethan stage by measurable distance from the centre of the house, has here become a judgmental relationship, echoing our response to the spatially related actors on the stage. In *All's Well That Ends Well* (I.iii) the Countess of Rossillion invites the audience to observe the condition of Helena's unhappy love as she passes at a distance on another part of the stage, even the balcony, unaware that she is being watched. As we all look at Helena, the older woman explains with compassion just how it is with the younger: 'Even so it was with me when I was young' (l. 123). In *King Lear*, Act I, scene iv, Goneril stands on her entrance in threatening silence, accusing her father by her very stillness and absence of words, until he emphasises her demeanour with an explosive, 'How now, daughter! what makes that frontlet on? You are too much of late i'th' frown' (ll. 197–8). Thus the momentous confrontation between father and daughter awaits the spectator's verdict on relative guilt. In *The Winter's Tale*, Act I, scene ii, Leontes first indicates his jealousy of Polixenes after that gentleman has innocently led Hermione away upstage – or somewhere out of his hearing – so permitting the husband to misinterpret the behaviour of his wife: 'Too hot, too hot! / To mingle friendship far, is mingling bloods' (ll. 108–9). We know that he is wrong, since we heard clearly enough their simple courtesies when he did not. Thus we are made sharply aware how the eyes – and human behaviour seen at a distance – cause mistakes to be made.

There are times when space seems to be almost visible, even self-conscious. Some forms of 'simultaneous staging' (the arrangement by which two things may happen on the stage at the same time) encourage the audience to perceive and evaluate both together. This simultaneity, incidentally, presents difficulties for the film and television camera but is easily assimilated by the human eye. The opening court scene in *King Lear* demonstrates a brilliant sequence of contrasting spatial images, with so much happening on the stage spatially that the test for Shakespeare's mastery of his craft is whether he has not bewildered the spectator by the riches of the scene.

First, the discussion between Gloucester and Kent that opens the play is not merely to announce the division of the kingdom: it is alive with a sinister kind of comedy, marked by the cruel laughter which separates Edmund from his father and showing how easy it is to divide the loyalty of families as well as kingdoms. Nevertheless, an audience makes this perception only if Edmund enters and stands apart from the older men, seeing their laughter enjoyed at his expense when they jest about his illegitimacy:

> **Kent** I cannot conceive you.
> **Gloucester** Sir, this young fellow's mother could.
> (I.i.12–13)

General mirth – until we see the grim expression on Edmund's face. He is eventually called over to be introduced: 'Do you know this noble gentleman, Edmund?' And now we hear the ice on Edmund's breath as he replies, 'My services to your Lordship' (l. 29). As the two parties are joined, the audience knows to hold them separate.

Second, Lear's throne (which may be presumed to be upstage centre from the evidence of Jonson's *Every Man in His Humour*, prologue, line 16, where he jokes about how the 'creaking throne comes down, the boys to please') must itself divide the stage again, between the sisters Goneril and Regan and their parties. For this part of the scene the most formal patterning is suggested, not only by the ceremonial occasion, but also by the outright rivalry of the sisters. Thus when Goneril speaks her smooth lines to Lear,

> Sir, I love you more than word can wield the matter;
> Dearer than eyesight, space and liberty ...
> (I.i.55–6)

the issue of division in the family comes across most powerfully if she faces, not so much her father, but her sister, placed directly across the width of the platform, and seems to address her. Again, when Regan speaks her formal statement of love, the issue is visually reinforced if she too faces across the platform, lobbing her words at Goneril:

> I find she names my very deed of love;
> Only she comes too short ...
> (I.i.71–2)

Once again we hear the icy tones of inbred hatred, and gesture and posture will match them.

Yet there is a third spatial statement made at this time. Three sisters on a square platform do not make for symmetry, and Cordelia is carefully placed on the perimeter of the platform for her two critical asides:

> What shall Cordelia speak? Love, and be silent.
> (I.i.62)

and

> Then poor Cordelia!
> And yet not so; since I am sure my love's
> More ponderous than my tongue.
> (I.i.77–9)

By her simpler words, her closer proximity to the house, and her more natural informality, sound and movement not only single her out but also identify her as the one to believe. Moreover, they also prepare the audience for the radical break in the apparent direction of the action, and for the next lesson in spatial exploration. To this point I take it that the audience has been chiefly an observer. At the first sign of direct address from the stage – that of Cordelia's 'asides' (the term, of course, is not the one that Elizabethans would recognise, so we must think of such lines merely as remarks intended to be heard as external comments presented outside the action) – the audience will be drawn into collusion with the speaker. Thus to this point we have separated Goneril and Regan, and now separate Cordelia. The only major character who remains unplaced in our regard is Lear himself. He remains on his throne, allowing essentially no distinction of feeling, unless it be that 'Now, our joy, / Although our last, and least ...' (I.i.82–3) marks the first change in him, since here it could be argued that he speaks more like a father and less like a monarch.

Fourth, then, when he speaks more like a father, any test of the Elizabethan platform will ease him from the formal upstage position and carry him downstage to greet his youngest daughter personally, affectionately. The naturalistic intimacy between father and daughter that follows in the shorter, more colloquial, broken lines ('Nothing, my Lord ...' 'Nothing? ...' 'Nothing' [I.i. 87–9]) has in production been conveyed by having Cordelia make the next move, even to sitting on Lear's knee. However, the intimacy that is shared with the house for this crucial exchange, one that addresses the leading motif of the play, is of greater importance. If the moment is played out in the centre of the house, not only are the actors able to speak their lines with more vocal and facial subtlety – and more realism – but the audience may receive the message about the bond of blood all the more forcefully for its being less formalised and more human.

It is interesting that Shakespeare's language usually signals the spatial relationships he appears to want between actor and actor, and between actor and spectator. Outstanding in its control of audience response and its differentiation between characters is the dialogue between Macbeth and Lady Macbeth during the scene of the murder of Duncan (*Macbeth*, II.i). In this remarkable piece of dramaturgy, the two principals, each in turn, move from soliloquy to dialogue as if to prepare for their increasing separation in body, mind, and spirit. With the prompting of a tolling bell and a screaming owl, each character passes from the unreal regions of the sick imagination to the realistic business of murder, from witchcraft and 'pale Hecate' to the grisly business of drugging the possets of Duncan's grooms and finding Macbeth's daggers laid ready.

Realism is at its peak in the scene when attention is drawn to the daggers and the blood on Macbeth's hands. Yet at this moment of greatest physical and visual horror, the dialogue suffers a striking change. As Lady Macbeth's lines grow shorter and more prosaic, her voice more shrill, so Macbeth's grow longer and more rhythmical, his voice more colourful.

> **Macbeth** There's one did laugh in's sleep, and one cried, 'Murther!'
> That they did wake each other: I stood and heard them;
> But they did say their prayers, and address'd them
> Again to sleep.
> **Lady Macbeth** There are two lodg'd together.
> **Macbeth** One cried, 'God bless us!' and 'Amen', the other,
> As they had seen me with these hangman's hands.
> List'ning their fear, I could not say, 'Amen',
> When they did say 'God bless us'.
> **Lady Macbeth** Consider it not so deeply
> (II.i.22–9)

It is clear that these two are moving in different realms of the mind. What may be less clear to the *reader* is that the lines also separate man and wife physically. On the one hand, Macbeth is off into his living nightmare, his feet not quite on the ground, moving into the neutral area of the platform, close to the centre of the playhouse, to the audience, and to the skies.

> Methought, I heard a voice cry, 'Sleep no more!
> Macbeth does murther Sleep', – the innocent Sleep;
> Sleep, that knits up the ravell'd sleave of care ...
> (II.i.34–6)

On the other hand, Lady Macbeth is powerless against the terrifying poetry of the murderer's mind, nor can she follow him into his private hell. She must remain where she is, unable to reach him, fixed and transfixed in the inner play. The audience, meanwhile, continues to share his thoughts to the end, rejecting those of his lady.

We have previously touched on a fourth use of responsive space, when a character is upstaged by another and temporarily denied the direct sympathy of the audience. Think of Beatrice's eavesdropping scene in *Much Ado about Nothing*, Act III, scene i, carefully arranged so differently from that of Benedick. Where Benedick commented upon what his deceivers were saying throughout, poor

Beatrice is allowed not a word. Thus Hero takes the opportunity to lambaste her friend with

> But Nature never fram'd a woman's heart
> Of prouder stuff than that of Beatrice.
> Disdain and scorn ride sparkling in her eyes … .
> (III.i.49–51)

Beatrice can only hear these words with pain, unable to respond, although we may know from her demeanour that she is upset. 'She is so self-endeared' is quite a challenge, and we may guess that Lady Disdain has a softer heart than she has shown before. When she is finally alone and free to address us, she does so in a joyful soliloquy of lyrical rhyming verse, closing upon her audience in a short confessional sonnet:

> What fire is in mine ears? Can this be true?
> Stand I condemn'd for pride and scorn so much?
> Contempt, farewell, and maiden pride, adieu!
> No glory lives behind the back of such.
> (III.i.107–10)

Her true and passionate nature is here revealed to everyone's satisfaction, and this time without laughing we confirm our impressions of her sincerity.

In this instance the upstaging has been redeemed. When Ulysses pronounces judgement on his victim Cressida in *Troilus and Cressida*, Act IV, scene v

> There's language in her eye, her cheek, her lip –
> Nay, her foot speaks; her wanton spirits look out
> At every joint and motive of her body,
> (IV.v.55–7)

it is left to the audience to choose between the man who has just engineered her rough treatment at the hands of the Greek army officers and the girl who was in tears when she was dragged from Troy and from Troilus. If we take Ulysses's words at their face value, we may well choose to recognise 'her wanton spirits' and think she simpers upstage to the exit – and so, indeed, have many critics and actresses unfamiliar with the ambiguous ways of the Elizabethan stage. However, if an audience senses the ambivalence, the 'indeterminacy', that so deliberately informs the problem comedies, it will claim the privilege of deciding for itself and will not believe everything it is told.

A fine instance of such spatial indeterminacy introduces that unusual tragedy of seesaw values, *Antony and Cleopatra*. The Roman soldiers Demetrius and Philo are granted the first lines of the play: they enter talking and talk their way downstage. There the audience can more readily hear the veteran Philo tell the rookie Demetrius of the problems that beset the army now that their general has taken up with his gypsy. And all this criticism of 'this dotage of our general's' may be assumed to echo the received idea of both Plutarch and the Elizabethan audience about Antony. Then, unexpectedly perhaps, we are commanded:

> Look, where they come:
> Take but good note, and you shall see in him,
> The triple pillar of the world transform'd
> Into a strumpet's fool: behold and see.
> (I.i.10–13)

The 'look where' tag directs all eyes to an upstage entrance where the subjects of the conversation may be seen. And the Folio has the unusually rich stage direction, '*Flourish. Enter Antony, Cleopatra, her Ladies, the Train, with Eunuchs fanning her*', as if the King's Men wanted to contradict Philo's censure of Antony visually, sensuously. The audience is confronted with a sharp incongruity, and its idea of the magnificent, legendary love of a weak, degenerate Antony notwithstanding, the play catches fire. It does so because we are shown a glimpse of both sides of the story, 'the bellows and the fan / To cool a gypsy's lust' as well as intimations of 'new heaven, new earth' (I.i.9–10, 17), the two not only contrasted in imagery and tone, but also divided by space. Our sympathies are evoked, balanced, and engaged – by the contradictory evidence of our eyes and ears on two parts of the stage.

Fifthly and finally, the Elizabethan platform encourages a stage space that demonstrates how well the eyes can deceive the ears. This kind of illusory space is implicit in every eavesdropping scene, every speech 'aside', every address in which the actor appears to step outside the inner action in order to embrace his audience. It was remarked how in *The Winter's Tale*, Act I, scene ii, Shakespeare arranged it that Hermione and Leontes be heard, then seen, alternately: a curious, mechanical, and highly experimental pattern by which the audience is invited to compare and accommodate the information of the ears with that of the eyes. When Leontes misreads the signs ('paddling palms, and pinching fingers' [l. 115], 'making practis'd smiles / As in a looking-glass' [ll. 116–17], 'to sigh, as 'twere / The mort o'th'deer' [ll. 117–18], 'Still virginalling / Upon his palm?' [ll. 125–6]), the audience knows his wife to be innocent. Yet it hears the heated words of Leontes's '*tremor cordis*' and has the urge to cry out advice at Hermione's puzzled 'He something seems unsettled' when she returns to that part of the stage where she can be heard as well as seen. At this moment Shakespeare anticipates Pirandello's manipulation of appearance and belief among the townspeople and the audience of *Cosi è, se vi pare*!

As with Pirandello, we are led to the edge of the irrational, and space becomes excessively self-conscious. *Othello* is a play rich in such spatial effects, for not only is the hero regularly upstaged by the villain (Iago's soliloquies begin with the first scene of the play, while Othello's first soliloquy proper is not heard until the last), but two of the major scenes of Othello's deception (Act III, scene iii, that of Cassio's request to Desdemona for his reinstatement, and Act IV, scene i, that of Othello's eavesdropping) use the full length or depth of the platform in order to stress the error of the eye. These are two notable scenes of experimental theatre.

During the Cyprus scene of Act II, scene i; the audience is prepared for spatial illusion to come. As Desdemona addresses Cassio, so Iago in his aside, certainly downstage of them, describes their innocent gestures and indicates how he will contrive to 'ensnare' Cassio:

> He takes her by the palm; ay, well said, whisper: as little a web as this will ensnare as great a fly as Cassio. Ay, smile upon her, do: I will catch you in your own courtesies … .
>
> (II.i.167–70)

Iago's threat is heard again a moment later in a second aside, this time undercutting the greeting of Othello and Desdemona:

> O, you are well tun'd now,
> But I'll set down the pegs that make this music,
> As honest as I am.
>
> (II.i.199–201)

Iago goes on to confirm his plan in the soliloquy at the end of Act II, scene i. Thus the audience is dragged into the ugly conspiracy and is cunningly put on the alert for further signs of the error of the eye.

The audience has not long to wait. As soon as Desdemona has given her assurance to Cassio, their dialogue conducted in intimate and urgent tones as they stand close together in one part of the platform, any audience might anticipate the husband's entrance in the classic sequence of comic cuckoldry.

> **Emilia** Madam, here comes my lord.
> **Cassio** Madam, I'll take my leave.
> **Desdemona** Why, stay and hear me speak.
> **Cassio** Madam, not now, I am very ill at ease,
> Unfit for mine own purpose.
> (III.ii.29–33)

Cassio's hurried exit and Desdemona's attempt to restrain him, perhaps by touching his arm, his hand, is 'guilty-like' by any convention of behaviour, and the two also present Iago with the opportunity to hint that all is not innocent, so that the audience soon hears in Othello's voice that a first doubt has been planted in his mind:

> **Desdemona** I have been talking with a suitor here,
> A man that languishes in your displeasure.
> **Othello** Who is't you mean?
> **Desdemona** Why, your lieutenant, Cassio, good my lord … .
> (III.ii.43–6)

He was of course almost sure who it was: all he needs now is to hear his wife seem to confess that it was indeed Cassio. And soon after we again hear the small voice of doubt and distress: 'when I love thee not, / Chaos is come again' (ll. 92–3). The jealous brain begins monstrously to misinterpret the smallest tone or gesture.

There follows the long and subtle scene of verbal temptation (III.iii), until Othello demands his 'ocular proof'. Iago will supply it in the scene (IV.i) where he can make barracks-room suggestions to Cassio about his mistress Bianca. He will laugh with him and have Cassio show how she falls about his neck, 'hangs, and lolls, and weeps' upon him, 'hales, and pulls' (ll. 137–8) him – all the time confident that on the other side of the stage Othello, observing but not hearing, will identify Desdemona with this Bianca. To Othello and to the audience every laugh will sound coarser, every gesture more obscene than it is, until the Moor is ready to kill. Iago has one moment of anxiety when, unexpectedly, the real Bianca approaches, for she is not at all the 'poor caitiff' of the earlier conversation, but a far more independent creature. However, as luck (and Shakespeare) would have it, she brings with her the very handkerchief that Othello gave Desdemona, and taking it to be 'some minx's token' (l. 151), she throws it in Cassio's face. For his part, Othello sees only what he wants to see, further incriminating evidence: 'By heaven, that should be my handkerchief' (l. 155). Thus Bianca's dangerous entrance has most conveniently exacerbated all his worst suspicions. So, again, space has served the play: in Cressida's words,

> The error of our eye directs our mind.
> What error leads must err; O, then conclude,
> Minds sway'd by eyes are full of turpitude.
> (*Troilus and Cressida*, V.ii.109–11)

Space at such times is seen and heard – but hardly invisible, scarcely silent. The days of the two-dimensional Victorian picture-frame stage are passing, and the proscenium-arch protesters who sustained the public debate that followed Tyrone Guthrie's thrust stages in Ontario, Chichester, and Minneapolis have fallen silent. It is everywhere acknowledged that the shape of the stage affects the acting and the response to it, even controls the play and the experience of it. Wherever Shakespeare is played in the Elizabethan way, the medium is the message, and we must now believe that actors are reassuming their former importance. Especially it is for us to learn to perceive the new old dramatic values. They have much to do with our rediscovery of spatial relationships between actor and audience; and the amazing fluctuation that space can create between, on the one hand, illusion and belief and, on the other, non-illusion and reality has yet to be experienced. Like Troilus, 'enkindled' by his eyes and ears, which he calls

> Two traded pilots 'twixt the dangerous shores
> Of will and judgement,
> (II.ii.65–6)

we the audience may hope to be at once more caught up in the essential spirit of the Shakespeare play and more aware and sensitive as its auditors.

From *Shakespeare and the Sense of Performance*, ed. Marvin Thompson and Ruth Thompson (London and Toronto, 1989), pp. 195–209.

NOTES

[Styan's essay first appeared in a collection of performance criticism dedicated to one of the critical movement's key figures, Bernard Beckerman. It offers a concise summation of the 'stage-centred' approach to Shakespeare that Styan himself had been instrumental in developing during the 1960s and 1970s. Strongly influenced by the theatre director Peter Brook's conception of the fundamental element of theatre being the 'empty space' of the stage, Styan's active reading discovers rich and suggestive continuities between verbal utterance, the spatial dynamics of the text as indicated by its explicit (and implicit) stage directions, and the configuration of the Elizabethan public playhouse. All quotations are from the Arden Shakespeare editions: *All's Well That Ends Well*, ed. G. K. Hunter (London, 1959); *Antony and Cleopatra*, ed. M. R. Ridley (1954); *King Lear*, ed. Kenneth Muir (1972); *Macbeth*, ed. Kenneth Muir (1951); Measure *for Measure*, ed. J. W. Lever (1965); *Much Ado About Nothing*, ed. A. R. Humphreys (1981); *Othello*, ed. M. R. Ridley (1958); *Romeo and Juliet*, ed. Brian Gibbons (1980); *Twelfth Night*, ed. J. M. Lothian and T. W. Craik (1975); *The Winter's Tale*, ed. J. H. P. Pafford (1963). Ed.]

1. Peter Brook, *The Empty Space* (London, 1968).

2

The Arrow in Nessus: Elizabethan Clues and Modern Detectives

ALAN C. DESSEN

Did you ever hear of a sleepwalker carrying a light?

Shakespeare's plays continue to fascinate – and puzzle – the modern reader. Actors, directors, editors, critics, and teachers all wrestle with the words that have come down to us in the quartos and the Folio, seeking clues to pluck out the heart of Hamlet's mystery or answer Lear's question: 'Who is it that can tell me who I am?' But anyone familiar with the wide range of interpreters and interpretations can attest that the solutions advanced or even the questions asked reveal as much about the modern detective as about the Elizabethan dramatist. Like Orlando bearing old Adam on his back, we too bring luggage with us to any reading of Elizabethan plays; or, to use Bernard Beckerman's image, when we pick up a book containing the printed words of a Shakespeare play we simultaneously put on a pair of spectacles 'compacted of preconceptions about what constitutes drama and how it produces its effects'.[1] To the modern reader, the luggage or spectacles of an earlier age may appear ridiculous. Thus, we can chuckle at Nahum Tate's decision 'to rectify what was wanting in the regularity and probability of the tale'[2] in *King Lear* by adding a love affair between Edgar and Cordelia and a happy ending, or we can look askance at Dryden's 'improvement' of *Troilus and Cressida* 'to remove that heap of rubbish under which many excellent thoughts lay wholly buried'.[3] But to recognise the assumptions and predispositions that control (and sometimes distort) *our* view of Elizabethan drama is far more difficult, even at times impossible, especially in our age of demystification in which the responses of the reader or the formulations of the theorist often take precedence over the 'intentions' of the author.

For an especially astute critique of the modern literary detective dealing with Shakespearean clues, consider James Thurber's 'The Macbeth Murder Mystery'.[4] At an English hotel, Thurber's narrator encounters an American lady addicted to murder mysteries at bedtime who discovers to her horror that inadvertently she has purchased *Macbeth*. Stuck with the bard, she grudgingly reads the tragedy and, as an experienced sleuth, becomes firmly convinced that Macduff rather than Macbeth is the murderer of Duncan. In her reasoning lies Thurber's insight. First, Macbeth could not be the murderer because: 'It would spoil everything if you could figure out right away who did it. Shakespeare was too smart for that.' Banquo was a suspect until he too was killed ('That was good right in there, that part'). Macbeth's suspicious behaviour in the banquet scene is attributed to his attempt to 'shield' Lady Macbeth, but she too must be innocent because, in the sleep-walking scene, she carries a taper. Says the American lady: 'Well, people who walk in their sleep *never carry lights*! ... They have a second sight. Did you ever hear of a sleepwalker carrying a light?' Rather, she declares Macduff the culprit because of his hyperbolic reaction to Duncan's death, for she notes that 'he comes running downstairs and shouts, "Confusion has broke open the Lord's anointed temple" and "Sacrilegious murder has made his masterpiece" and on and on like that.' Our amateur detective observes shrewdly: 'All that stuff was rehearsed ... You wouldn't say a lot of stuff like that, offhand, would you – if you had found a body? ... You wouldn't! Unless you had practised it in advance. "My God, there's a body in here!" is what an innocent man would say.'

With a fine comic touch, Thurber here demonstrates how the introduction of irrelevant evidence and inappropriate questions can distort a Shakespearean scene or character or problem. Thus, his American lady brings her lore about sleep-walkers, her awareness of mystery story conventions, and her sense of realism about language and human reactions under stress to bear upon a poetic tragedy where a sleep-walker *can* carry a taper and an innocent figure, confronted with the murder of his saintly king, *can* state that 'most sacrilegious murder hath broke ope / The Lord's anointed temple'. At such moments in an Elizabethan play, another kind of literary or theatrical logic – call it symbolic or imagistic or presentational – can take precedence over the interpretative logic or generic expectations supplied by the devotee of Agatha Christie (or Henry James or Henrik Ibsen or Sigmund Freud or A. C. Bradley).

To see such interpretative logic in conflict on stage, consider a moment from the Oregon Shakespearean Festival production of *King Lear* in 1976. Here, in a rendition of Act III, scene iv, Denis Arndt as Lear took upon himself the role of a lecturer with Poor Tom as his visual aid ('consider him well') in order to raise an essential question ('is man no more than this?') by placing particular emphasis upon nakedness ('uncovered body', 'the thing itself', 'unaccommodated man', 'a poor, bare, forked animal'). At the same time, Ron Woods as Tom was building his characterisation upon his iterated line 'Tom's acold' and was therefore shivering, 'playing cold', grasping at anything that would provide warmth. As a result, at one performance the two actors engaged in a strenuous struggle for Tom's blanket (his only possession other than a loin-cloth), with Lear trying to pull it off in order to display a naked or nearly naked figure (to establish his thesis) while Tom, with equal vigour, sought to pull the blanket around him (to gain warmth). Tom won – perhaps at the expense of the larger implications of Lear's speech.

Note that the two actors were responding to two different sets of signals that then led them in two different directions. Woods, as a modern actor conditioned by the logic of naturalism, was reaching out for appropriate stage business to resolve the question: how would a nearly naked man obviously suffering from the cold 'behave' in a storm? In contrast, Arndt was drawing upon previous speeches about naked wretches in the pitiless storm and was therefore treating Tom as a theatrical expression of images crucial to this part of the play ('is man no more than this?', can 'man' be reduced to this?). The two different kinds of interpretative logic (physiological-naturalistic versus imagistic-symbolic) are not necessarily incompatible but were at odds in this wrestling match where Poor Tom as stage image linked to the particular coordinates of this scene did not mesh comfortably with Poor Tom as a 'man' or 'character' responding to blasts of cold. The actor's choice, moreover, to play 'cold' rather than 'nakedness' may be a subtler version of what I am terming the *logic* of Thurber's American lady, who 'knows' that in 'the real world' sleep-walkers do not carry candles and thanes who discover dead bodies do not react in highly imagistic blank verse.

To see such a logic of interpretation in action in yet a third arena, let me turn now to two problems involving stage directions – one omitted, the other inserted. First, at the moment that Romeo threatens to commit suicide in Act III, scene iii, the second or 'good' quarto of 1599 (presumably the version closest to Shakespeare's draft) provides no stage direction, but the first or 'bad' quarto of 1597 (presumably based upon an actor's memory of some production) reads: '*He offers to stab himself, and Nurse snatches the dagger away*' (Giv). Some modern editors incorporate the signal from Q–I into their texts (usually putting it in square brackets to show it is not to be found in Q–2), but in his recent New Arden edition Brian Gibbons rejects the Nurse's intervention as 'neither necessary or defensible'. Rather, for this editor 'this piece of business looks like a gratuitous and distracting bid on the part of the actor in the unauthorised version to claim extra attention to himself when the audience should be concentrating on Romeo and the Friar'.[5] Given his sense of what 'the audience should be concentrating on', Gibbons therefore relegates the Nurse's intervention to his textual notes and footnotes. No distractions here.

Like Poor Tom 'playing cold' or the American lady reading *Macbeth* as a murder mystery, this editor is invoking a logic of interpretation that then determines for him what evidence shall be included or excluded, what is deemed 'necessary' or 'defensible' as opposed to 'gratuitous' or 'distracting'. Since many readers concentrate upon the text rather than the notes, such an editorial decision (especially in this prestigious series) can have a greater impact upon future interpreters than an equivalent choice by an actor or critic. Granted, if an Arden editor omits such a signal, it has not ceased to exist: other editors will make different decisions; some readers take the notes into account; other readers go back to facsimiles of the earliest texts. But this editor's decision (noted with approval by at least one reviewer)[6] has made it easier for future interpreters of this scene to ignore the Q–1 stage direction – indeed, has made it more likely many will not know of its existence.

The reader may well ask: why all the fuss? In what sense can the Nurse's intervention be seen as meaningful or consistent or

'Shakespearean'? In response to Gibbons, one scholar has noted that, later in the play, we learn 'that Romeo carried his dagger scabbarded on his back', so, given proper positioning on stage, the Nurse could readily have prevented his access to the weapon, perhaps with 'a genteel hammerlock'.[7] For me, the Q–1 version makes excellent sense in imagistic or symbolic terms. After Mercutio's death, Romeo had cried out: 'O sweet Juliet, / Thy beauty hath made me effeminate / And in my temper soft'ned valor's steel!' (III. i.111–13). Then, after Romeo's aborted attempt at suicide, the Friar's long moralisation starts:

> Hold thy desperate hand.
> Art thou a man? Thy form cries out thou art;
> Thy tears are womanish, thy wild acts denote
> The unreasonable fury of a beast.
> Unseemly woman in a seeming man!
> And ill-beseeming beast in seeming both!
> (III. iii.108–13)

The spectator who sees Romeo's self-destructive violence interrupted by the Nurse and then hears the Friar's terms (e.g. 'Art thou a man?'; 'Thy tears are womanish'; 'Unseemly woman in a seeming man') is thus confronted with the question: what kind of man *is* Romeo at this point in the play? Like other moments of stage violence, the woman's intervention here may set up a powerful and meaningful stage image at the heart of the tragedy. What may seem by one logic of interpretation 'gratuitous and distracting' or 'out of character' or 'unbelievable' may, by a somewhat different logic, appear imagistically or symbolically consistent or meaningful. Indeed, how *would* a dramatist in the mid 1590s (the age of *The Faerie Queene, Doctor Faustus*, and *Titus Andronicus*) have acted out on stage the 'womanish' behaviour of his protagonist?

For a second example, consider the context of one of the most famous moments in Shakespeare, Macbeth's 'to-morrow, and to-morrow, and to-morrow'. The scene starts with the entrance of Macbeth, Seyton, and soldiers. Seven lines later a stage direction calls for '*a cry within of women*' (V. v.7. s.d.); Macbeth asks 'What is that noise?' and Seyton responds: 'It is the cry of women, my good lord'. After a powerful short speech ('I have supped full with horrors') Macbeth asks again: 'Wherefore was that cry?' to which Seyton responds: 'The Queen, my lord, is dead' (ll. 15–16), a revelation that elicits the famous speech. The Folio, however, provides no exit and re-entry for Seyton between his two lines, so the only authoritative text gives us no indication how he finds out that the queen is dead. Few editors (or directors or critics) can abide such an untidy situation (especially since the original texts *are* erratic about indicating exits and entrances), so the Pelican, Riverside, Signet, and New Arden editions (to cite only four) include an exit for Seyton after his first line and an entrance before his second (with the insert usually, but not always, enclosed in square brackets). A director may have Seyton exit or may have him send off a lesser functionary who then returns or may have Seyton walk to a stage door, confer with someone off-stage, and return to Macbeth. As Gibbons might argue, the focus here is upon Macbeth, not Seyton, so the editor must decide what is 'necessary' and what is 'distracting'. If we are to understand that Lady Macbeth has died at the moment of the cry (which would then rule out Seyton knowing of her death at the outset of the scene), the announcer of the news presumably must have some means of learning the news. Therefore, our prevailing logic of interpretation calls for an exit or some other visible means of getting the news on stage.

Without further evidence, we will never know whether or not such an interpretation is correct.[8] Regardless, given the widely shared assumptions about what is 'necessary' to make such a scene 'plausible', editors undoubtedly will continue to insert the two additional stage directions, a self-fulfilling action that in turn validates the interpretation and keeps us comfortable. But how valid *is* this logic of interpretation? Can we imagine the scene as presented in the Folio? Macbeth would ask his first question ('What is that noise?') and get the answer ('It is the cry of women'). No one leaves the stage; Seyton remains by his side. After his ruminations about fears and horrors, Macbeth asks again: 'Wherefore was that cry?' and Seyton responds: 'The Queen, my lord, is dead'. In this rendition, the audience cannot help seeing that Seyton (to be pronounced *Satan*?) has no normal (earthly?) way of knowing what he knows. But he *does* know. Macbeth may be too preoccupied to notice the anomaly, but, if staged this way, the spectator cannot help being jarred. Indeed, the anomaly then becomes a major part of the context for the nihilistic comments that follow. Such a staging (which adds nothing but rather takes the Folio at face value) strikes me as eerie, powerful, perhaps quite unnerving. A focus upon *how* Seyton knows of the death almost inevitably leads to the addition of stage business that can provide a practical explanation for that 'how', but such literal-mindedness may, in fact, end up masking a truly distinctive Jacobean effect linked to a mystery behind that 'how'. After all, how do Enobarbus and Iras die in *Antony and Cleopatra*? How does Henry VI know of the murder of his son in *3 Henry VI*, V. vi? Or, much closer to home, how do the witches know what they know in this play? In this, Seyton's last specified appearance, are we being encouraged to grasp larger meanings in his name? Most important, where does one draw the line between 'editing' and 'interpreting' such a moment?

That my two examples of editorial logic have to do with stage directions is no coincidence. Every Shakespeare play has its share of much discussed problems involving which *words* were intended by the author. Thus, in his third soliloquy at the end of Act II, does Hamlet compare himself to a 'scullion' (a kitchen wench) or a 'stallion' (a male prostitute) or (perhaps looking forward to Cleopatra's 'salad days') a 'scallion' (the delectable reading from the 'bad' quarto)? Even in a play like *Macbeth* which survives in one rather than three versions many such decisions must be made. But the editor's rigour in decisions about the prose and poetry is rarely matched by an equally careful treatment of stage directions. Rather, like many critics and teachers, editors regularly envisage Elizabethan plays as literary texts rather than theatrical playscripts, with predictable results. Those readers (e.g., theatrical professionals) who do read the plays as scripts often end up viewing the original effects through invisible barriers set up (often unwittingly) by the modern editor. Thus, the actor or director, although bringing valuable know-how to the reading of Elizabethan playscripts, is nonetheless conditioned both by the logic of the editor and the prevailing assumptions of much twentieth-century theatre (as with Poor Tom playing cold) with significant results for contemporary productions. The Nurse's intervention or Seyton's missing exit may puzzle or provoke the theatrical professional as much as the editor or critic. [...]

Let me clarify my working assumptions. To avoid the trap epitomised by the American lady's wrenching of *Macbeth* or the tug-of-war at the Oregon *King Lear*, the modern interpreter should make every possible effort to sidestep inappropriate assumptions, conventions, or expectations. A major part of this effort involves conceiving of the plays as staged events and consequently viewing the surviving documents as theatrical scripts rather than literary texts (thereby drawing upon the province of the theatrical professional) but with the understanding that the logic of the staging then (as with the Nurse's intervention as a 'womanish' side of Romeo or Seyton's possible continued presence) may differ significantly from the logic of staging or 'realism' now (thereby drawing upon the province of the critic or historian). Any inferences or conclusions, moreover, should be based upon the original evidence (thereby drawing upon the province of the editor), but that includes the original stage directions, not the adjustments made by editors and other scholars who may not be sympathetic to theatre then or now.

To some readers, my assumptions or precepts may sound straightforward, even self-evident, but, in fact, they create many problems [...] and considerable controversy. Critics, editors, theatrical professionals, stage historians, teachers – all constituent parts of the enormous 'Shakespeare industry', all confident that they know perfectly well what they are doing – often show minimal patience with or tolerance for alternative views. Attempts to build bridges are not always welcomed. My claims, moreover, posit a large role for the historian of drama who should be providing firm evidence about the original staging and conventions, a role that has not always been carried out successfully, both because of the nature of the evidence and, at times, some questionable assumptions on the part of the practitioners. So Shakespeare studies move (and will continue to move) merrily along – on parallel tracks to infinity.

But if we *start* with the assumption that there is much we will never know (e.g., what the stage at the Globe actually looked like to a spectator), we may be able to ascertain what *can* be discovered or recovered. [...]

A particularly disturbing feature of any study of staging and stage practice is that, quite simply, we have no way of knowing how much we do not know. When a word unknown to modern philologians survives in a Shakespeare play (e.g., the 'prenzie' Angelo, Caliban's 'scamels'), the critic or actor at least is aware of a gap in our knowledge (or a textual crux) and can consult learned notes in editions or journals. Similarly, we know we are missing something when we hear Pistol twice call out 'have we not Hiren here?' (2 *Henry IV*, II. iv.145, 158–9), apparently a famous line from a lost play, as well known then as 'To be or not to be' now. Again, when Hamlet tells Rosencrantz: 'Ay, sir, but "while the grass grows" – the proverb is something musty' (III. ii.329–30) or when Lady Macbeth castigates her back-sliding husband for 'letting "I dare not" wait upon "I would", / Like the poor cat i'th'adage'

(I. vii.44–5), we know that Shakespeare is expecting us to fill in the blanks with a proverb well known then albeit obscure today ('while the grass grows, the horse starves'; 'the cat would eat fish yet dare not wet its feet'). A reader without access to notes or Tilley's dictionary of proverbs[9] may have some difficulty making full sense out of these moments, but no alert reader will be unaware that something beyond the words themselves is being invoked or assumed, something presumably accessible to most of the original audience.

But when one turns to the stage practice and theatrical conventions of the past, especially in the plays of Shakespeare (which seem to speak to us so readily across the wide gap of time), the historian or director or critic or editor can never be sure when we are talking the same language, when we are sharing the same assumptions. To be sure, few readers today have difficulty with soliloquies, asides, disguises, eavesdropping scenes, even perhaps alarums and excursions (i.e., regular and recognisable features of Elizabethan plays), but even these well-known practices can cause problems for some sensibilities. Thus, several scholars have challenged modern 'realistic' assumptions about the aside. In his seminal study of the Globe plays, Bernard Beckerman notes that 'many asides give the actor neither time nor motivation for creating verisimilitude'. We often assume that, to deliver an aside, a Richard III or Hamlet or Othello must be distanced from the other figures on stage, but, drawing upon examples from *Pericles* and *Othello*, Beckerman argues that 'the Globe players, in the staging of asides, did not think in terms of creating an illusion of actuality but of relating the crucial elements of the narrative to each other'.[10] Or, as Ernest L. Rhodes has noted, 'the important thing was not the distance but the signal for the "aside", regardless of whether it was given by a movement on the stage, a gesture, by a special tone of the voice, or by all of these'.[11] The modern sensibility may expect some visible separation between the speaker and potential listeners, but if the deliverer of the aside is quite close to the other actors, the emphasis may fall not upon his deceptive speaking but rather upon their faulty listening, an effect demonstrably present in many moral interludes and used adroitly for sardonic comic purposes repeatedly in *Volpone*. Is, then, the gap between aside speaker and listener 'real' or conventional or symbolic?

To confront this and other such questions one must first arrive at a working definition of 'theatrical convention', so let me turn to the useful discussion of that term by Raymond Williams.[12] A convention, for Williams, 'is simply the terms upon which author, performers and audience agree to meet, so that the performance may be carried on'. Such agreement, he notes, 'is by no means always a formal or definite process' but rather 'is largely customary, and often indeed it is virtually unconscious'; this consent, moreover, 'must usually *precede* the performance, so that what is to be done may be accepted without damaging friction'. Those attuned to a set of conventions (e.g., 'that the speech and action should as closely as possible appear to be those of everyday life') often do not recognise their conventions as such, rather equating their familiar procedures with 'what a play is like' or 'the sort of thing a play tries to do', yet, as Williams notes, what could be more illogical than seeing actors who supposedly 'represent people behaving naturally, and usually privately', standing in front of 'a large audience, while all the time maintaining the illusion that, as characters, these persons are unaware of the audience's presence'. Similarly, an actor 'can speak to us, acknowledging his most private thoughts, and we will agree that while we hear him from the back of the gallery, he cannot be heard by a man a few feet away from him, or waiting in the wings'. Although in the cold light of day we might question these and other effects, in the theatre 'we do not challenge them. We accept; we agree; these are the conventions'.

Consider the many cinematic conventions to which we give such unthinking consent. To audiences today, cinema may represent the epitome of realism, yet if we can, for a moment, examine our own assumptions, what is 'real' about sitting in a darkened auditorium, watching figures larger than life (especially in 'close-ups') projected onto a flat screen and seen through camera angles that often do not correspond to our normal viewing range, while listening to voices, not from the lips of the speakers, that boom around us in stereophonic sound accompanied by music from a full orchestra? Yet 'We accept; we agree; these are the conventions'. Again, modern readers of Elizabethan plays may chuckle at the narrative shorthand provided by a choric figure like Time in *The Winter's Tale* or a stage direction like *exit at one door and enter at another* (to indicate a quick change in time or locale), but at the cinema that same individual will have no difficulty recognising moving calendar pages as the passage of time, accepting necessary exposition from the headlines of newspapers, or inferring the whole of a journey from seeing a figure get on a plane in one airport and get off in another. Granted, the camera can provide far more detail for the viewer of cinema or television than could be presented on the Elizabethan stage, but complex events (a long journey, the flight of an arrow) still require a selectivity in presentation that enlists our conventional responses, while in any medium exposition of essential information without some form of narrative shorthand proves very cumbersome.

One of my goals [...] therefore is to reconstruct or recover some Elizabethan playhouse conventions in the hope of determining more fully the terms upon which dramatists, actors, and spectators 'agreed to meet'. My emphasis is not upon familiar devices that function relatively smoothly in modern productions (e.g., the soliloquy, the aside, impenetrable disguise) but rather upon techniques or procedures that appear to us odd, illogical, or intrusive. In such anomalies may lie important clues to the basic assumptions that characterised theatregoers in the age of Shakespeare.

To clarify such assumptions, however, is no easy matter. The original playgoers have left us little evidence; the extant comments from the dramatists about their craft (e.g., various prefaces, Heywood's *Apology for Actors*) are not especially revealing or instructive. Certainly, the most telling insights are to be found in the choric passages of *Henry V*. In the justly famous Prologue, Shakespeare's spokesman apologises for the limits of 'this unworthy scaffold' in conveying 'so great an object' as Agincourt; still, the players can 'on your imaginary forces work' if the viewers are willing to 'suppose', to 'make imaginary puissance' by dividing one man into a thousand parts, to 'think, when we talk of horses, that you see them / Printing their proud hoofs i'th'receiving earth', in short, to 'piece out our imperfections with your thoughts'. Again, the Chorus to Act III pleads with the audience to 'suppose', 'behold', 'do but think', 'grapple your minds', 'work, work your thoughts, and therein see a siege', and, finally, 'still be kind, / And eke out our performance with your mind'. Before Agincourt, the Chorus to Act IV apologises in advance for disgracing this great event 'with four or five most vile and ragged foils, / Right ill-disposed in brawl ridiculous', but asks the audience: 'Yet sit and see, / Minding true things by what their mock'ries be'. Repeatedly, Shakespeare asks his audience to accept a part for the whole, to supply imaginatively what cannot be introduced physically onto the open stage.

This apologetic stance, especially when coupled with the strictures of purists like Sidney and Jonson, would seem to suggest severe constraints upon what could be introduced onto the Globe stage. But given the available conventions or shared assumptions (at least in the public theatres), such limits seem to evaporate. For example, consider battle scenes, surely among the most difficult to realise effectively on any stage. Sidney could mock 'two Armies ... represented with four swords and bucklers';[13] Jonson could sneer at the players who 'with three rusty swords, / And help of some few foot-and-half-foot words, / Fight over *York*, and *Lancaster's* long jars: / And in the tiring-house bring wounds, to scars'. Shakespeare himself, as already noted, was conscious of the danger of lapsing into the 'brawl ridiculous' in presenting Agincourt through only 'four or five most vile and ragged foils'. Nonetheless, rather than avoiding battle scenes, the Lord Chamberlain's Men and the other companies found practical solutions. As Alfred Harbage observes: 'The audience did not see the battles so much as hear them. What it saw was displays of skill by two or occasionally four combatants on that small sector of the battlefield symbolised by the stage.' In addition, the players made adept use of *alarums* or off-stage sound effects ('a gong insistently clanging, trumpets blaring recognisable military signals, then steel clashing, ordnance firing') and *excursions* ('individual pursuits and combats onstage').[14] Thus, from *Captain Thomas Stukeley: 'Alarum is sounded, diverse excursions, Stukeley pursues Shane O'Neill and Neil Mackener, and after a good pretty fight his Lieutenant and Ancient rescue Stukeley, and chase the Irish out. Then an excursion betwixt Herbert and O'Hanlon, and so a retreat sounded*' (ll. 1170–5). Through such theatrical synecdoche, the whole of a battle is to be imagined or inferred through the parts displayed, an approach to mass combat well suited to a large platform stage and limited personnel.

Not all Elizabethan spectators, however, were willing to make this imaginative leap and 'be kind' to the 'imperfections' or 'mock'ries' presented on the open stage. Sidney, for one, argues that 'many things may be told which cannot be showed' if dramatists would only observe 'the difference betwixt reporting and representing'.[15] Some popular dramatists did substitute a Chorus for the sweep of staged action, as in *Henry V* or *I The Fair Maid of the West* where Heywood's Chorus laments: 'Our Stage so lamely can express a Sea / That we are forc'd by *Chorus* to discourse / What should have been in action' (II, 319). Elsewhere, dramatists often used dumb shows to bring complex events on stage, as in *Edmond Ironside* where the Chorus would prefer to have the audience 'see the battles acted on the stage' but since 'their length will be too tedious / Then in dumb shows I will explain at large / Their fights, their flights and Edmond's victory' (ll. 970–3). But most popular drama before and after Sidney's strictures ranged widely in space and time (e. g., Shakespeare's *I Henry VI, Antony and Cleopatra, Pericles*, and *The Winter's Tale*) and brought on stage exciting events that would seem to pose insuperable difficulties. Thus, in his argument on behalf of the classical *nuntius* Sidney remarks: 'I may speak (though I am here) of *Peru*, and in speech digress from that to the description of *Calicut*; but in action I cannot represent it without *Pacolet's* horse.'[16] Yet in the closing moments of *The Travels of the Three English Brothers*, John Day does introduce a version of Pacolet's horse: a prospective glass that enables the three brothers and their father, widely dispersed in different countries, to see and communicate with each other. Despite the position taken by figures like Sidney and the practical limitations of the stage, Elizabethan dramatists, players, and audiences clearly relished big scenes and effects that would seem to us to burst the bounds of the unworthy scaffold.

As a representative example, consider a 'mission impossible' sequence from Fletcher's *The Island Princess* (VIII, 106–18) where Armusia and his men rescue the King of Sidore from a supposedly impregnable island. First, Fletcher shows us the wicked Governor taunting the king in his prison; next, Armusia and his group appear '*like Merchants, arm'd underneath*' to reveal that they have rented a cellar adjacent to the Governor's storehouse of gunpowder. With their departure the confident Governor enters with a captain; in rapid succession follow an off-stage explosion, a bell ringing, a citizen shouting 'fire, fire', the returning captain with news of the castle and its wealth in danger, more citizens, a call for buckets, and a mass *exeunt*. Armusia and his man appear for a few lines ('Let it flame on') followed by a brief appearance of captain and citizens ('more water, more water'), perhaps with buckets (none are specified). Then: '*Enter Armusia and his company breaking open a Door*'; they discover the king, break his chain, drive off the guards, and depart for their boat. The sequence concludes with comic comments from some citizens and their wives, followed by a final appearance of the Governor and his men to recount what has happened. The key to the successful plot and rescue is the diversion, but neither the fire nor the quenching of the fire can be shown directly on the Elizabethan stage. But through a combination of sound effects, vivid reports, exits and entrances, and alternating scenes Fletcher has provided all the excitement of such a fire as an appropriate and telling context for the daring rescue. In a good production, a spectator presumably would 'believe' in the fire and the stratagem without actually witnessing the flames, burning buildings, and a bucket brigade throwing water (effects possible in cinema or nineteenth-century theatre).

Or consider *Fortune by Land and Sea* where Heywood brings onto the platform stage a battle between two ships at sea (VI, 410–18). After '*a great Alarum and shot*', the two pirates, Purser and Clinton, enter with prisoners from their most recent conquest. Once the stage has been cleared, young Forrest appears '*like a Captain of a ship, with Sailors and Mariners, entering with a flourish*'; a boy is told to 'climb to the main-top' to 'see what you ken there'; '*Above*', the boy calls out 'a sail' and shouts down details; Forrest instructs his gunner, steersman, master, and boatswain; '*a piece goes off*' when the pirates raise their colours (as reported by the boy above). Again, with the stage cleared, Purser and Clinton return '*with their Mariners, all furnished with Sea devices fitting for a fight*'; they urge on their gunner ('Oh 'twas a gallant shot, I saw it shatter some of their limbs in pieces'), and debate strategy. Again, Heywood switches to Forrest exhorting his men not to spare the powder. Finally, '*a great Alarum, and Flourish. Enter Young Forrest and his Mates with Purser and Clinton with their Mariners prisoners.*' As in *The Island Princess*, the key to the effect lies in the combination of alternating scenes and appropriate signals: the boy above, nautical language, costume (e.g., Forrest '*like a Captain of a ship*'), and sound effects, along with the reported action. There is no evidence that shots are actually fired on stage (although there is considerable talk of guns and gunnery), but there is frenzied activity, much noise, and presentation of '*Sea devices fitting for a fight*', all appropriate for two ships in battle at sea.

My two examples from Fletcher and Heywood display the problems posed by fire and water on the Elizabethan stage and the solutions found if such moments were to be represented rather than reported.[17] Remember too the shipwrecks so important for romance plots but so difficult to present at the Globe. In itself, a storm at sea posed no greater difficulty than a storm on land, calling for sound effects and appropriate acting and dialogue. Thus, Pericles is to enter '*a-shipboard*' (III. i.o.s.d.) and describe the storm for the audience; this storm and its equivalent in *The Tempest*, Act I, scene i, are then followed by the speeches of figures on shore recounting what has happened. But to provide an actual shipwreck on the open stage is another matter indeed. Thus, at the outset of *The Tempest* Shakespeare provides a shouting match between the boatswain and the courtiers, mariners who enter '*wet*' and crying 'all lost', hasty exits, '*a confused noise within*', and Gonzalo's 'we split, we split, we split!' In contrast, Heywood (ordinarily the dramatist least inhibited by the limits of the unworthy scaffold) at least twice conveys a shipwreck by concentrating upon the recently completed action. Thus, in *The Captives* Palestra is to enter '*all wet as newly shipwrecked and escaped the fury of the seas*' (ll. 653–4), while in *The Four Prentices of London* a reported shipwreck is followed by dumb shows that display Godfrey '*as newly landed and half naked*', Guy '*all wet*', and Charles '*all wet with his sword*' (II, 176–7). The stage direction from *The Thracian Wonder* is worth quoting at length, if only for its insights into 'playing wet': '*Enter old Antimon bringing in Ariadne shipwrecked, the Clown turning the child up and down, and wringing the Clouts. They pass over the Stage. Exeunt. Enter Radagon all wet, looking about for shelter as shipwrecked. Enter to him Titterus, seems to question him, puts off his Hat and Coat, and puts on him, so guides him off. Exeunt. Storm cease*' (B4v). In these three examples (as opposed to *The Tempest*, I. i), the spectator has been shown not the action itself (the shipwreck) but the results or effects of that action (figures '*as shipwrecked*' or '*as newly landed and half naked*' or '*all wet*'). To borrow terms from *Henry V*, the viewer is being asked to 'work, work your thoughts, and therein see a siege', a shipwreck, a diversionary fire, or a battle at sea, thereby 'Minding true things by what their mock'ries be'.

Let me conclude with a particularly revealing moment, Heywood's rendition of the death of Nessus the centaur in *The Brazen Age* (III, 180–2). Here, one would suppose, is an event too complex to be enacted on the open stage, for it involves (1) Nessus carrying Dejanira on his back across a river and (2) Hercules then shooting an arrow across that river to kill the centaur. How does Heywood do it? First, after the departure of Nessus and Dejanira, Hercules, alone on stage, describes for the audience their progress through the water ('well plunged bold centaur') but then must rage impotently as he witnesses the attempted rape and hears his bride cry for help (four times). Finally, Hercules announces: 'I'll send till I can come, this poisonous shaft / Shall speak my fury and extract thy blood, / Till I myself can cross this raging flood.' The stage direction then reads: '*Hercules shoots, and goes in: Enter Nessus with an arrow through him, and Dejanira.*' Moments later, 'after long struggling with Evenus' streams', Hercules reappears to 'make an end of what my shaft begun'. To depict a figure on one side of a river shooting a figure on the other side, Heywood has resorted to rapidly alternating scenes, reported action, off-stage sounds, and, most important (in his version of what in our age has become a stock cinematic effect), a presentation of the initiation and then the immediate resolution of the central event ('*Hercules shoots ... Enter Nessus with an arrow through him*') rather than the full sequence (the complete flight of the arrow and the striking of its target). If the choric passages from *Henry V* provide the 'theory' behind the open stage (e.g., that the audience is expected to use their imaginary forces to 'eke out our performance with your mind'), the arrow in Nessus provides a telling demonstration of the resulting theatrical practice. The spectator sees (1) the shooting of the arrow and (2) the result but then must supply (3) the connection between the two (I am assuming that Nessus enters immediately at another door), including any sense of the river and the distance involved. For the scene to work, the actors must provide the timing and energy, the audience, the imaginative participation.

To readers concerned primarily with Shakespeare's major plays, my examples from Heywood, Fletcher, and lesser dramatists may appear unrepresentative, tangential, even bizarre. But Shakespeare also provides an arrow-shooting scene, one with a decidedly allegorical emphasis (*Titus Andronicus*, IV. iii), just as he provides off-stage sea battles (e.g., 2 *Henry VI*, IV. i, *Antony and Cleopatra*, III. x, IV. xii), storms, and various spectacular effects. My goal in invoking such moments is not to reduce Shakespeare's plays to their lowest common denominator but rather to establish what effects were possible, even likely, on the open stage and what assumptions were shared then by dramatist, actor, and spectator. What *were* the terms upon which they agreed to meet? And how are we to recognise them? Perhaps we will never be able to recover more than a fraction of what was shared then, but even that fraction may help us avoid indulging in the kind of misguided modern detective work based upon Elizabethan clues epitomised in extreme form by Thurber's American lady.

And herein lies the value of taking seriously the arrow in Nessus. Initially, this stage direction may seem quaint or silly, worthy only of amused contempt, but we should remember that Heywood, like Fletcher and Shakespeare, was a working professional linked to a specific theatrical company who not only knew his craft well but also knew his theatre from the inside, both its potential and its limits. If we chuckle at the arrow in Nessus, we are implicitly asserting our superiority to a 'primitive' dramaturgy ('how could anyone be expected to believe that?') and, in the process, revealing more about ourselves (e.g., how we read playscripts) than about the Elizabethans. If we are not responsive to this and other such moments (e.g., Jupiter descending on an eagle, Gloucester's 'suicide' at Dover Cliffs), are we not in danger of reconceiving the plays to suit our sensibilities, of rewriting the clues to suit our solutions? Certainly, I would not defend *The Brazen Age* as a long lost masterpiece, but it *is* highly representative of one major strain in Jacobean drama (i.e., the kind of sensational play associated with the Red Bull playhouse) and can thereby tell us much about *their* assumptions and predilections. Are we to characterise the theatre or theatrical conventions of another age by the moments that make the best immediate sense to us, that cause us the least discomfort, or, in contrast, can we best understand a theatre other than our own by concentrating upon those moments that do cause us problems and therefore make us conscious of the gaps between then and now (e.g., the wearing of masks in classical drama, the parting of the Red Sea in a Corpus Christi play)? For me, the key to understanding what is distinctive about drama in the age of Shakespeare lies in the anomalies, the surprises, the moments that make us aware of the full stretch of the dramaturgy. To confront the plays squarely, in short, is to confront the arrow in Nessus.

From Alan C. Dessen, *Elizabethan Stage Conventions and Modern Interpreters* (Cambridge, 1984), pp. 1–18.

NOTES

[Alan C. Dessen's study of Elizabethan stage conventions takes as its starting point the contention that a contemporary reader or spectator often misreads Renaissance theatrical texts as a result of their conditioning in realist techniques of spatial and scenic representation, narrative exposition, and character development. Invoking Raymond Williams's definition of theatrical conventions as the terms upon which dramatists, actors and audiences 'agree to meet', Dessen focuses upon devices that may now appear bizarre, ludicrous or incomprehensible in order to stress the Elizabethan drama's estrangement from realism, and argues that a properly historical and theatrical understanding of it will confront its strangeness rather than attempt to explain it away. All quotations from Shakespeare in the extract are from *The Complete Pelican Shakespeare*, ed. Alfred Harbage (Baltimore, MD, 1969). Ed.]

1. Bernard Beckerman, *Dynamics of Drama* (New York, 1970), p. 3.
2. Nahum Tate, *The History of King Lear*, Regents Restoration Drama Series, ed. James Black (Lincoln, NE, 1975), p. 1.
3. John Dryden, 'Preface, the Grounds of Criticism in Tragedy', *Of Dramatic Poesy and Other Critical Essays*, ed. George Watson (London and New York, 1961), vol. 1, p. 240.
4. James Thurber, *The Thurber Carnival* (New York and London, 1945), pp. 60–3.
5. Brian Gibbons (ed.), The Arden Shakespeare *Romeo and Juliet* (London and New York, 1980), p. 180.
6. George Walton Williams, 'The Year's Contributions to Shakespearian Study: Textual Studies', *Shakespeare Survey*, 34 (1981), 188.
7. Alan Brissenden, '*Romeo and Juliet*, III. iii. 108: The Nurse and the Dagger', *Notes and Queries*, NS, 28 (1981), 126–7.
8. The Padua *Macbeth*, a Folio text apparently annotated for use in a seventeenth-century amateur performance, does add to or expand the original stage directions, especially in Act V, but does not indicate an exit and re-entry for Seyton here. See G. Blakemore Evans (ed.), *Shakespearean Prompt-books of the Seventeenth Century*, 5 vols (Charlottesville, VA, 1960), vol. I, Part i.
9. Morris Palmer Tilley, *A Dictionary of the Proverbs in England in the Sixteenth and Seventeenth Centuries* (Ann Arbor, MI, 1966).
10. Bernard Beckerman, *Shakespeare at the Globe 1599–1609* (New York, 1962), pp. 161–2.
11. Ernest L. Rhodes, *Henslowe's Rose: The Stage and Staging* (The University Press of Kentucky, 1976), p. 164.
12. Raymond Williams, *Drama from Ibsen to Brecht* (London, 1968), pp. 12–16. For more general treatments of 'convention' (not limited to theatrical contexts), see David K. Lewis, *Convention: A Philosophical Study* (Cambridge, MA, 1969); and Lawrence Manley, *Convention 1500–1750* (Cambridge, MA and London, 1980). In an early classic study, M. C. Bradbrook defines convention 'as an agreement between writers and readers, whereby the artist is allowed to limit and simplify his material in order to secure greater concentration through a control

of the distribution of emphasis' (*Themes and Conventions of Elizabethan Tragedy* [Cambridge, 1935; rpt. 1960], p. 4). For a provocative study with an emphasis upon 'character' and 'reality' see Robert R. Hellenga, 'Elizabethan Dramatic Conventions and Elizabethan Reality', *Renaissance Drama*, NS, 12 (1981), 27–49.

13. Sidney, 'An Apologie for Poetrie', in *Elizabethan Critical Essays*, ed. C. Gregory Smith, 2 vols (Oxford, 1904), vol. I, p. 197.

14. Alfred Harbage, *Theatre for Shakespeare* (Toronto, 1955), p. 52.

15. Sidney, 'Apologie', p. 198.

16. Ibid.

17. For other 'difficult' scenes involving fire and water, see Heywood's rendition of Horatius at the bridge (*The Rape of Lucrece*), Fletcher's version of the battle at sea (*The Double Marriage*), Nero looking on while Rome burns (*The Tragedy of Nero*), and, perhaps strangest of all, the on-stage rescue by a ship of a man marooned on a rock (*The Hector of Germany*).

3

The Rhetoric of Performance Criticism

W. B. WORTHEN

> ... My own major interest has always been Shakespeare in the theatre; and to that my written work has been, in my own mind, subsidiary. But my experience as actor, producer and play-goer leaves me uncompromising in my assertion that the literary analysis of great drama in terms of theatrical technique accomplishes singularly little. Such technicalities should be confined to the theatre from which their terms are drawn. The proper thing to do about a play's dramatic quality is to produce it, to act in it, to attend performances; but the penetration of its deeper meanings is a different matter, and such a study, though the commentator should certainly be dramatically aware, and even wary, will not itself speak in theatrical terms.[1]

I would like to pause briefly over these remarks, taken from the preface to G. Wilson Knight's *The Wheel of Fire*, in order to raise the general question of the relation between 'text' and 'performance' in Shakspearean 'performance criticism'. An 'actor, producer and play-goer', Knight candidly describes the difficulty of assimilating commentary on the dramatic text to the 'dramatic quality' that can be seized only in performance. Yet while Knight finds this 'dramatic quality' to be producible only in the language of the stage, he also finds that 'theatrical technique' is incapable of penetrating to the 'deeper meanings' available to 'literary analysis'. This is an arresting limitation. It seems that critical commentary can disclose the text's 'deeper meanings' precisely because it is not coextensive with the text it represents. Performance, on the other hand, is naturalised to the drama, and so exhausts the play's 'dramatic quality' at the moment the text is staged. Conceived not as a discourse for representing the text but as a 'technique' for realising the drama onstage, performance can only reiterate the text in its own technical terms. As a result, 'performance criticism' – the 'literary analysis of great drama in terms of theatrical technique' – fails to approach the play's 'deeper meanings' because the 'theatrical technique' it imitates is not itself seen to be critical, invasive, interpretive. 'Performance criticism' becomes an expendable enterprise, offering neither the 'meanings' of literary criticism nor insight into the truly 'dramatic quality' provided by performance.

Knight trains our attention on a basic problem in dramatic criticism, one that has now preoccupied Shakespeare studies for decades: how to relate the signification of the dramatic text to the practices of performance. What is surprising, though, is that the extensive 'tradition' of performance criticism – reaching, it has been argued, from Granville-Barker's *Prefaces to Shakespeare* and the early work of M. C. Bradbrook through the more recent work of John Russell Brown, J. L. Styan, Bernard Beckerman, Michael Goldman, and others – has been more successful in reifying Knight's polarity between text and performance than in suspending it.[2] The cultural authority of 'Shakespeare' (which includes but exceeds Shakespeare's plays) has shaped the text/performance question in Shakespeare studies, marked as it is by the desire to identify and conserve the authority of the text in performance. Despite an impressive body of scholarship, in some respects performance criticism remains stalled at Knight's impasse, bound by an opposition between a 'subsidiary' critical practice and a conception of performance – and so of performance criticism – natural to the 'detextualised' practices of the theatre.[3] This covert, perhaps unrecognised, opposition has prevented performance criticism from developing an acknowledged complex of aims, methods, theoretical consequences, and principles of persuasion. The text/performance dichotomy, and the interpretive priorities and assumptions it governs, stands at the centre of the disciplinary ambiguity that characterises performance criticism *as* criticism. More important, it prevents performance criticism from pursuing what I take to be its justifying critical agenda: to locate the space and practice of criticism in relation to the practices of performance.

We need only recall Lamb's criticism of the role of Lear ('essentially impossible to be represented on a stage') and Hunt's remarks on Kean's Othello ('the masterpiece of the living stage'), Jonson's and

Shakespeare's attitudes toward play publication, or Aristotle's discrimination between drama (plot, character, diction, thought) and spectacle, to be reminded that text and performance have long seemed to compete for legitimacy as means of representing the drama.[4] In our era the critical derogation of performance is usually, and somewhat unfairly, charged to the widespread influence of the New Criticism. New Criticism treated the drama in terms of its normative literary genre – the lyric – and so presented the dramatic text as a verbal icon. Applying its powerful interpretive technology to formal, verbal, thematic, and generic features taken to be determined by the text, New Criticism necessarily discredited stage performance – as well as criticism speaking 'in theatrical terms' – as extrinsic to a play's literary design. While New Critical practice sharply discriminated against stage performance as a means of interpreting the dramatic text, performance did have an oddly important function in New Critical thinking. Despite its investment in the text as a closed, organically coherent system, the 'heresy of paraphrase' implicit in much New Critical writing and pedagogy points to the reader's engaged performance of the poem as one that should exceed and enrich the formal, verbal, and thematic determinations of critical analysis. Of course, New Criticism placed strict limitations on the validity of interpretation generated by reading-as-performance. For as performance, reading was naturalised to the text's internal dynamics, seen as a mode of recovering meanings rather than as a means of producing the text in a different order of signification. Unlike reading, in this sense, stage performance enlarges on the text, forces it to speak in languages that often exceed the determinations of the words on the page. 'In acted drama', Brooks and Heilman remind their readers, 'we have costumes, settings, and "properties"; but drama as literature has no such appurtenances.'[5] To the New Critical temperament, theatrical performance and a criticism derived from it must seem ungrounded, a kind of interpretive free play. [...][6]

'Performance criticism' seeks to replace 'textual' interpretation with 'performance' and its criticism as a means of representing the drama's truly 'dramatic quality'. But the persistence of the 'text against performance' question points to an ongoing interdependence between 'performance' and 'literary' critical modes. Performance criticism can define a 'sense of the authentic' precisely because it regards performance as preserving an authentic text; this 'text' is, of course, the product of the 'literary' critical practice it often claims to dislodge.[7] Many versions of performance criticism avowedly locate performance (and so 'performance criticism') as supplemental to the designs of the text, mapping the text's meanings onto the histrionic and pictorial relationships of the stage. I am thinking here of most treatments of 'subtext' in Shakespearean characterisation, metadramatic and metatheatrical criticism, iconographical readings of stage imagery, and what might be called 'directorial criticism' – the idealised description of how a Shakespeare play might orchestrate the conventions of the Elizabethan theatre on the modern stage in order to recover 'the Shakespeare experience'. James H. Kavanagh rightly implies that the assumptions about both text and performance saturating this 'ostensibly alternative "stagecraft" commentary' tend 'to produce a kind of paraliterary ideological discourse', one that casts the stage in a lapsed relation to the authority of the 'literary' text.[8] By displaying the privileged status of textual to performance signification, such criticism not only extends New Critical attitudes toward the drama but also sidesteps the definitive challenges that a performance criticism ought to address: how the text is traced and transgressed both by theatrical and by critical strategies for producing it as drama.

These versions of Shakespearean performance criticism have been, and should continue to be, deservedly influential in our thinking about text/performance relations; in many respects they represent the most scrupulous engagement with the problems of how texts operate in performance that we have available to us. But by grounding meaning – even performed meaning – in the text, such criticism itself runs the risk of being repudiated by the more polemical version of performance criticism that I wish to address here (and which forms the body of work I will refer to as 'performance criticism' in the remainder of this essay). The kind of criticism I have in mind grounds itself in the drama's theatrical 'origin' as a means of displacing textual interpretation, either by limiting interpretation to the presumed capacities of Elizabethan performance practice or, more often, by contextualising the play within a universal definition of the purposes, forms, and meaning of enactment. This more insistent 'performance criticism' also accepts the New Critical valuation of a 'text against performance' but simply reverses the terms of the question, urging the priority of the lively and spontaneous performance over the 'impractical' insights reached by criticism (even, many times, the insights of 'iconographic' or 'directorial' criticism). As Richard David has it, 'It is for this reason that half (I sometimes think all) the subtleties exposed by commentators are not, as actors would say, "practical"'; if 'meaning' can't be played, it 'cannot be integral to the drama as drama'.[9] As an object of inquiry, 'performance' is marked out as a special zone of individual expression, a kind of wild semiology set apart from the institutional practices that govern criticism and that inform signifying practices in the culture at large.

This brand of performance criticism has driven the wholesale adoption of the 'theatrical dimension' in Shakespeare pedagogy and criticism. Yet despite the salutary effects of conceiving Shakespearean drama as theatre, in practice this mode of performance criticism has significant liabilities and limitations. Granted, John Russell Brown's complaint (of 1962) that 'Critics, trained in literary disciplines, are apt to think that theatrical experience is coarse and vulgar' has been fully replaced by Richard David's 'commonplace of criticism' that 'Shakespeare's plays were written for the theatre, and only in the theatre develop their full impact'.[10] But has this 'shift from page to stage, from analysis of the plays as literature to a new interest in the plays as performance',[11] produced a substantive change in our thinking about text/performance? Writing in the 1984 *Shakespeare Quarterly* special issue devoted to teaching Shakespeare, Homer Swander takes a path-breaking position: 'To read a script well is to discover what at each moment it tells the actor or actors to do'; 'Shakespeare's words, deliberately designed by a theatrical genius for a thrust stage with live actors and an immediately responding audience, cannot be satisfactorily explored or experienced in any medium but his own.'[12] In order to understand what the text 'tells an actor or actors to do', however, we must regard 'acting' as both an interpretive and a signifying practice, articulating a dialogic relationship between the text and the *mise-en-scène*, and between the *mise-en-scène* and the audience. How does acting reproduce a text? How does the actors' training enable them to conceive the text as *telling* them to *do* anything in particular? How does a range of perceived acting opportunities constitute a strategy for reading the play *as* actable, as representable to an audience in the theatre? A similar line of questioning might, of course, be trained on directors, designers, and so on, but that's not the point. As the history of theatre demonstrates, stage performance always requires a highly formalised body of activities: techniques for training and preparation; conventions of acting and staging style; habits of audience disposition, behaviour, and interpretation. Richly diverse and historically localised, these practices articulate the text as 'acting' within the wider range of signifying behaviour specific to a given theatre and culture. Swander's view of 'dramatic quality' appears to oppose the New Critical priority of text-to-performance but in fact duplicates it: while the text produced by criticism is irrelevant to the stage, the performance-text speaks directly to the actors through a privileged 'technique', one that retains textual authority precisely by emptying 'performance' of its interpretive, textualising, ideological function.

John Russell Brown is more blunt about it: 'Readers and critics have become increasingly aware that the plays were written for performance and reveal their true natures only in performance.'[13] A shaping force in performance criticism, Brown is careful to recognise the historical specificity of acting, the difference between Shakespeare's actors and our own. Recently, for example, he reminds us that 'modern actors are not those Elizabethan and Jacobean actors for whom Shakespeare wrote his plays and that they bring to rehearsals many prejudices and skills which Shakespeare could not have imagined and lack others that he took for granted'; indeed, he concludes that 'the same argument can be levelled against any reading of the plays. No one person can reconstruct a historically accurate response, even if we could know what that might be.'[14] Fair enough. But Brown's recognition leads not to an inspection of modern acting's historical and cultural contingency but to an effort to essentialise the relation between modern acting and the authority of Shakespeare. For, like Knight perhaps, Brown assigns the difference between Elizabethan and modern acting to the level of technique, a stylistic difference that only masks the fundamental identity between all modes of performance, governed as they are by the inherent qualities of Shakespeare's text:

> Perhaps Elizabethan actors were cruder or more eloquent, or more formalised and less lifelike, than their modern counterparts, but every actor who steps onto a stage has to bring a whole self into play and must relate what is spoken to what is there, palpably, before the audience. No actor can cheat for very long; incomplete performances, or those which have some elements at odds with others, will be recognised for what they are by audiences and by fellow actors. *We need have little doubt that modern actors are responding to qualities inherent in Shakespeare's text*; if they did not, they would find acting in his plays a troublesome labour and not a great pleasure.[15]

Garrick, Irving, and Olivier each applied a different histrionic technology to their roles, methods of interpretation and of signification that not only required different acts of attention from their audiences but conveyed markedly different ideologies of action, character, and meaning. To preserve the unchanging 'true natures' of Shakespeare's texts in performance, Brown must present the true nature of performance as equally inert, unaffected by alterations in the condition of the stage, in the social function of theatre and theatricality, in styles of acting on and offstage – regardless of how deeply acting may be implicated in local conceptions of the subject, the self, human identity and action: 'His theatre was different from any we know today, but the essential act of performance was the same.'[16]

Although it questions the adequacy of 'literary' interpretation in order to advance stage-oriented readings, this sense of performance casts the *mise-en-scène* as a vehicle for reproducing the authority of the text, a text whose 'dramatic quality' is both determined and recovered through a universal and transparent stage technique. To put it more generally, such 'performance criticism' naturalises the *mise-en-scène* as an ideal zone of realisation, iterating meanings 'written for' its operation, rather than conceiving it as a rhetoric for strategically producing the drama as theatre. Despite the claim that it legitimates performance as a mode of inquiry independent of both 'literary' criticism and its 'text', performance criticism of this kind represses the rhetorical character of performance and so conceals its relation to other, similarly institutional, means of producing textual significance.

Some consequences of this conception of 'performance' – that actors 'realise' the text rather than produce it – are dramatised by the highly regarded television series 'Playing Shakespeare'. The aim of the series is not, of course, to provide access to live Shakespearean theatre, to the kind of event that performance criticism should legitimately address. Indeed, rather than staging Shakespearean performance, 'Playing Shakespeare' stages 'performance criticism' itself and richly illustrates how the assumptions of performance criticism sustain critical, interpretive, and pedagogical practice. Playing the part of avuncular critic/director, John Barton repeatedly urges his actors to discover the 'infinite' interpretive freedom at their disposal through a scrupulous reading of 'the text' and its 'ambiguities'. And yet any viewer of the series must feel that the performances and Barton's direction are far from infinite in their variety. Indeed, Barton's illustration of the divergence between criticism and theatre provides an arresting instance of the ideological complicity between his directorial practice and the 'literary' notions he repudiates. In the 'Set Speeches and Soliloquies' episode Barton invites David Suchet to read a convoluted passage of criticism 'from one of the world's leading theatrical magazines'. The passage begins,

> This ambiguity is one of the significant aesthetic counterparts of the broad philosophic drift defining the modern age ... In theatre, *Hamlet* predicts this epistemologic tradition ... The execution of the deed steadily loses way to a search for the personal modality of the deed ...

and continues on for a few more heavily edited sentences.[17] The passage is hardly amusing; it is, of course, the manner in which it is produced in Barton's lecture/performance that makes it funny, that determines its performed meaning for us. In part the text's emphatically 'academic' quality seems inflated, pretentious in contrast to Barton's ingratiatingly low-key style. But the passage becomes funnier in Suchet's delivery, for he not only hectors us, he speaks in what – to me at least – sounds like an oddly aggressive, distinctly American accent, one perhaps touched by a trace of Brooklynese – 'duh leading uhsthetic problem'. This is, in fact, a notable instance of the 'textualising' function of performance style. The choice of dialect here can hardly claim to arise solely from the text. Instead, the dialect suggests that this voice speaks in the wrong accents, accents that mark its critical perspective – its origin in America, and in 'literary' study – as unspeakable in the powerful, legitimating sonorities of the RSC style. How the passage becomes textualised by performance largely determines how we will decode it, and so determines what we will take it to mean. Spoken in the wrong accent, it must be saying the wrong thing.

Barton then turns to Michael Pennington, about to deliver Hamlet's 'To be, or not to be' soliloquy, and says, 'Michael, come and follow that'. Pennington first gives an underplayed, obviously 'intellectualised' reading, one that seems to illustrate the unsatisfying results of following the dictates of an overabstract and literary conception of the part. Then Pennington gives the soliloquy a second try. Following Barton's direction to 'share it with us', to 'open himself to his audience', Pennington gives a lively reading, broadening his range of movement, and making explicit contact with the audience offstage. In other words, Pennington produces the speech through our contemporary conventions of Shakespearean stage characterisation: a concentration on psychological motivation complicated by a degree of openness to the theatre audience, the post-Brechtian compromise between 'realistic' and 'theatrical' characterisation typical of the RSC since the mid-1960s. The results here are, however, confusing, despite Barton's enthusiasm and the elegance of Pennington's enactment. For Pennington's performance, oddly enough, seems to conform to the thematics of character described by the vulgar American. Both Pennington and his 'Hamlet' seem engaged in a 'search for the personal modality of the deed' in the public confines of the stage, a search typical of 'the leading aesthetic problem of the actor in the modern theatre – the interpretation of action through characterologic nuance'.[18] (This reading is actually emphasised by the 'textualising' work of the camera, which after showing Pennington full-length in front of an approving audience, shortly closes to a head shot, stressing the interiority of Pennington's performance.) The point here isn't that the critic is really in the right, or that Pennington's performance 'illustrates' such critical conclusions about *Hamlet*. It's that theatrical practice – the production of 'character' as an effect of 'acting', in this case – is not an unconstrained means of realising the text but a practice related to other modes of cultural transmission, signification, and interpretation. The acting that Barton praises as a matter of 'common-sense rather than of interpretation' clearly owes its 'common-sense' to its ideological redundancy, the degree to which the actor's rhetoric of characterisation comports with practices for identifying 'character' – as well as the 'self' and 'acting' – available in the culture at large. By regarding his own direction and the actors' training as transparent techniques for the preservation of textual 'ambiguity', Barton specifically represses acting and direction as *theory*, as a way of locating the theatre's production of meaning in relation to the signifying practices that the stage shares with film, television, sports, social behaviour in general, or even with criticism.

Performance criticism of this kind claims for 'performance' an exclusive access to the 'dramatic quality' of the text, while at the same time subverting its claims as signifying practice by insisting on the 'freedom' of performance from the signifying formalities that make 'meaning' possible and determinable. Yet, the 'test question' of such criticism – 'Can this be played?' – dramatises the impasse we come to when we regard 'playing' as the realisation of an immanent textual significance.[19] For the idea that performance *can* test criticism risks the priority of the stage that performance criticism has worked so hard to claim. Such a test implies a kind of redundancy between critical and performed 'meaning', as though writing and acting were able to render the same message through entirely different means of articulation. The 'test' serves to confirm only those 'meanings' already assimilable to the privileged presentation of the performer. This redundancy, however, seems more likely to threaten the priority of performance, since it suggests that the stage tests 'meanings' already formulated elsewhere, either as a feature of its own technique or in an unstaged engagement with the play (such as reading, criticism). This belatedness creates the possibility that a test might work in both directions at once: it would subject the insights of criticism to the physical immediacy of the *mise-en-scène* and also subject the mute languages of the stage – acting, design, costume, direction – to rhetorical criteria of coherence, integration, and theoretical rigour, testing the production's retextualisation of the drama as performance. One example of such a testing might be a scene in which a line of business establishes the stage referent of a line of speech, as in Donald Sinden's business with the sundial in John Barton's 1969 *Twelfth Night*. Sinden describes how he used a piece of business (adjusting the sundial to conform to the time on Malvolio's watch) to provide a referential context for a series of lines: '"Why everything adheres together" (glance at sundial) "that no dram of a scruple" (look at watch) "no scruple of a scruple" (back to sundial) "no obstacle" (look at watch). Check "sunbeam" to sundial and adjust it until correct time is shown during – "no incredulous or unsafe circumstance".'[20] In her fine article 'Re-viewing the Play', Miriam Gilbert notes 'the way in which the "business" actually fits the language, taking off from "everything adheres together" and then finding a concrete example where things don't adhere together until the stone is shifted'.[21] To 'test' such a 'fit', though, might well require us to develop a fuller and more specific account of the production's systematic means of relating the dramatic text to its physical milieu onstage. Is this a real 'discovery' about the play or a funny gimmick unrelated to the production's engagement with the play as a whole? To answer such a question would be, so to speak, to subject performance choices to the 'test of criticism'.

Let me try to suggest what is at stake here. Regarding performance as realisation represses the institutional practices already inscribed in the theatre, in gesture and intonation, in the body and its behaviours, the 'textualising' formalities that render theatre significant. In so doing, we disqualify the processes that produce meaning in the theatre as legitimate objects for our attention and scrutiny. Indeed, we dramatise the degree to which we are still firmly in the grip of the rhetoric of theatrical naturalism, with its characteristic erasure of the machinery of theatrical production from our view. Yet a variety of such discourses necessarily intervenes between the text and its stage production, much as it does between the text and its production as reading experience or as critical activity. Terry Eagleton has remarked that 'text and production are distinct formations – different material modes of production, between which no homologous or "reproductive" relationship can hold. They are not two aspects of the same discourse – the text, as it were, thought or silent speech and the production thought-in-action, articulate language; they constitute distinct kinds of discourse, between which no simple "translation" is possible.'[22] But to say that text and performance are incommensurable is, I think, again to miss the point that the text is 'against performance' of all kinds, to the degree that it necessarily differs from *any* discourse that represents it – reading and criticism as well as acting. Text and performance are dialectically related through the labour of enactment, in which the instruments of representation – both literary and theatrical, critical and performative – 'transform the "raw materials" of the text into a specific product, which cannot be mechanically extrapolated from an inspection of the text'.[23] The production of the text's 'meanings' in the theatre requires the application of a complex machinery of interpretation and of signification, whose adequacy – like the machinery of criticism – cannot be 'mechanically extrapolated' from the text because it is engaged in making the text, producing it as theatre. Where homology may be possible, then, is not between text and performance, nor between the results of 'literary' interpretation and of stage production. Much as the effect of performance is not itself immediately assimilable to 'criticism', so too our readerly 'ideas' about the dramatic text are not illustrated in a direct manner in the theatre. Performance criticism should look instead to the relationship between the practices that we use to stage the text as 'drama', both as criticism and as theatrical performance.

Our ability to read a text as 'drama', then, is enabled by the practices that allow us to read it both as literature and as theatre. Such a sense includes not only the strategies that allow us to read the text as instigating the behaviours we recognise as 'acting', but also the interpretive habits that guide our performance as readers and critics. This contingency could be illustrated in a number of ways. One version of performance criticism might trace the relationship between textual criticism and stage performance as means of producing the dramatic 'text'. The extensive controversy surrounding contemporary Shakespearean editing can only be touched on here. Yet in an important sense, textual and performance criticism share – or might come to share – an interest in determining how 'the text' has been produced as a cultural artifact, and how the process of production inscribes itself into – and perhaps constitutes – the 'text' it represents. To regard the text at the moment of its insertion into social discourse doesn't, of course, imply that editorial choices can or should be limited to what is performable. For as A. R. Braunmuller argues, while textual opacities often depend for their resolution on what the editor thinks is happening in the dramatic action and in its stage enactment, such decisions often rely on a romanticised, overly narrow, or simply outmoded understanding of stage practice.[24] A familiar framework of conventions defines what 'works' in the theatre. Editors also produce a text in relation to interpretive and signifying conventions that legitimate certain versions of 'the text' as authoritative, and so legitimate what such texts can say.[25] Like the *mise-en-scène*, the *mise-en-page* places the text and its production at issue; in this regard performance criticism might take Shakespearean textual criticism as a paradigm. For not only does this controversy locate the act of reading as a social behaviour potentially related to other performances, it raises in a cogent and powerful manner the central issue still eluding performance criticism: the problematic relation between the text's origin, its initial production, and its reproduction throughout history. [...]

Finally, [...] performance criticism might ask how acting in a particular historical mode – the American Method, for instance – textualises 'character' as performance. Performance criticism might address the relation between criticism's production of 'character' analyses, the reading/interpretive practice implied in Method actor-training and preparation, and the ways that Method signification articulates interpretive activities for its audience, enabling the spectators to read (and so to write) the script of 'character'. Method acting renders a certain kind of interpretation legitimate by qualifying the subjects of characterisation – the 'character' and the performing actor – in particular ways. It leads us to find 'character' at the subtextual level, to view its most important activities as impulsive or reactive, to feel as though 'character' is discovered only through indirection, and to privilege events that seem to have a certain degree of expressive immediacy as authentic and motivational. 'Character', like the acting that produces it, is progressive, developing through the operation of desire toward a particular goal, a motivational 'objective'. This goal, like the fiction of continuous 'character' itself, can only be recognised from a transcendental – or voyeuristic – perspective, by an audience who is itself not subject to such staging, such disclosure.

If I am right in thinking that Stanislavskian attitudes toward acting and character suffuse American acting, then there's little point in trying to repudiate the Method as a vehicle for Shakespearean drama: we can hardly imagine acting not imbued with these values of 'truth', interior fidelity, subtextual vitality, character coherence, and so forth. Yet the rhetoric of the Method is at once a mode of representation and a mode of suasion. Insofar as the Method remains inscribed by the practices of the proscenium stage, it provides a strategy for constituting character 'objectively', as an object overseen by an unacknowledged, absent audience. Stanislavsky's attention to 'public solitude', and the Method's concentration on the actor's ' private moments', are both, in this sense, means for training the actor to create character before – not with, not for, not among – a silent majority of disembodied spectators. These practices clearly textualise character in ways probably undesirable – even unimaginable – on Shakespeare's more open, public, and interactive stage. As epilogues, soliloquies, and various versions of direct address to the audience imply, enactment of 'character' in the Renaissance may have been a more collaborative or even collusive activity, one in which the seam between actor and character may well have been visible ('indicated', in Method terms) for good effect – patronage, crowd management, and so on. In this sense, then, to naturalise the structure of dramatic roles to the practices of the Method obscures certain potentialities of Shakespearean characterisation, the possibility of representing 'character' as a strategy of mediation, one that transpires between stage and audience and so responds to the 'given circumstances' both of the play and of the theatre that sustains it. Both requiring and reifying the absent audience, Method acting manifests the ideological terrain of the naturalistic theatre from which it is drawn, and so subjects actor, 'character', and spectator to its relations of legitimate interpretation.

To describe how the theatre subjects texts and performers to its process is a daunting challenge, one that performance critics have pursued with energy and success. But to make such insight valuable, we need to locate its claims as criticism. The first move in such a venture would be to displace the enervating polarisation of 'criticism against performance' (the subtext, so to speak, of the 'text against performance' controversy), in that our access to the text is always through its performance, a performance continually taking place offstage – as reading, education, advertising, criticism, and so on – before any stage performance is conceived. Shakespeare performance criticism seems inexplicably isolated from the theoretical and methodological inquiries that might help to direct it, isolated in many instances even from the new historicism's general interest in theatrical and cultural representation. Indeed, as James R. Siemon remarks, 'Among the factors that make performance-oriented criticism of Elizabethan drama of such potential importance, none seems more promising than the evidence of Renaissance interest in those features that qualify all signifying activity as performance and thereby render it so much more complex than analyses of rhetorical strategy, poetic device, propositional content, or the "character" of the speaker can suggest.'[26] Performance criticism is defined by its attention to 'signifying activity as performance'; for this reason it should more tenaciously undertake to expose what Kenneth Burke might have called the 'lie' at the heart of theatre.[27] This would mean understanding the rhetoric implicit in our conceptions of performance and in performance practice throughout history, the 'body of identifications' that sustains acting and directing, and that informs our critical, interpretive, and signifying practice outside the theatre as well.[28] Theatrical production writes the drama into stage practice. Performance criticism should reveal the affiliations between this writing and the very different acts of inscription that make the theatre readable. To understand the drama, we need to understand all the ways that we make it perform.

From *Shakespeare Quarterly*, 40: 4 (1989), 441–55.

NOTES

[In this slightly edited version of an essay which offers a critique of the tradition of performance criticism which is exemplified by the first two essays in this volume, W. B. Worthen examines the enabling assumptions and rhetorical strategies which impute certain kinds of performative authority to the Shakespearean text as innate or essential qualities. Citing both academic criticism and the testimony of practitioners, Worthen argues that stage-centred criticism tends to universalise a naturalistic, character-centred acting practice. By appealing to an authorially sanctioned theatricality fully immanent in the text, it also affirms its continuity with the traditional modes of literary criticism it ostensibly seeks to displace. Ed.]

1. G. Wilson Knight, *The Wheel of Fire*, fourth edn (London, 1949), p. vi.
2. See Marvin and Ruth Thompson (eds), *Shakespeare and the Sense of Performance: Essays in the Tradition of Performance Criticism in Honor of Bernard Beckerman* (London and Toronto, 1989), pp. 13–23.
3. On the 'detextualisation' of the body, 'the transfer of meanings from language to nonhuman forces in "nature"', see Harry Berger, Jr, 'Bodies and Texts', *Representations*, 17 (1987), 144–66.
4. Charles Lamb, 'On the Tragedies of Shakespeare, Considered with Reference to Their Fitness for Stage Representation', in *The Works of Charles Lamb* (London, 1818); Leigh Hunt, *Theatrical Examiner* No. 338 (4 October 1818), rpt. in *Prose of the Romantic Period*, ed. Carl R. Woodring (Boston, 1961), pp. 229–40, 383–4.
5. Cleanth Brooks and Robert Heilman, *Understanding Drama* (New York, 1945), p. 25. For a brief history of the development of New Criticism's treatment of Shakespearean drama, see Charles H. Frey, *Experiencing Shakespeare: Essays on Text, Classroom, and Performance* (Columbia, 1988), pp. 130–3.
6. I am much indebted to Dolora Wojciehowski for suggesting this qualification.
7. See Marvin and Ruth Thompson, 'Performance Criticism from Granville-Barker to Bernard Beckerman and Beyond', in *Shakespeare and the Sense of Performance*, p. 15.
8. James H. Kavanagh, 'Shakespeare in ideology', in *Alternative Shakespeares*, ed. John Drakakis (London, 1985), p. 147.
9. Richard David, *Shakespeare in the Theatre* (Cambridge, 1978), pp. 16, 17.
10. John Russell Brown, *Shakespeare's Plays in Performance* (London, 1966), pp. 223–37, esp. p. 224; David, *Shakespeare in the Theatre*, p. 1.
11. Sherman Hawkins, 'Teaching the Theatre of Imagination: The Example of *1 Henry IV*', *Shakespeare Quarterly*, 35 (1984), 517–27, esp. p. 519.
12. Homer Swander, 'In Our Time: Such Audiences We Wish Him', *Shakespeare Quarterly*, 35 (1984), 528–40, esp. pp. 529, 540.

13. John Russell Brown, *Discovering Shakespeare: A New Guide to the Plays* (New York, 1981), p. 1.

14. John Russell Brown, 'The Nature of Speech in Shakespeare's Plays', in *Shakespeare and the Sense of Performance*. pp. 48–59, esp. p. 57.

15. Ibid., p. 58, italics added.

16. Brown, *Discovering Shakespeare*, p. 8.

17. John Barton, *Playing Shakespeare* (London and New York, 1984), p. 101, Barton's ellipses. Indeed, Barton elides three passages which in the original occur in three separate paragraphs covering two pages of text; Barton's target is, in fact, much more directly interested in the relationship between text and performance than Barton's heavily edited quotation would suggest to a listener or to a reader: 'As for staging, the theatre of modern realism thrusts the actor into the very centre of the theatrical event. Like Paganini, Shakespeare, in the writing of *Hamlet*, casts the performer as virtuoso, a role elusively part of, yet apart from, the play's central personage. *This* treachery plagues every staging of *Hamlet* and *exemplifies the leading aesthetic problem of the actor in modern theatre – the interpretation of action through characterologic nuance and rarefaction*' (italicised portions quoted by Barton and read by Suchet); see Donald M. Kaplan, 'Character and Theatre: Psychoanalytic Notes on Modern Realism', *Tulane Drama Review*, 10 (1966), 93–108, esp. p. 103.

18. Barton quotes Kaplan in *Playing Shakespeare*, p. 101.

19. David Samuelson, 'Preface' in *Shakespeare: The Theatrical Dimension*, ed. Philip C. McGuire and David A. Samuelson (New York, 1979), p. xv.

20. Philip Brockbank (ed.), *Players of Shakespeare: Essays in Shakespearean performance by twelve players with the Royal Shakespeare Company* (Cambridge, 1985), p. 62.

21. See Miriam Gilbert, 'Re-viewing the Play', *Shakespeare Quarterly*, 36 (1985), 609–17, esp. p. 612.

22. Terry Eagleton, *Criticism & Ideology* (London: Verso, 1978), p. 66.

23. Ibid., p. 65. In the passage I have quoted here, Eagleton assigns such transforming labour to 'the theatrical instruments (staging, acting skills and so on)'; I am suggesting that comparable labour is undertaken in any act that produces the text, such as reading.

24. See A. R. Braunmuller, 'Editing the Staging/Staging the Editing' in *Shakespeare and the Sense of Performance*, pp. 139–49. For a frank, and provocative, discussion of the editor's role in the determination of stage directions, see Stanley Wells, *Re-Editing Shakespeare for the Modern Reader* (Oxford, 1984), ch. 3.

25. See Jerome J. McGann, *A Critique of Modern Textual Criticism* (Chicago, 1983), p. 75.

26. James R. Siemon, review of R. Chris Hassel, Jr's *Songs of Death: Performance, Interpretation, and the Text of Richard III, Shakespeare Quarterly*, 40 (1989), 105.

27. Kenneth Burke, *A Rhetoric of Motives* (Berkeley, CA, 1969), p. 23.

28. Ibid., p. 26.

4

Bifold Authority in Shakespeare's Theatre

ROBERT WEIMANN

I

Shakespeare's dramaturgy is deeply embedded in the social institution of the Elizabethan theatre. If, as Stephen Greenblatt has suggested, Shakespeare's plays 'offer no single timeless affirmation or denial of legitimate authority', and if, instead, his 'language and themes are caught up, like the medium itself, in unsettling repetitions, committed to the shifting voices and audiences, with their shifting aesthetic assumptions and historical imperatives, that govern a living theatre',[1] then surely Shakespeare's uses of authority must be traced in the actual circumstances and in the shifting strategies of that theatrical institution itself. The theatre is central to an understanding of Shakespeare's uses of authority in that as a cultural and economic institution, in the very terms of its rise and subsistence, it incorporated some altogether unresolved issues and conflicts among different authorities in Tudor legislation and administration. Existing on the one hand under the shadow of the city's protests, restrictions, and repressive gestures, and on the other hand under the gracious, airy canopy of royal and aristocratic benevolence, the theatre was thrown back upon its own resources in coming to terms with, and even thriving on, the underlying clash of these differing authorities, civic and royal, bourgeois and aristocratic. Such resilience was possible in part because the public theatres were situated in a unique place in the cultural landscape of Elizabethan

England: namely, the Liberties of London, the area beyond the city walls, seen as the most licentious, most unruly, and juridically the least defined of sites, existing in the very teeth of the contradictions between city, court, and county. The Liberties, as Steven Mullaney has shown, were 'ambivalent zones of transition between one realm of authority and another', an 'ambiguous realm' in its own right, 'a borderland whose legal parameters and privileges were open-ended', and so 'equivocally defined' that this virtually ungoverned area constituted, as the lord mayor suggested to Burghley, a truly 'incontinent rule'[2] in the topography of Elizabethan power relations. Resonant with long-standing traditions of late-ritual sport and release, game and pastime, this area of communal festivity and temporary release was appropriated by unsanctioned social groups – entrepreneurs, actors, and playwrights – who all defied the traditional economic demarcations and actually seemed to thrive on social mobility and the decline of guild regulations and privileges.

As these groups designed, set up, and used a large wooden architecture of unlicensed pleasure and intense communication, the mingle-mangle traffic in these buildings was no longer 'contained by the customary antitheses of rule and misrule, order and disorder, everyday and holiday'.[3] 'By its own logic, a commercially funded, secular, professional, shareholding enterprise tended to constitute conditions of discursive practice that in several important respects differed from those governing the dominant rules of discourse and ideology in Elizabethan England. Contrary to the sanctioned models of authorising political, ecclesiastical, and juridical types of discourse, the theatre could not but acknowledge as authoritative the provision of pleasure, the efficacy of communication, the distribution of information and news-value, and the functions of social release and collective memory. In integrating (densely) spectacle, gesture, and language, movement and articulation; in projecting a hodge-podge of social interests and national expectations, this theatre broke with those fixed and determined correlations of theatrical signs and ideological meanings that were sanctioned in part by the lingering authority in humanistic discourse of neoclassical rules.

The new constellation of authority in this theatre was openly revealed when an actor named William Shakespeare began to appropriate the academically privileged 'rare wit' of university-trained playwrights, so that – as Robert Greene disapprovingly noted – 'an absolute *Johannes fac totum*' could now exceed whatever 'past excellence' and 'admired inventions' were previously thought to be legitimised by an Oxford and Cambridge education.[4] For Shakespeare to be called 'an upstart Crow, beautified with our feathers', and to be scornfully hailed as *factotum* was significant enough. The natural metaphors of envy and distaste against 'those Anticks', mere players from the country, and, even more, against that actor-dramatist serving the 'pleasure of such rude groomes' were by themselves revelatory in their undertone of insecurity and threatened privilege. Even more important, the shifting grounds of authorial function were revealed when the authority of class and education had to be summoned against the sheer capacity for bombasting out a blank verse like 'the best of you'. What Greene most resented (next to a harshly felt bitterness at being 'forsaken') was a mode of theatrical legitimation by which a versatile concurrence of hitherto separate activities appeared sufficient to guarantee public success in the theatre. If we read '*Johannes fac totum*' as 'a Jack of all trades, a would-be universal genius' and, even, as 'one who meddles with everything' (*OED*), then the academically sanctioned authority of possessing 'rare wit' and owning the fine arts ('*our* feathers') may be seen as defending itself against the impurity of a different location of writing that must have appeared contaminated by its greater proximity to such unliterary and unlearned institutions as those served by common players.

To make the composition of blank verse coextensive with its reproduction on the stage and, even worse, with its impersonation by plebeian actors, appeared scandalous to one who, in articulating his personal disappointment, emphasised social distance between poets and players. Since Shakespeare was not a university-trained writer and since, *factotum*-wise, he combined acting with writing for the common stage, he presumably did not, for his work in the theatre, consider the possession of 'rare wit' and the ownership of academically attested fine arts authoritative in themselves. In other words, as Timothy Murray put it, Shakespeare's work in the playhouse preceded the 'transference of textual property rights and intellectual authority from the communal structures of the ... theatre to the private domain of the author and subsequent possessor' of his text – a transference that was to result, as early as 1616, in the publication of *The Works of Benjamin Jonson*. In Shakespeare's theatre, the mode of authorising discourse was as yet different from that defined in *Leviathan* where 'he who owneth his words and actions is the AUTHOR: In which case the Actor acteth by Authority'.[6]

It is true that Shakespeare's Prologue to *Henry V* does invoke a 'muse', but the muse is not summoned to promote the workings of a 'genius' nor to engage the inspired 'imagination' of the epic poet and thus, as with poets from Spenser to Milton, to authorise his writings.[7] Since outside the theatre the marketable value of the author's 'rough and all-unable pen' (*Henry V*, Epilogue. l. 1) appeared negligible, and inside the theatre the author himself was not one 'who owneth his words and actions', the noteworthy thing about authority in the Globe was the way it resided in proximity to the actual process of theatrical production and communication. Authority in this theatre, as we shall see, needed to be validated by the audience and was unlikely to result without the cooperative effort of the audience's 'imaginary forces' (*Henry V*, Prologue. l. 18). At the same time, there is a connection between the ensemble quality of 'this great account' (l. 17) and the fact that, as never before and rarely after, it was possible to 'suit the action to the word, the word to the action'. What is more, Hamlet's formula (III.ii.17–18) must have tended to sanction such a richly achieved synthesis of spectacle and poetry, gesture and language as was itself a correlative of collective effort and multiple authority: unlike the Prologue to *Troilus and Cressida*, such intertwining of 'action' and 'word' must have presupposed the 'confidence / Of author's pen [and] actor's voice' (ll. 23–4) alike, a confidence that shareholding interests and the institutionalisation of diverse faculties appeared fully to vindicate.

Even though, as recent criticism suggests, the killing off of Falstaff at the beginning of *Henry V* and the shareholding arrangement associated with the move to the Globe in the same year of *Henry V*'s production (1599) may have precipitated the triumph of the 'commodification of culture' over the traditional cultural economy of 'gifts and wagers' (as associated with Richard Tarlton and William Kemp);[8] the shareholding principle – which was not peculiar to the Globe – did have advantages: for example, it ensured a distribution of authority to those several talents who, through their various proficiencies, contributed to the achievements of the Chamberlain's Men. If Kemp, as in *Kemps Nine Daies Wonder*, resisted 'any suggestion that you can produce entertainment for exchange',[9] he may himself have been not quite consistent, having previously served as one of 'the sharer members'[10] of Lord Strange's Men. From the point of view of the theatrical location of authority, it is of course difficult to decide whether the shareholding arrangement at the Globe collided with (or whether it developed further from) the previously held author-function. If Shakespeare ceased to be the youthful *factotum*, he may still have retained his versatile capacity for serving several functions in that 'great account'. This, at any rate, would have nicely accorded with the ensemble process of distributing theatrical authority to several quarters – through which process the '*tygers hart*' had prospered from the beginning of his self-authorised ascent to the heaven of theatrical invention. For a mere upstart actor to have snatched the right for himself 'to bombast out a blanke verse as the best of you' was to use and exploit to the full those conditions of proliferating discourse and social mobility without which the rich 'mingle-mangle' (including the mingle-mangle of theatrical authorities) was scarcely possible. But since, as Walter Cohen has convincingly argued, 'the theatre was a composite formation in which disparate modes coexisted and intertwined',[11] this 'hodge-podge' form must have been one by which cultural bastards and theatrical *factota* thrived. Such form was constituted of (and in its turn promoted by) diverse ways of legitimating an astonishingly durable confederation of 'author's pen' and 'actor's voice'.

Finally, such mingle-mangle conditions of authorisation were of course part of that wider constellation in social, political, and cultural history of which the theatre was a product as well as, in several ways, a producer. If we were to analyse this constellation – impossible task here – we would have to read the topography of the theatre not just in terms of the juridical immunity of Shoreditch, Newington Butts, and Bankside, but in relation to that wider landscape marked by the transitional historical circumstances of a heterogeneous economy and a post-feudal and pre-bourgeois settlement in politics and religion. In particular, the issue of authority in the theatre would have to be related to that growing sense of uncertainty characteristic of the last years of Elizabeth's reign, with the question of the succession in suspension.

As recent social historians have shown, the acceleration of social change in the nineties began to reveal disturbing cracks in the Tudor alliance. In these years there emerged some early antagonism among the ways of legitimating social and communicative action, especially as the 'horizontal expansion of county government' came increasingly in collision with that 'vertical growth in power' by which 'the Elizabethan regime sought to intervene increasingly in the running of local communities, wherever possible absorbing functions previously performed on an informal, seigneurial or neighbourly level'.[12] In the case of the town of Norfolk, for example, where after 1572 a previously powerful network of patronage was uprooted, 'two conflicting views of county government tended to polarise the gentry into coherent and reasonably stable groups', with the effect that the 'conflict between "court" gentry and "county" gentry intensified during the 1590s'.[13] No less important, these early years of decline in the Elizabethan settlement opened up a widening gulf between professed ideas and social practice, an 'enormous gap' – as Joel Hurstfield has described it – 'between the constitution and the political reality; between those who wielded authority and those who merely legalised its use'.[14] In such a situation, 'frequent debates about who did what and on whose authority'[15] must have been widespread among those involved in or affected by the business of governing county and country. It seems impossible not to assume that the theatre, so much in the forefront of public awareness, was not resonant with these trends and even helped to precipitate events when theatrically using and transforming them on what remained, in the newly erected Globe, the 'incontinent rule' of the platform stage.

II

At this point it may be helpful to glance at the wider context of Tudor uses of the word 'authority', if only because we can thereby gain a sharper focus on the kind of unsanctioned social energy and licence the large public stages were able to project into their dramatic significations of the same word. Let me here refer again to the contemporary language of jurisdiction, in which it was possible for William Lambarde, indefatigable justice of the peace, author, and ever-faithful servant of the Crown in Kent, so to address his 'good neighbours and friends' at the Quarter Session at Maidstone, 1 April 1600:

> ... such is nowadays the bold sway of disobedience to law that it creepeth not in corners but marcheth in the open market ... yet how few are there found amongst us that will use the bridle of authority which they have in their own hand and cast it upon the head of this unruly monster.[16]

'Authority' in such discourse clearly serves as an unquestioned instrument of rule; it is, as Lambarde says elsewhere, 'already given' to the justices.[17] In Lambarde's discursive practice (as well as, surely, in his non-discursive actions), authority is asserted as something given prior to the act of representation and jurisdiction and even prior to the performance of violence and punishment through which 'authority' – always already available – is merely applied or used like a 'bridle' on the unruly and disobedient. In order to underline what is perhaps the most crucial difference between Lambarde's and Shakespeare's uses of 'authority', it may be said that in juridical discourse the same authority that is represented is also representing. In Lambarde's text representation of authority presupposes an altogether fixed and closed relation between signifier and signified, a mode of signification that in its turn posits *and* supports a static view of society as an unchanging entity.

But the point that needs to be made is not simply that Lambarde in his language and his violence is worlds apart from the representation of authority in Shakespearean drama. The point to be examined is that sanctioned uses of authority like Lambarde's were in fact widely prevalent and that, not surprisingly, they were inscribed in some of the dominant texts in the pre-Shakespearean theatre. A morality play like *The Tyde taryeth no Man* provides us with a particularly illuminating instance, in that here the representation of authority is, as it were, actually folded out upon itself through an allegorical figure bearing this very name. 'Authority', with the help of 'Correction', enters the play to have its Vice, 'Courage', arrested and punished. In this play, the allegorical representation of Authority provides several theatrical correlatives to the political and juridical acts of representation in the discourse of Justice of the Peace William Lambarde. In the first place, the character Authority uses, and is supported by, images of physical force, as when he says to the figure of Correction:

> Draw neare Correction and thine office doe,
> Take here this caytife vnto the Jayle.[18]

Quite unambiguously, Authority is represented as in alliance with the 'office' delegated to pursue justice and correction. Authority has the officially sanctioned power to enforce through his 'commaundement'. Second, Authority is conceived of as representing, and addressing himself to, a previously established order existing prior to his own act of representing and defending that order through force. As the play draws to a conclusion, Authority feels empowered to pledge to Christianity:

O Christianity vnto vs draw neare,
That we thy abused estate may redresse.
And as freely as this power vnto vs is lent,
Here we now by force of the same:
To thee fayt[h]full few do here condiscent,
That thou Christianities estate shalt frame.
(sig. G. iiii.[v])

Again, 'this power' is 'freely', originally, and unquestioningly given; insofar as the 'estate' of Christianity is abused, it needs only to be redressed 'by force of the same' power which 'vnto vs is lent'. It is lent to those forces of correction and authority that would 'condiscent' – as if out of heaven – ever ready to guide and support the allegorical 'faythfull few'. Authority, in other words, is viewed as preordained and as already there; in the play he needs only to be *found* and established in order to have his regime ensured.

This brief excursion into a highly selective pre-Shakespearean representation of authority must here remain quite pragmatic and oversimplified (there is not even room enough to examine the subversive potential of Courage and related farcical figures of Vice); yet this must suffice as a context in which to view the altogether different uses of authority in Shakespeare's theatre. The difference in question can perhaps best be defined by recalling that the Shakespearean theatre was marked by divergent rather than integrated authorities, and that, consequently, authority would rarely be presented in alliance with power (or 'Correction'). No less important, the conditions of 'incontinent rule' in the Liberties of London made it difficult for any single source of authority to be considered as unambiguously given. As distinct from both the orthodox representations of vice and virtue and the juridical differentiation between the justice and the thief, one salient fact about the nature of authority in Shakespeare's theatre needs above all to be emphasised; authority in this theatre is not something unified or conclusive; it is not given, as it were, at the beginning of the play in performance but is implicated in the process – in the effect of, in the response to, the dramatic production itself. In Shakespeare's theatre the uses of mimesis were remarkably open-ended; they were bound up with a multiplicity of divergent social and cultural functions by which altogether different authorities could quite effectively be negotiated in the very form and pressure of the theatrical performance.

III

Under these conditions theatrical representation became itself a site for what in a crucial scene in *Troilus and Cressida* is called 'Bi-fold authority' (V.ii.148). Using and developing further a terminology which elsewhere I have discussed at some length,[19] I suggest that the Elizabethan platform stage – far from constituting a unified representational space – can itself be said to have provided two different, although not rigidly opposed, modes of authorising dramatic discourse. One, the *locus*, was associated with the localising capacities of the fictional role and tended to privilege the authority of what and who was *represented* in the dramatic world; the other, the *platea*, being associated instead with the actor and the neutral materiality of the platform stage, tended to privilege the authority of what and who was *representing* that world.

In line with this distinction, let me suggest that the *locus*-centred authority of what was represented tended to be defined spatially, socially, and linguistically in terms of a certain verisimilitude, decorum, aloofness from the audience, and representational closure. For instance, in Shakespeare's drama we have the throne as the representational *locus* of privileged royalty; we have the bed as a *locus* of patriarchal power and female sacrifice, the tomb as a *topos* of family dignity and piety; we have the widest conceivable spectrum of language used as a mirror of chastity, honour, courage, and warlike resolution; we have a full repertoire of signs and significations of the house and household and the power therein of parental authority. The representational structure, function, and effect of such *loci* was to a large extent already inscribed in Tudor histories and in Shakespeare's fictional narrative sources; they were part of a dominant or nascent ideology and served, emblematically or symbolically, as widely used figures and figurations of the current relations of power.

Such *locus*-centred presence (that which was visually shown and verbally re-presented) was considerable, so much so that the Elizabethan theatre was not, by any stretch of the imagination, a subversive institution, hostile to the Tudor balance of socioeconomic forces old and new. On the contrary, let me say without the usual qualification that in the Shakespearean theatre dramatic representations of juridical, political, and ecclesiastical authority could be made to carry great weight and meaning – 'meaning' in the sense that, with considerable efficacy, the audience was made to accept impressive moments of illusion and significations effecting the already-given closure between what was represented and what was representing.

However, if the *locus*-centred authority of what was represented could be amply confirmed, that same authority could also be deeply and profoundly challenged, and such challenge was, more often than not, geared to whatever *platea*-dimension Shakespeare's stage tended to retain or, sometimes, revitalise. For instance, in *Hamlet*, the mirror of representation, faithfully held up to a previously inscribed image of virtue or vice, showing each her own feature, could be altogether deflected from its customary *locus* of verisimilitude and decorum. Through a modified use of *platea*-functions, the mirror of representation, the rules of decorum, the language of privilege could be challenged or confronted by a different 'impertinent' or 'antic disposition' of dramaturgy. On such a *platea* occasion 'Th' expectancy and rose of the fair state, / The glass of fashion and the mould of form', together with 'that noble and most sovereign reason' (III.i.155–6, 160) could be 'blasted with ecstasy' (l. 163) under the mantle of an assumed madness, a highly indecorous convention of audience-related acting and speaking. The 'glass of fashion' and courtly virtue, far from showing 'her own' already-given image, could be quite distorted by a whole set of socially, spatially, and verbally encoded forms of theatricality. Among these, wordplay and 'impertinency' loom large, as does the ordinary and sometimes quite deflating language of the proverb. Even more important, conventions of disguise and, of course, clowning, together with reminders of misrule and topsy-turvydom, all help to counterpoint the represented images of authority. In most cases, such impertinent, indecorous, anachronistic comedy of place and disguise could involve a subversion of the dominant uses of authority and could, in doing so, make use of devices from what used to be called the extra-dramatic 'aside' to the more highly integrated uses of the play-metaphor to invite a rich spectrum of audience awareness. As a matter of course, such *platea*-directed mimesis could never be strictly representational; there remains in bright daylight the social occasion inside the public theatre, the materiality of things on the scaffold stage, the unmistakable contours of known actors, and, finally, the awareness of the theatrical occasion in the dramatic language itself. The play-metaphor reveals the actor (the real person who is representing) behind the role (the fictional person who is represented); moving between these two different types of identity (and authority), the poor player, like the one cited in *Macbeth*, could be overwhelmed by the 'borrowed robes' of kingship and the other irreducible materials of theatrical work and signification. In his attempt to negotiate two differing locations of authority in the theatre, the actor was not allowed to be quite absorbed in symbolic meaning, and so remained – at least in his metaphorical use of language – in touch with that bustling space of theatrical 'sound and fury' which, as neutral matter, was literally 'signifying nothing'.[20]

IV

It is this unique capacity of the Shakespearean stage for simultaneously widening and closing the gaps between role and actor, between the site of dramatic illusion and the real place of and on the stage, with which the chorus in *Henry V* is concerned. Using, as does the Prologue to Lyly's *Midas*, a culinary metaphor, the chorus asserts the authority of the theatre vis-à-vis the intractable site of representation in this revealing phrase: 'we'll digest / Th' abuse of distance, force a play' (II.Prologue. 31–2). The theatre's authority is no longer that of the rules of dramatic unity. The unity of place in particular is broken up, and the distance between 'this cockpit' and 'the vasty fields of France' has become much larger, involving much more symbolising and signifying activity. On the platform stage such activity was at the heart of the representational process as it localised and neutralised the space between the imagined *loci* of Southampton and France on the one hand, and, on the other, the awareness of 'this unworthy scaffold' inside 'this wooden O'.

By digesting the 'distance' between these two basic levels and locations of authority, the platform stage was able not simply to have 'the scene ... transported' (II.Prologue, 34–5) from the London Globe to Southampton but also to traverse the difference between real actors and their imagined dramatic identities. Such would have been impossible except for the bifold capacity of Shakespeare's theatre to project and dissolve the scene, to merge and to rupture theatrical signs and their meanings, to digest both the use and the 'abuse' of distance.

When I say the use *and* abuse of distance, I am of course suggesting a reading of the chorus in *Henry V* that, again, assumes that the 'unworthy scaffold' in the newly erected Globe did not provide a unified space for representation. Instead, let me propose a reading of the chorus as a singular and quite extraordinary attempt to redefine and master the bifold location of time, place, and authority in the Shakespearean theatre. I am of course only too well aware of the fact that to choose *Henry V*, with its resounding theme of martial triumph and national unity, is to bring my focus on 'bifold authority' in the Shakespearean theatre into confrontation with what is undoubtedly the most formidably difficult text in Shakespeare's whole oeuvre. But then, since this chorus is unique, it may, as it were, here provide a test case, albeit an exceptional one, for what happens to the *locus* and *platea* conventions as Shakespeare, taking leave of the chronicle play tradition, is about to move on to the problem plays and to the tragedies.

To anticipate my reading, I would like to suggest that in *Henry V* the traditional complementarity of place and *locus* appears to be redefined in terms of a relationship that, in the words of the Prologue, is established between 'this unworthy scaffold' and 'the swelling scene'. Somewhere between these two, the chorus – as Prologue and throughout the play – against increasing odds attempts to strike a continuing balance between the representational needs and strains of an historiographical subject matter and the social institution of theatrical place. In fact, the chorus can be said to embrace both these differing grounds of authority at the point where their conflicting claims are being negotiated.

What is most remarkable about the chorus is that the authority of the *locus*-centred discourse of patriotic historiography appears so devastatingly triumphant that on the surface the complementary uses of theatrical place are minimised. In terms of its representational efficacy, the *platea*-function is either disparaged as 'unworthy scaffold' or reappropriated with a view to controlling and stimulating the celebration of national unity and popular royalty. There is a fanfare note in the trumpet of the chorus, as when the ravishing appeal of the iambic language is effectively carried to the speech that opens Act II, where 'all the youth of England are on fire, / ... and honour's thought / Reigns solely in the breast of every man' (II.1, 3–4). And yet, in the most stirring speech of them all, as the chorus to Act IV articulates the patriotic fervour of 'brothers, friends, and countrymen' (l. 34), the tensions between 'the swelling scene' and 'this unworthy scaffold' remain quite unresolved and culminate unexpectedly in these lines:

> Where – O for pity! – we shall much disgrace
> With four or five most vile and ragged foils,
> Right ill-dispos'd in brawl ridiculous,

The name of Agincourt. Yet sit and see,
Minding true things by what their mock'ries be.
(ll. 49–53)

At this crucial moment the awareness of theatrical realities serves as a convenient vehicle of common sense, counterpointing the jubilant memories of 'Agincourt' with an unambiguous sense of place in the Elizabethan public playhouse. The chorus, at the height of its powers, serves as a down-to-earth reminder of the reality of that which is representing. The ferocious weapons of victory are theatrically transcribed into 'four or five most vile and ragged foils'; the glorious battle itself becomes a 'brawl ridiculous'. This, indeed, is a peculiar way to 'digest / Th' abuse of distance'. Signifying the signs of the signs of glory can indeed 'disgrace' the discourse of historiography through the 'incontinent rule' of unsanctioned interpretation, especially when a mixed and somewhat licentious audience is, in no uncertain terms, urged to assist. At this point the 'imaginary forces' of 'mean and gentle all' can become an unpredictable element in the production of theatrical meaning. To tell such audiences, 'For 'tis your thoughts that now must deck our kings' (Prologue. l. 28) is, to say the least, to expand the margin of indeterminacy and to express considerable confidence in, even bestow authority on, the signifying capacities of a good many ordinary people.

Here the alleged 'imperfections' of the scaffold stage, like other institutionalised realities of the newly open Globe theatre, are introduced on a note of exceeding modesty. The Prologue in fact has seemed almost to denigrate everything theatrical; he is excessively apologetic about the order of that which, in 'this cockpit', is representing while, at the same time, acknowledging the overwhelming authority of what is represented. The note of humility seems strongest where the site and the signs of the theatre are made to appear 'unworthy' of what is to be fully signified, as when the question is asked, how 'can this cockpit hold / The vasty fields of France?' (ll. 11–12). What is apologised for is, apparently, the severely limited space available for faithful representation, the imperfectly achieved continuity on the barren platform between theatrical signs and historiographical meaning.

And yet, as we read again the opening lines of the Prologue, the humble apology for 'this unworthy scaffold' seems strangely at odds with the stirring confidence in the dramatic powers of 'invention' to serve and inspire 'the swelling scene';

> O for a Muse of fire, that would ascend
> The brightest heaven of invention!
> A kingdom for a stage, princes to act,
> And monarchs to behold the swelling scene!
> Then should the warlike Harry, like himself,
> Assume the port of Mars; and at his heels,
> Leash'd in like hounds, should famine, sword, and fire
> Crouch for employment. But pardon, gentles all,
> The flat unraised spirits that hath dar'd
> On this unworthy scaffold to bring forth
> So great an object. ...
>
> (ll. 1–11)

To appropriate 'A kingdom for a stage' and to make 'princes ... act ... the swelling scene' seems competent enough. This concept, rather than rehearsing the traditional element of complementarity between *locus* and *platea*, appears to emphasise the expansive force of localising and visualising the stage at large. As such, 'the swelling scene', I suggest, connotes the unfixed, performative thrust of drama in production, involving self-propelled modes of theatrical signification, the unsettling capacity of the theatre for disrupting the fixture between signs and their meaning – in short, the movable, audible, visible extension in the use of signs, symbols, localities in rapid succession and interaction. If my reading is not altogether off the mark, then 'the swelling scene' has plenty of authority to represent 'princes', 'monarchs', even a whole 'kingdom'. This is how the role of the king is projected: 'Then should the warlike Harry, like himself / Assume the port of Mars'. Here the swelling force of theatrical signification appears perfectly entitled and, indeed, powerful enough to encroach upon the received symbols of authority and to expand, as it were, the represented role of the king, so that the actor, in addition to doing the role of Harry, is visualised as assuming yet another role, a mythological one: 'the port of Mars'. The unfixing, expanding thrust of 'the swelling scene' makes the king himself ascend the brightest heaven of theatricality.

When the space of kingdoms and the title of a prince can so freely be negotiated on this scaffold stage, surely it seems possible to assume that the self-representation of the theatre in the language of the chorus has more performative thrust and fulfils more nearly the function of a dramatic role than is commonly acknowledged. In particular, there is reason to believe that this thickly performed account of the relationship of dramatic text and scaffold stage appears strangely unreliable and even confusing: whatever fruitful interaction existed between writing and stagecraft, between the allegedly 'rough and all-unable pen' and the theatrical potential of the platform stage, is suppressed rather than articulated.

But before we proceed to grapple with such highly conspicuous areas of silence and contradiction, let me hasten to emphasise the complexity and acknowledge the multiplicity of functions associated with the Prologue. For one thing, his silence may be said to involve some complicity with the later choruses, as he helps to ensure success, applause, response, communication on behalf of the drama in performance. In this view the humble emphasis on all the 'imperfections' of the platform stage must have helped to engage the audience in that cooperative and unifying effort by which all 'ciphers to this great account' appear humbly willing to contribute to some ensemble effect in what is a truly epic work of the theatre. And there is of course not the slightest doubt that the audience's sense of, and participation in, this ensemble occasion becomes especially important when the play itself is about to rehearse (not to say resurrect) a festival sense of English unity and patriotism (with, perhaps, some contemporary resonance of Essex preparing for his Irish expedition). While this epic dimension of revitalised unity may well be understood to serve, as late as 1599, a conservative concern about the twilight of the Elizabethan settlement, it also and at the same time does not preclude a popular and perhaps even slightly egalitarian perspective on the social uses of drama. In this context, the metaphorical definition of the theatre as 'cockpit' serving 'mean and gentle all' seems revealing: the language of popular sport and pastime appears appropriate enough. But the site of game and entertaining struggle called *cockpit* provides more than an abbreviated simile for the relative shape of the Globe *en miniature*. For the harmless enough shape of 'this wooden O' allows for a peculiar figure of wordplay revealing 'this cockpit', with its 'unworthy scaffold' for what, in this text, it actually is: 'a crooked figure'. True enough, 'a crooked figure may / Attest in little place a million' (ll. 15–16). The theatre, modestly inscribed in the figure of an O, is a mere nought: this reiterates the *topos* of worthlessness, but at the same time so expands and swells the meaning of a sign that the value of a nought is thrust to the million range. Even so, the scaffold stage, like the number nought, is a *crooked* figure, and not to be trusted: as the Elizabethan mathematician Baret noted in *A brief Instruction of Arythmetike* (1580), the cipher or number zero 'is no Significatiue figure of it selfe, but maketh the other figures wherewith it is ioined, to increase more in value by their place'.[21] This describes precisely the platform stage, which, without localising signs, is a neutral place, 'no Significatiue figure of it selfe'. It seems as if 'this wooden O', the 'cockpit', the unsanctioned 'scaffold', does after all retain a place which is nothing but a place: the communal space for a social occasion, a cultural institution called theatre. The reality of the *platea*, of playing *with* rather than *for* an audience, of laughing *with* rather than *at* the player, continues to persist in the imagery and the forceful movement that the Prologue delivers in the swelling scene of its own performance.

Seen in his 'double dealing' function, the Prologue negotiates his own version of the clash, in this theatre, between authorities representing and authorities represented. To read this clash merely in terms of a fixed difference between an incompetent platform and the overbearing weight of historiographical authority clearly distorts the purpose of the Prologue. Rather, its opening function has to do with how and on what grounds 'this unworthly scaffold' can presume to engage 'so great an object' in contemporary discourse. For that, the crooked figurations in the Prologue's own language point the way. To say that warlike Harry 'Assume[s] the port of Mars', only to have 'famine, sword, and fire' follow at his heels is 'by outward signes to shewe' him 'otherwise' than represented in the Tudor myth of history: otherwise than in the overwhelming form and pressure of historiography.[22] The authority of royalty in the drama is not equally given, but has to be theatrically contested, and this contest, in order to succeed, calls for some 'imaginary puissance' (l. 25). As the context of the phrase suggests, power and authority in the theatre are inseparable from a responsive audience whose 'imaginary forces' are invited to endorse the authority of what is represented – but only on the condition that they participate in the order of that which is representing.

Such 'puissance', derived from an assisting audience, is needed to authorise the alleged 'imperfections' (l. 28) of the scaffold stage. It is because the scaffold's 'imperfections' are established so emphatically that the audience cannot but supply 'thoughts that now must deck our kings' (l. 28). The demand for the audience to 'deck' royalty seems to point to the need for an act of cooperation that sanctions a hitherto unauthorised popular and, in part, unliterary imagination; among other things, it sanctions the topical uses of a self-fashioned memory, harking back to a piece of advice offered by a scurvy politician of a father in *2 Henry IV* on how 'to busy giddy minds / With foreign quarrels' (IV.v.213–14).

Such public intervention in the order of the represented is, in seeming modesty, again acknowledged when the 'imperfections' of this cockpit are used to *confine* the representations of 'mighty men'. This, then, is what the 'unworthy scaffold' can do to the mighty and the glorious:

> In little room confining mighty men,
> Mangling by starts the full course of their glory.
> (*HV*, Epilogue. ll. 3–4)

Here the authority of might and 'glory' so collides with the alleged ineptitude of the scaffold stage that the dominant figures in historiographical discourse are deeply affected if not (in the wider meaning of 'mangling') spoiled, disfigured, mutilated. The chorus, in humbly attempting to explain, if not to apologise for, such treatment, by implication projects the 'little room' as one where the locality of high office, the *locus* of glorious action, the 'full course' of war-like deeds, can effectively be defined or even thwarted by theatrical place. Its strength is that of an 'unworthy scaffold' where the representation of political power can literally be confined and mangled by the imperfect power of theatrical representation.

This, of course, must remain an altogether provisional reading of *Henry V* as long as the text of the chorus is not carefully related to what the play itself does or does not do to the collision of authority of historiographical discourse.[23] This, clearly, is not the place to pursue such a reading of the play at large, except perhaps to remind ourselves that the element of humility in the language of the chorus strangely echoes what Eric Auerbach calls the *sermo humilis* in the midst of heroic matter.[24] In the play there are indeed such unsanctioned figures as, for example, honest soldier Michael Williams, who in his own way presents the king with 'a black matter', 'a heavy reckoning ... when all those legs and arms and heads, chopp'd off in a battle, shall join together at the latter day and cry all, "We died at such a place"' (IV.i.143, 134–7). If ever 'at such a place' such anguish was articulated, it was not, as in this swelling scene, a cry for legitimation. The scene brings together the sentiment, even the empathy, associated with a *locus* of such true feeling as 'passeth show'. And yet the occasion is dark, the scene an irreverent place in the camp, the main actor in disguise. *Locus* and *platea* are brought together in a platform scene digesting the abuse of distance, including the distance between king and commoner, with the divisive issue of authority written large across this 'scene individable, or poem unlimited'. As the disguised king attempts to authorise his foreign policy, pleading 'his cause being just and his quarrel honourable' (ll. 126–7), honest soldier Williams has the curt reply: 'That's more than we know' (l. 128).

V

At this point and in conclusion, the question may be asked whether this redefinition and use of 'distance' in the process of theatrical representation remains exceptional in the epic context of the last of Shakespeare's Elizabethan history plays or whether it opens up a perspective on a more highly experimental and self-conscious use of the *platea* projection of complementary authority. To answer this question, one would need to look at those plays, following close upon *Henry V*, where divided uses of authority appear most centrally to involve a changing use of *locus* and *platea* conventions, as especially in *Hamlet, Troilus and Cressida*, and *Measure for Measure*. While in these plays traditional modes of correlating theatrical space, language, and social status begin to collapse or at least show signs of strain, the supple art of crossing from *locus* to *platea*, and vice versa, continues right into the great tragedies as a mode of constituting, articulating, and performing 'bi-fold authority'.

Since there is a space only for glancing at one more text, my choice, almost predictably, is Lear addressing Gloucester:

> Thou hast seen a farmer's dog bark at a beggar? ... And the creature run from the cur? There thou mightst behold the great image of authority; a dog's obey'd in office.
>
> (IV.vi.154–9)

Gloucester in his blindness is told to 'Look with thine ears' and is advised to 'see ... with no eyes'; when he replies he can see things 'feelingly', then this language itself re-enacts the incontinent rule of topsy-turvydom by which the signs of authority are subjected to a 'handy-dandy' use of signs. When Lear sheds his 'lendings' (III.iv.107) and in imagination has his boots pulled off ('Harder, harder! So' [IV.vi.173]), these precious signs of status and authority are dismantled, and Lear proceeds to embrace a beggar's experience and knowledge of 'how this world goes'. The outrage of the senses that is reflected in Lear's language – reminiscent of Bottom's 'The eye of man hath not heard, the ear of man hath not seen' (*MND*, IV.i.209–12) – helps to project a 'most rare vision' of authority indeed.

The handy-dandy language of the beggar-king embodies a *platea* occasion and distances whatever *locus* of illusion, office, house, and time would otherwise accompany the presence of a king. In conjunction with the convention of madness, this language helps to undermine whatever representational status the *locus* of royalty would normally demand on the platform stage. Much as Hamlet uses his 'antic disposition' to distance the princely authority associated with the *locus* of royal status, so Lear in his *Figurenposition* disrupts the authority of order, degree, and decorum.[25] The resulting effect on his signifying practice is quite unsettling and is conducive to great indeterminacy and irreverence. As, in his language, Lear re-enacts some saturnalian 'change [of] places', the difference in class between 'justice' and 'thief' collapses: 'See how yond justice rails upon yond simple thief. Hark in thine ear: change places, and, handy-dandy, which is the justice, which is the thief?' (IV.vi.151–4). Simultaneously, in this one phrase a whole set of sanctioned social and juridical, lexical and semantic differences are challenged through recourse to those topsy-turvying uses of language that in Shakespeare's drama first emerge in the *Figurenposition* associated with Jack Cade's phrase, 'then are we in order when we are most out of order' (*2 Henry VI*, IV.ii.185–6).

The noteworthy thing, however, is that at this stage the *platea* occasion does not involve non-representational and non-sensical release but, somewhat in the fashion of *Henry V*, comes to be suspended in a 'swelling scene' that combines an unlocalised *Figurenposition* with representational matter. Thus, the disruption of decorum in the mirror of royalty is, paradoxically, complemented by some newly representational perspective on the hitherto suppressed or inarticulate experience of the poor naked wretch. As the language of authority is transcribed into images of bare force and repression, 'the great image of authority' is made to signify the experience of the victims rather than that of the spokesman of Tudor authority. As in the popular voice of soldier Michael Williams, the bifold nature of authority is articulated on the level and in the order of what is represented; only this time the voice is that of a beggar-king, a crooked, Janus-faced figuration of two authorities in one, each warring upon the other. As in Troilus's vision of 'madness of discourse' (V.ii.146), the representation of experience enters into and helps change the incontinent rule of the *platea* in action.

This, finally, is what the dramatic inversion of the senses can reveal (*Lear*, IV.vi.151): the suppressed knowledge of 'how this world goes' (ll. 147–8). The eye, the most noble organ in Renaissance specular psychology, was blind to this vulgar spot of silence and oliteration, never ever able to hear the harsh sound of the farmer's dog bark at a beggar who, as Poor Tom – another victim of authority – is represented as one who 'drinks the green mantle of the standing pool; who is whipp'd from tithing to tithing, and stock-punish'd, and imprison'd' (III.iv.132–4) – imprisoned by those who use the bridle, not to say the whip, of authority. As in the madness of Lear, the raving space of *platea*-licence helps destabilise a little brief authority in the language of degree, priority, and place, but – in doing so – provides a new *locus* for signifying (and appropriating for the theatre) hitherto unrepresentable divisions in human kind, order, and legitimation.

From *Shakespeare Quarterly*, 39:4 (1988), 401–17

NOTES

[In this essay Robert Weimann returns to the dialectical (*platea* and *locus*) model of Elizabethan dramaturgy first developed in his *Shakespeare and the Popular Tradition in the Theater* (1967; English translation 1978) in the light of the New Historicist work of the 1980s. Weimann's work, which has a more direct and unambiguous relationship with Marxism than that of the New Historicists, offers a detailed sociology of theatrical institutions, practices and forms, and plays upon the various meanings of authority, authorisation and authorship to disclose the professional and institutional forces regulating theatrical practice and dramaturgical form, technique and effect. Weimann focuses upon *Henry V* as an exemplary instance of a text self-consciously engaged in negotiations between the competing claims of the play's subject-matter and the social energies of the playhouse itself. The concept of 'bi-fold authority' indicates that the divided representational space of the stage opened up a potentially abrasive dialogue between the drama's official function and the ambiguously subversive activities of the theatre. Quotations are from the Arden Shakespeare *King Henry V*, ed. J. H. Walter (London, 1954). Ed.]

1. Stephen Greenblatt, *Renaissance Self-Fashioning: From More to Shakespeare* (Chicago, 1980), p. 254.
2. Steven Mullaney, *The Place of the Stage: License, Play, and Power in Renaissance England* (Chicago, 1988), pp. 21, 49.
3. Ibid., p. 49.

4. *Greene's Groatsworth of Wit*; the relevant text is duplicated in S. Schoenbaum's *William Shakespeare: A Documentary Life* (New York, 1975), pp. 115–16.

5. Timothy Murray, *Theatrical Legitimation: Allegories of Genius in Seventeenth-Century England and France* (New York, 1987), p. 96.

6. Thomas Hobbes, *Leviathan* (1651; rpt. New York, 1950), p. 135.

7. See John Guillory, *Poetic Authority: Spenser, Milton, and Literary History* (New York, 1983).

8. Colin MacCabe, 'Abusing Self and Others: Puritan Accounts of the Shakespearean Stage', unpublished paper presented at the Chapel Hill conference 'Representations of Authority', March 1988. This refers to and appears substantiated by David Wiles, *Shakespeare's Clown: Actor and Text in the Elizabethan Playhouse* (Cambridge, 1987), chs 1–4.

9. Ibid.

10. Cf. Carol C. Rutter (ed.), *Documents of the Rose Playhouse* (Manchester, 1984), pp. 24, 72.

11. Walter Cohen, *Drama of a Nation: Public Theater in Renaissance England and Spain* (Ithaca, NY, 1985), p. 180.

12. Peter Clark, *English Provincial Society from the Reformation to the Revolution: Religion, Politics and Society in Kent, 1500–1640* (Hassocks, 1977), p. 144.

13. H. Hassell Smith, *County and Court: Government and Politics in Norfolk, 1558–1603* (Oxford, 1974), pp. 333, 277.

14. Joel Hurstfield, *Freedom, Corruption and Government in Elizabethan England* (London, 1973), p. 25.

15. Hassell Smith, *County and Court*, p. 334.

16. Conyers Read (ed.), *William Lambarde and Local Government: His 'Ephemeris' and Twenty-nine Charges to Juries and Commissions* (Ithaca, NY, 1962), pp. 143–4.

17. Ibid., p. 80.

18. George Wapull, *The Tyde taryeth no Man* (London, 1756), sig. G.iii.v.

19. See Robert Weimann, *Shakespeare and the Popular Tradition in the Theater* (Baltimore, 1978), pp. 73–85, 215–46.

20. Such has been cogently argued by Malcolm Evans, *Signifying Nothing: Truth's True Contents in Shakespeare's Text* (Athens, GA, 1986), pp. 133ff.

21. Cited in J. H. Walter (ed.), *The Arden Shakespeare: King Henry V* (London, 1954), p. 6.

22. For Holinshed and Hall and also for Daniel's 'panegyric of Henry V', see Geoffrey Bullough (ed.), *Narrative and Dramatic Sources of Shakespeare*, vol. 4 (London, 1962), pp. 349ff.

23. For a stimulating study, see Günter Walch, 'Tudor-Legende und Geschichtsbewegung in *The Life of Henry V*: Zur Rezeptionslenkung durch den Chorus', *Shakespeare Jahrbuch*, 122 (1986), 36–46.

24. Eric Auerbach, *Mimesis: The Representation of Reality in Western Literature*, trans. Willard Trask (Garden City, NY, 1953), pp. 131–8.

25. The strategy of *Figurenposition* has been cogently studied by Michael Mooney in two essays, '"This Luxurious Circle": *Figurenposition* in *The Revenger's Tragedy*', *ELR*, 13 (1983), 162–81; '"Edgar I nothing am": *Figurenposition* in *King Lear*', *Shakespeare Survey*, 38 (1985), 153–66.

5

'To Represent such a Lady'

KATHLEEN McLUSKIE

I

The constant, witty play around the sexuality of men and women on and off the stage creates [...] complex resonances through the use of boy actors to play all women's roles. This practice calls into question the relationship between the actor and his role, the nature and limits of theatrical representation and the connection between the theatre and the world beyond. Of necessity it stands in the way of a simple correlation between the theatrical representation of women and their treatment either in social formations or in other forms of ideological construction. Among both Elizabethan commentators and theatre historians the discussion of boy actresses circles around the dividing point between the theatre and the world, either locking them into the world of representation or seeking to generalise from them about the nature of male and female sexuality. The two positions are seen as mutually exclusive. Jensen, for example, firmly asserts:

> Like any convention in any art form, the use of boy actors in female roles was a practice that audiences accepted without confusion or feelings of sexual ambivalence.[1]

In this view, theatrical convention is seen as a form of translation in which the reality of the narrative is reproduced on the stage – in such a way as to close off or suppress any irrelevant thoughts about the actors or the nature of their activity on the stage. 'Convention' is seen as a stable controller of meaning, mediating between a stable text and a stable reality.

The opposite point of view sees theatrical representation as open to a knowing awareness of its own activity and is seen at its most extreme in Lisa Jardine's claim that homosexual attraction towards the boy players was a primary pleasure for Elizabethan theatregoers.[2] This interpretation sees performance as paramount, suppresses entirely the narrative which is being enacted and focuses exclusively on the relationship between performer and audience. Boys dressed as women acting out a narrative are seen as the same as boys dressed as women in a tavern or on the street.

Part of the difficulty and confusion which attends these discussions is a product of Elizabethan confusions in a similar discussion. The boy actresses could not be 'like any convention in any art form' for theatrical representation in general and boy players in particular were, for the Elizabethans, a source of anxiety and heated debate. The whole business of theatrical representation violated notions of decorum and degree and in particular the practice of boys playing women transgressed the primary boundary between male and female. Moreover, there was biblical authority for objection to that practice in the injunction against cross-dressing, so the question recurs with wearisome regularity in all the contemporary discussions of the antitheatrical prejudice.[3]

Like the modern discussions, the arguments of the antitheatrical polemicists wilfully confused the requirements for putting a narrative on stage with behaviour in real life. The defenders of theatre were quick to point out the distinction:

> nor do I hold it lawfull to beguile the eyes of the world in confounding the shapes of either sex, as to keepe any youth in the habit of a virgin, or any virgin in the shape of a lad, to shroud them from the eyes of their fathers, tutors, or protectors, or to any other sinister intent whatsoever. But to see our youths attired in the habit of a woman, who knowes not what their intents be? Who cannot distinguish them by their names, assuredly knowing they are but to represent such a Lady at such a time appoynted.[4]

Heywood sought to protect the theatre by insisting on the limits of its specificity and the purity of its intentions. He distinguishes between the dangerous cross-dressing for nefarious purposes in the real world and the stable representations of women fixed by the boundaries of narrative and the stage.

Heywood's position and that of the 'convention' critics clearly has a good deal of common-sense support. The fictions of

Elizabethan drama would have been rendered nonsensical if at every appearance of a female character – say Ursula the pig woman or the Duchess of Malfi – their gender was called into question. Nevertheless the conditions in which that stability prevailed and the process by which it was sustained bear some investigation.

The clearest sexual indicators which could 'represent such a Lady at such a time appoynted' were voice and costume. The boy players had unbroken voices and the examples of women's costumes from Henslowe's inventory suggest that considerable trouble and expense went into providing appropriate costumes for those playing women's parts.[5] These indicators seem to have been sufficient in themselves and not merely aids to the boy player's suitability for representing a woman. Flute the bellows mender in *A Midsummer Night's Dream* is, after all, told that his incipient beard is no bar to an adequate representation of 'the lady that Pyramus must love':

> That's all one: you shall play it in a mask;
> and you may speak as small as you will.
> (I.ii.45–6)

Pictorial representations of scenes from Elizabethan drama, moreover, portrayed women characters as women without any hint of sexual ambiguity. As R. A. Foakes's collection of illustrations has shown, the representation of women in pictures of the Elizabethan stage drew on contemporary iconographic traditions. Arethusa in the title page to *Philaster* is shown with fully exposed breasts, and Zenocrate in the woodcut in the third edition of *Tamburlaine* depicts 'a conventional representation of a richly dressed woman'.[6] The theatre, like other modes of signification, drew on familiar signifiers of sexuality as it did for those of class or profession or royalty. These signifiers drew on the real world or the permanent attributes of the actors who bore them only in so far as those elements in the real world themselves depended upon familiar systems of signification.

In plays where representation of fictional characters is produced by emblem and symbol, where the acting style evidently proceeds by a set of formal encounters, the difficulty of incorporating a stable representation of women was not great. The signification of 'woman' is entirely contained within the text and in no way depends on the personality or gender of the actor in question. If we return to *A Midsummer Night's Dream* we can see that Quince and his fellows are dealing with just such stable categories. Bottom asks 'What is Pyramus? A lover, or a tyrant?' and is confident that he could play either: it is a simple extension of his confidence for him to feel that 'An I may hide my face, let me play Thisbe too. I'll speak in a monstrous little voice' (I.ii.46). Bottom's self-confidence is based on his perception of the fixed relationship between character, action and narrative which had been created by the literary and dramatic traditions which the Elizabethan dramatists inherited.

When dramatic narrative moves away from these simple oppositions, however, the players' roles require a different kind of dramatic control, as Bottom and his mechanicals find out when they try to control the difficult and shifting relationship between the representation of a narrative and the perceptions of the audience. They debate how to control the limits of their fiction so as not to affright the ladies with their lion and invoke the real phases of the moon to overcome the technical difficulties of stage lighting. The range of solutions that they suggest spans the spectrum of representation from the static emblem which requires a special gloss – 'this lanthorn doth the horned moon present' (V.i.230) – to the channelling of the world outside the fiction:

> You may leave a casement of the great chamber window where we play open; and the moon may shine in at the casement.
>
> (III.i.52–4)

A good deal of the humour of the mechanicals' play in *A Midsummer Night's Dream* depends upon the recognition that their fixed and conventional notions of representation are becoming out of date. Indeed the effect of the play within the play is to ensure the greater reality – of the main action. Their style of acting, associated with earlier emblematic and rhetorical drama, came to be an object of mockery in contrast to the apparently spontaneous, internally constructed notions of character and action developed in later plays.

But this spontaneous, internally constructed notion of character was itself the result of careful dramatic control – particularly in the case of women characters. In Shakespeare's romantic comedies, for example, the discussions of femininity, and the role of cross-dressing in the plots seem always to be inviting and at the same time denying a metatheatrical awareness of the true identity of the actor playing the woman's part. The 'realishness' of the boy players' femininity was asserted not only by the self-enclosed, self-referential visual and verbal indicators but by its contrast with what it was not. The cross-dressing of Shakespeare's romantic heroines is thus used partly as a means of resolving plot but also as a means of asserting their true femininity. Their characters as women are seen as something essential and internal and not a simple result of their clothes. In *The Two Gentlemen of Verona*, for example, when Julia plans her pursuit of her true-love, she has this exchange with her maid:

> **Lucetta** But in what habit will you go along?
> **Julia** Not like a woman, for I would prevent
> The loose encounters of lascivious men;
> Gentle Lucetta, fit me with such weeds
> As may beseem some well reputed page.
> **Lucetta** Why then your ladyship must cut your hair.
> **Julia** No, girl; I'll knit it up in silken strings
> With twenty odd conceited true-love knots –
> To be fantastic may become a youth
> Of greater time than I shall show to be.
> **Lucetta** What fashion, madam, shall I make your breeches?
> **Julia** That fits as well as 'Tell me, good my lord,
> What compass will you wear your farthingale?'
> Why even what fashion thou best likes Lucetta.
> **Lucetta** You must needs have them with a codpiece madam.
> **Julia** Out, out, Lucetta, that will be ill favour'd.
> **Lucetta** A round hose, madam, now's not worth a pin
> Unless you have a codpiece to stick pins in.
> **Julia** Lucetta, as thou lov'st me, let me have
> What thou think'st meet and is most mannerly.
> (II.vii.40–58)

Part of the wit of this complicated exchange depends upon the realisation that Julia and Lucetta are both played by 'fantastic youths' in costume; however, it also plays on the inappropriateness of male dress for a female heroine – 'that fits as well as "Tell me, good my lord, what compass will you wear your farthingale?"' Moreover, the joke about the empty codpiece may have a satiric resonance at the expense of gallants in the audience, but it also clearly indicates that, within the fiction, Julia lacks the primary sexual signifier. The overall effect of the sequence, like Rosalind's frequent references in *As You Like It* to the woman's heart which lies beneath her doublet and hose, is to insist on the true and essential character of Julia's femininity, a fictional identity which transcends her clothes.

Bawdy jokes about the connection between clothes and sexual identity are developed into a complete scene in *The Roaring Girl* when Moll Cutpurse is fitted for breeches by a tailor:

> **Tailor** I forgot to take measure on you for your new breeches.
> **Moll** What fiddling's here? would not the old pattern have served your turn?
> **Tailor** You change the fashion, you say you'll have the great Dutch slop, Mistress Mary.
> **Moll** Why sir, I say so still.
> **Tailor** Your breeches then will take up a yard more.
> **Moll** Well, pray look it be put in then.
> **Tailor** It shall stand round and full, I warrant you.
> **Moll** Pray make 'em easy enough.
> **Tailor** I know my fault now, t'other was somewhat stiff between the legs, I'll make these open enough, I warrant you.
> (II.ii.73–87)

These instances could be seen merely as the necessary development of a convention but for the fact that transvestite heroines almost all appear in plays where questions of sexual identity are only one point on a spectrum of questions about identity, action and representation. In *The Two Gentlemen of Verona*, Valentine's character as a lover is determined by the list of special marks which his servant mockingly itemises:

> ... first you have learn'd, like Sir Proteus, to wreath your arms like a malcontent; to relish a love song, like a robin red-breast; to walk alone, like one that had the pestilence; to sigh like a schoolboy that had lost his ABC; to weep like a young wench that had buried her grandam; to fast like one that takes a diet; to watch, like one that fears robbing; to speak puling, like a beggar at Hallowmas.
> (II.i.17–25)

Speed's list of similes shows that each attribute is precisely *not* like a lover's. It is only when taken together that they produce the correct diagnosis: the representation of a lover or a tyrant or a woman is part of a system of representation rather than the result of a single conventional attribute.

The situation is even more complicated when the category woman is part of a system of representation rather than the result of Sylvia, which causes Julia to question how far the differences between them are the product of 'true' distinctions or simply differences of representation:

Here is her picture; let me see, I think
If I had such a tire, this face of mine
Were full as lovely as is this of hers;
And yet the painter flatter'd her a little,
Unless I flatter with myself too much.
Her hair is auburn, mine is perfect yellow;
If that be all the difference in his love,
I'll get me such a colour'd periwig.
Her eyes are grey as glass, and so are mine;
Ay but her forehead's low and mine's as high.
What should it be that he respects in her
But I can make respective in myself,
If this fond love were not a blinded god?
Come shadow, come, and take this shadow up,
For 'tis thy rival.

(IV.iv.180–93)

Julia does not compare herself to Sylvia but to Sylvia's picture: the realities are irrelevant, the representations are all. At that moment the shadow of Julia, disguised as a page, can only compare unfavourably with the flattered shadow of Sylvia, dressed in the tires of formal portraiture.

The fact that there is a further, extra-diegetic, reality, in which Julia is not a lady at all but a boy, need not enter into the awareness at this point: it does not do so, for example, in modern productions in which Julia is played by a woman. Indeed, to introduce the ambiguities of gender at this point would muddy an elegant opposition.

II

Questions of role playing and acting need not lead beyond the narrative to a notion of metatheatre; they can be used to privilege the act or role played by the narrative hero or heroine as the one that has 'that within which passes show'. The convention helps to hold the action of the play within the narrative so that the boy player – or any other player – will only 'represent such a Lady at such a time appoynted'.

Nevertheless, the implications of these discussions of acting and playing are further complicated by their use in literary descriptions of 'real life'. The list of women's parts which Heywood gives in the prefatory verses to *An Apology for Actors* makes no concession to the fact that these women would be played by boys. They are simply part of a pre-existing moral typology:

She a chaste Lady acteth all her life
A wanton courtezan another plays.
This covets marriage loue, that, nuptial strife
Both in continual action spend their days.

The moral typology not only provides character but determines narrative, and notions of decorum determine the relationship between the two.

Behind all such discussions lay the trope of the *theatrum mundi*,[7] the notion that there was a vital, if ill-defined, connection between the theatre and the world. In the Induction to *Antonio and Mellida* this question is addressed with precise reference to the roles of lover, tyrant and woman:

Feliche Why, what must you play?
Antonio Faith, I know not what, an hermaphrodite, two parts in one; my true person being Antonio son to the Duke of Genoa, though for the love of Mellida, Piero's daughter, I take this feigned presence of an Amazon, calling myself Florizel and I know not what. I a voice to play a lady! I shall ne'er do it.
Alberto O, an Amazon should have such a voice, virago-like. Not play two parts in one? away, away; 'tis common fashion. Nay, if you cannot bear two subtle fronts under one hood, idiot go by, go by, off this world's stage. O time's impurity!
Antonio Ay, but when use hath taught me action to hit the right point of a lady's part, I shall grow ignorant, when I must turn young prince again, how but to truss my hose.
Feliche Tush, never put them off; for women wear breeches still.
(Induction, 67–80)

Alberto's comments reassure Antonio that he has only to look to the world in order to see how to play a part. However, the world beyond the play which he invokes is not the real world of variety and inconsequentiality but the constructed world of satiric commonplace. As in other examples of the *theatrum mundi*, the comparison is not between acting and truth so much as between competing fictions. Since the world can only be defined in terms of its significations, the actor has to turn to those signifying systems in order to represent the truth of the fiction he enacts.

This is seen even more clearly in the Induction to *The Taming of the Shrew*, where the comedy plays on the limits of competing fictions. The Lord's page plays the woman's part in the elaborate deception worked on Sly but he soon has to establish the limits of his role. Sly responds to the news that he has a wife by claiming his conjugal rights. The page's only self-protection – short of exposing the fiction completely and destroying the joke – is to retreat hurriedly into a further elaboration of the fiction to save his/her honour:

> Thrice noble lord, let me entreat of you
> To pardon me yet for a night or two,
> Or if not so, until the sun be set,
> For your physicians have expressly charged,
> In peril to incur your former malady
> That I should yet absent me from your bed.
> I hope this reason stands for my excuse.
> (Induction 2, 116–22)

Yet Sly was convinced of the page's femininity less because of the boy actor's truth to life than because they both inhabit the same fictional world. The Lord who is directing the show instructs his servants in the most effective and convincing presentation of their fiction:

> Sirrah go you to Barthol'mew my page
> And see him dressed in all suits like a lady.
> That done, conduct him to the drunkard's chamber,
> And call him 'madam', do him obeisance.
> Tell him from me – as he will win my love –
> He bear himself with honourable action,
> Such as he hath observed in noble ladies
> Unto their lords, by them accomplished.
> Such duty to the drunkard let him do,
> With soft low tongue and lowly courtesy,
> And say 'What is't your honour will command
> Wherein your lady and your humble wife
> May show her duty and make known her love?'
> And then with kind embracements, tempting kisses,
> And with declining head into his bosom,
> Bid him shed tears, as being overjoyed
> To see her noble lord restored to health,
> Who for this seven years hath esteemed him
> No better than a poor and loathsome beggar ...
> (Induction 1, 102–20)

The page's woman's part will be achieved by the appropriateness of his costume and the other servants' behaviour towards him but, most importantly, it will be effected by his dialogue and gestures.

The more difficult matter of his tears, however, will require a technical trick:

> And if the boy have not a woman's gift
> To rain a shower of commanded tears,
> An onion will do well for such a shift,
> Which in a napkin, being close conveyed,
> Shall in despite enforce a watery eye.
> (Induction 2, 121–5)

Paradoxically, the Lord's description of the trick draws the most explicit analogy with the supposed 'real' world, but his sense of 'woman's gift' is itself entirely literary. The young boy actor has none of the stereotyped attributes of a 'real life' woman so he must resort to the techniques of duplicitous women rendered familiar by such fabliaux tales as Dunbar's *Twa Merrit Wemen and the Wedo*[8] or by the woman in 'The Boke of Mayd Emlyn' who, after she had pushed her husband down a well, attended his funeral where

> A reed onyon wolde she kepe
> To make her eyes wepe
> In her kerchers.[9]

The key to effective mimesis lay not in close observation of the real world but in imitating fictional antecedents.

The distinction between men and women on stage and off consisted of a series of related and intertwined distinctions, all governed by and informing convention. They ranged from a simple unquestioned statement – 'this is a man', this is 'such a Lady at such a time' – to a complex set of moral categories. In social life the distinction between maleness and femaleness is paramount and in narrative or fictional life it carries the same central importance. But it cannot be known with certainty. The primary, physiological, distinction could not, of course, be represented on the stage.

In plays where the difference between a man and a woman is of crucial narrative importance, the distinction is either simply effected by *fiat*,[10] or by a displaced revelation, the removal of a hat or a wig. However, these narrative questions of maleness and femaleness can only provide the initiative or the resolution of a plot. For a woman character to be adequately represented on the stage, the category of woman must be disintegrated into the components of the moral typology – chaste lady, courtesan, married love, nuptial strife – which equally depend upon systems of signification.

More complete frustration with the system of signification is evident in *Much Ado About Nothing*. Claudio, having rejected Hero on their wedding day, attempts to justify his action by interpreting the signs for the assembled company. He asserts:

> She's but the sign and semblance of her honour.
> Behold how like a maid she blushes here.
> O what authority and show of truth
> Can cunning sin cover itself withal!
> Comes not that blood as modest evidence
> To witness simple virtue? Would you not swear,
> All you that see her, that she were a maid
> By these exterior shows? But she is none:
> She knows the heat of a luxurious bed;
> Her blush is guiltiness, not modesty.
>
> (IV.i.32–41)

No blush at all need have come from the boy player; within the drama he is merely an emblem to be read according to different models of reality. Claudio's model of reality is based on the imagery and typology of misogynist satire with its talk of 'pamper'd animals that rage in savage sensuality' and is a discourse shared by misogynists throughout the drama; its value and power depended on the status of the man who used it. Knowledge of the 'true' gender of the boy player may complicate but it cannot simply deny the complexity of these questions of significance. The frustrated critic may wish, like the puppet in *Bartholomew Fair*, simply to lift the skirts and expose the reality behind the signification but the result, as in Jonson's play, would simply be a disconcerted silence. For the question of the theatrical representation of femininity cannot be restricted to the physical; gender has never been coterminous with biological sex. When dramatists tried to complicate 'the woman's part', they took on board the moral and social definitions which in their fixity could always be challenged by the flux of action both fictional and real.

III

These conclusions about how gender and sexuality were represented in Elizabethan drama cannot, nevertheless, provide any clear guidance as to how players were perceived by their contemporary audience. It may be, as the moralists asserted, that the boys were subject to homosexual exploitation by the adult players[11] or were the object of their audience's homosexual lust. If that was the case it is remarkable that no specific charge of homosexuality was ever brought against an actor or a boy player. Even the scandal over the abduction of Henry Clifton's son[12] involved only the social difference between a chorister in the Chapel Royal and 'the base trade of a mercynary enterlude player'. Moreover, the clamour of antitheatrical attack is not the only, or even the most reliable, sound of response to the Elizabethan theatre: the institution was defended by the highest in the land, and even municipal attempts at control are delivered in the more measured tones of a concern for public order, with apparently little anxiety about sexual mores or the nature of representation.[13]

Nevertheless, the boy actresses do seem to have generated a disproportionate amount of fuss, a fuss which cannot be accounted for simply as misguided prejudice or a failure to understand the nature of representation. In its fervour and its language, the attack on the boy players echoed attacks on other forms of social change, providing an example of what Stuart Clark has described as 'the periodic social need to relocate moral and cultural boundaries by means of accusations of deviance'.[14]

In their attack on the boy players, however, the moralists had chosen the most difficult and most shifting of moral and cultural boundaries – the relationship of clothes to sex. At its most extreme, the case was simple: as Philip Stubbes wrote:

> Our apparell was given as a signe distinctive, to discern betwixt sexe and sexe, and therefore one to weare the apparell of an other sex, is to participate with the same and to adulterate the veritie of his owne kinde.[15]

Clothes, as Stubbes acknowledged, were signs. They were signs, Stubbes and others were sure, of a natural and unchangeable phenomenon: sex was 'the veritie of his own kind'. However, as in the theatre, these 'verities' could not extend very far. Stubbes had to go on to make a further distinction in kind; not between male and female but between needful and excessive modes of dress:

> when they have all these goodly robes upon them, women seeme to be the smallest part of themselves, not natural women, but

> artificiall women, not women of fleshe and bloud, but rather Puppits, or Mawmets consistyng of ragges and cloutes compact together... .[16]

Stubbes's slide into metaphor indicates the impossibility of talking about clothes without invoking pre-existing moral categories, the most influential of which is the distinction between the natural and unnatural.

A similar confusion pervades the 'Homily Against Excess of Apparell'. It begins generously enough by accepting that God 'alloweth us apparell not only for necessity's sake but also for an honest comliness'. However, 'honest comliness' is soon having to be set against 'fine bravery' which will be an inducement to 'wanton, lewd and unchaste behaviour' and distinguished further from the necessary adornment appropriate to high degree.[17] For women the case was even more complicated, for in moral and metaphoric terms it seems they needed no clothes at all:

> Let women be subject to their husbands and they are sufficiently attired ... .[18]

What was clearly most important of all was the 'difference in apparel between an honest matron and a common strumpet'.[19] As in the discourses of satire, the distinction between male and female in fact mattered less than the moral and social distinction between chaste and unchaste, noble and common. In spite of the evidently serious and didactic purpose of the Homily, its conviction that it was addressing real social ills, it cannot escape from the rhetoric of complaint and the categories of decorum:

> many a one doubtless should be compelled to wear a russet coat which now ruffleth in silks and velvets, spending more by the year in superfluous apparell than their fathers received for the whole revenue of their lands... .[20]

The signs of morality, since they were established by custom and not by nature, were notoriously unstable. They were, moreover, under pressure from a different tradition in which nature is best seen stripped of all customary embellishment. The reductive logic and static oppositions of this kind of writing could easily be overturned by the common-sense wit of the new generation of satirists such as Henry Fitzgeffrey:

Socraticke Doctors, Catoes most austeer
Roule up the Records of Antiquity,
To frame Abridgements for youth's Liberty.
Accuse Wit's folly, Time's strange alterations;
The vaine expence of cloth consuming fashions
When their allowance was (themselves can tell)
At least unto a Codpiece halfe an Ell
...
As if a Frounced, pounced Pate coo'd not,
As much Braine couer, as a Stoike cut.
Or practicke Vertue, might not lodge as soone
Under a Silken, as a Cynicke gowne.[21]

A pair of pamphlets responding to the androgynous fashions of the turn of the century conducted the debate in familiar terms. *Hic Mulier* took the line from decorum, calling on 'the powerful Statute of apparell' to:

> lift up his Battle Axe, and crush the offenders in pieces, so as every one may be knowne by the true badge of their bloud or Fortune.[22]

The defensive reply, *Haec Vir*, challenged the simple fit between sartorial signifier and moral signified and asked

> ... because I stand not with my hands on my belly like a baby at Bartholomew Fayre, that moue not my whole body when I should, but onely stirre my head like Iacke of the Clocke house which hath no ioynts, that am not dumbe when wantons court me, or because I weep not when injury gripes me, like a worried Deere in the fangs of many Curres, am I therefore barbarous and shameless?[23]

However, before we can take these iconoclastic inversions as true statements of youthful defiance or feminist self-assertion, we have to note that they merely involve choosing a different set of oppositions and metaphors with which to score debating points in a contest which repeats itself throughout the period. It was a contest, moreover, which embodied anxiety about the sexual and social definition but which could only reveal its elusive and contradictory nature.

IV

In subsuming questions of gender into the moral and social typologies of sumptuary regulation Elizabethan commentators on the stage and on social mores were able to avoid direct confrontation with questions of sex and gender. Nevertheless, on a few occasions, the gender ambiguity which the convention of boys playing women allowed was given the literary and theatrical space to tease out more complex ways of seeing the boundaries of gender and sexuality. One of the best known of these is Shakespeare's sonnet 20, which celebrates the 'Master Mistress of my passion' and dramatises the problem of male and female signification in the fullest possible way.

In the opening lines the gender of the beloved addressed is not entirely clear:

> A woman's face, with Nature's own hand painted
> Hast thou, the Master Mistress of my passion.

Nevertheless she/he is defined through an opposition to conventional female moral categories: she/he has

> A woman's gentle heart, but not acquainted
> With shifting change, as is false woman's fashion;
> An eye more bright than their's, less false in rolling
> Gliding the object whereupon it gazeth.

A figure with the opposite to women's attributes has to have something male about him, and indeed is

> A man in hue, all hues in his controlling
> Which steals men's hearts and women's souls amazeth.

The force of that *moral* opposition between men and women is, however, complicated by the third quatrain. In spite of the unfeminine virtues which the beloved possesses.

> For a woman wert thou first created
> Till Nature as she wrought thee fell adoting
> And by addition me of thee defeated
> By adding one thing to my purpose nothing.

The sonnet turns on the difference between the beloved's feminine beauty, which can be verbally but not physically distinguished from the false beauty of other women. Since the lover's face is 'with Nature's own hand painted', by implication 'false woman's fashion' is not natural but social. The logic of Nature's painting is thwarted by the addition of the primary sexual signifier: 'one thing to my purpose nothing'. This 'addition' is the only difference between a young man and a woman but it is sufficient to change not only the young man's gender but all the moral signification that goes with it. However, by the end of the sonnet the poet realises that the only purpose of maleness is the relationship, both natural and social, of sex:

> But since she prick'd thee out for women's pleasure,
> Mine be thy love, and thy love's use their treasure.

The truth at the heart of the beloved's beauty is 'one thing to my purpose nothing'. The categories of sexuality are artificially constructed but they carry nevertheless the most serious social taboos. Once again the emphasis is on familiar moral categories but the poem shows an awareness that men and women might be created out of an overlapping system of differences and, more dangerously, that these physical attributes might inspire love regardless of their ascription to a particular gender.

That rather more threatening possibility of physical passion which is not appropriately directed is raised, albeit lightheartedly, in *The Maid's Metamorphosis*, performed by the children of Pauls in 1600.[24] The play combines the story of Ascanius' thwarted love for Eurymine, and her adventures in the forest where she has fled from her murderers, with a conflict between Juno and Iris, played out on the fates of the unfortunate lovers. This combination of different styles and ways of resolving the action allows strange clashes which raise interesting questions about the literary and theatrical conventions governing combinations of the sexes. Having escaped from death, Eurymine takes up a pastoral existence, keeping sheep in the forest, where she encounters Apollo. He tries at first to seduce Eurymine to be his lover and, when she refuses, attempts 'with proffered force a silly Mayd to touch'. In order to prevent the rape, Eurymine asks Apollo to show his power by transforming her into a man. Apollo grants her request but, out of spite, says that he will change only her body and not her desires:

> I graunt thy wish, thou art become a man:
> I speake no more then well performe I can,
> And though thou walke in chaunged bodie now,
> This pennance shall be added to thy vow:
> Thy selfe a man, shalt loue a man, in vaine:
> And louing, wish to be a maide againe.
> (III.ii.223–7)

Apollo's spite is caused by his own thwarted passion for the boy Hyacinth and raises questions about the relationship between sexuality, gender and sexual desire. It seems to support the essentialist view that since Eurymine is a woman she can only love men. However, since she will be a man when she does so, it is clearly not impossible for men to love men. Sexual desire is thus located both in the essential characteristics of one gender and in the contingent desirability of the beloved.

The situation is further complicated when Ascanius comes to the forest in search of his beloved. He is dismayed to find that she has been transformed into a man. He is outraged by the suggestion that he might be 'haunted with such lunacie' (IV.i.153) as to love a boy, but his comic page, Ioculo, tries to resolve the difficulty by suggesting that the problem is a metaphorical one:

> Women weare breetches, petticoates are deare.
> And that's his meaning, on my life it is.
> (IV.i.118–19)

However, this simple retreat into the metaphors of misogynist satire is explicitly prevented by the action of the play. It uses the *fact* of Eurymine's transformation to investigate further the connections between homosexual friendship and heterosexual desire, playing on the ambiguous use of the word 'love' and the familiar opposition between true identity and 'habit' in both the social and the sartorial senses:

> **Eurymine** How gladly would I be thy lady still,
> If earnest vowes might answere to my will?
> **Ascanius** And is thy fancie altered with thy guise?
> **Eurymine** My kinde, but not my minde in any wise.
> **Ascanius** What though thy habit differe from thy kind:
> Thou mayest retain thy wonted louing mind.
> **Eurymine** And so I doo.
> **Ascanius** Then why art thou so strange?
> Or wherefore doth thy plighted fancie chaunge?
> **Eurymine** *Ascanius*, my heart doth honor thee.
> **Ascanius** And yet continuest stil so strange to me?
> **Eurymine** Not strange, so far as kind will give me leave …
> (V.i.17–26)

The dialogue continues to turn on friend and love and sex until Ascanius reluctantly concludes 'Then haue I lost a wife' and Eurymine confronts him:

> But found a friend, whose dearest blood and life,
> Shal be as readie as thine owne for thee:
> In place of wife, such friend thou hast of mee.
> (V.i.47–50)

The possibility of resolving these difficulties by a homosexual attachment is not allowed within the scope of this story, and the problem is eventually solved by Apollo relenting and declaring baldly 'she is a maide again'. In the same process, he reveals that Eurymine is in truth the long-lost daughter of Aramanthus and so the social bar to her marriage with Ascanius is removed to ensure the final happy ending.

In one sense this comic circling around questions of gender and sexual identity is a displacement of the real barrier to the lovers' union, Eurymine's obscure birth. Identity in this play is bound up not only with gender but also with status, but these are presented as narrative rather than social problems. The lovers' problems are merely the narrative framework on which the other dramatic pleasures of the play, the songs and the comic turns of the witty pages, are grafted. The lovers' despair can be treated as another comic episode precisely because they inhabit a magical story world in which gender identity or social status are dramatic counters available for the dramatist to play with in making his play. As a social idea the notion of gender instability is at least unnerving and at most subversive: in dramatic play it enables wit and bawdy and turns of plot which finally can be held in place and restored to safety by narrative closure. When in *Twelfth Night* Viola finds herself loving a man who thinks she is a boy and being beloved by a woman, she can sigh 'O time, thou must untangle this, not I / It is too hard a knot for me t'untie', we know that Time is in the hands of the dramatist, who will restore rightful sexual relations when the full dramatic potential has been fulfilled.

Sexual identity was available for 'play' of this kind partly because of the tradition of tales of metamorphosis. Heywood in his *Guneikeon* tells the story of Iphis, whose female sex was concealed by her mother to save her from her father's vow to murder any girl children. There was no difficulty in disguising her sex, for

> The habit of a Boy she wore
> And it had such a face,
> As whether she were Boy or Gyrle,
> It either Sex would grace.

When she/he came to marriageable age a bride was chosen for her who was in every way suitable:

> they were bred together, brought up and schooled together, and as they had like instructions, so they had like affections, they were paralleld in love but not in hopes.

The mother prays to Jupiter, who intervenes directly and saves the situation by turning Iphis into a man as he leaves the marriage ceremony.

In retailing the finale of the story, Heywood moves from prose narrative to verse, claiming to quote from 'Ovid my maister'. The transformation he describes lists the signifiers of masculinity: the longer strides, the darker complexion, the broader shoulders and even shorter hair. Though the necessary, fundamental physiological change also occurs, it is included in 'she feeles about her something grow' which could equally extend to all the other physical changes. As a tall tale of divine intervention the story is deftly enough handled, but Heywood tries to claim some historical authenticity for it with accounts of parallel modern stories. He refers to accounts of children who 'have been mistaken for daughters, and so continued some yeeres' until the truth is discovered at 'the age of twelve, or thereabouts' when male sexual organs appear. Heywood, however, does not see the transformation as one of physiological development. For him the change is occasioned by the child's becoming 'able to distinguish of good or evil (being capable of passions, and subject to affections) whether Loue or Time have produced these strange effects I am not certaine'. Love and Time as modes of causation fit well into narrative patterns of tales of metamorphosis on or off the stage: they fulfil the literary pleasures of suspense and surprise and hold at bay the moral and social panic which ensued on the rare occasions when real cases of homosexuality or transexuality appeared to challenge these familiar ways of talking about sexual identity before the courts of early modern Europe.[25]

The ambiguities around sexual identity may have seemed particularly pointed in the reign of a homosexual king. David Seville has suggested that Day's *Isle of Gulls* was a direct commentary on the sexual intrigues of the Jacobean court.[26] The comic movements of the plot certainly turn on sex and disguise and involve the hero, Lysander, disguising himself as an Amazon so that he can court his beloved Violetta. The Duchess falls in love with the Amazon and suggests that s/he might pretend to be a man but still enjoy the behaviour open to women:

> Seeme coy, look nice and, as we woemen use
> Be mild and proud, imbrace and yet refuse.

To complicate the action, the Duke falls in love with the Amazon too and the action consists of a series of complicated encounters until the rightful sexes are appropriately paired off.

Given the prevalence of the comic conventions which the play uses, it seems unnecessary to insist on a particular satiric application. It consists of a series of satiric set pieces in which the pages are constantly employed to mock the action and call the seriousness of the whole endeavour into question. It is probably most appropriate to place the play in the genre of parodic comedy produced by boy players in the early years of the century.[27] Nevertheless it indicates the theatre did provide a number of conventions through which even potentially dangerous matters to do with the sex could be explored.

These ways of talking about sex intertwine in an even more complex way with the image of the theatre in Francis Osborne's observations of the King's unseemly conduct towards his favourites at court:

> the love the King shewed was as amourously conveyed as if he had mistaken their sex, and thought them ladies; which I have seene Sommerset and Buckingham labour to resemble in the effeminateness of their dressings ... [James] ... kissing them after so lascivious a mode in publicke, and upon the theatre, as it were, of the world ... prompted many to imagine some things done in the tyring house that exceed my expressions. ...[28]

The connection between behaviour in the theatre and the tiring-house which Osborne suggests, may reflect the actual behaviour of actors and their young apprentices. However, it also provides an elegant and witty image with which we could both mask and expose the scandal of the King's behaviour. The King's conduct is an 'act' in the theatre of the world which may or may not represent a reality in the off-stage world of the tiring-house. Moreover, the reality which it may have represented could not be named: it is enough that the sexuality is lascivious; the young men to whom it is directed are suitable objects because they are effeminate and are effeminate because they are suitable objects for a man's lust.

Similarly, in the world of the commercial theatre the meaning of boys playing women had to be negotiated in every case. It was not fixed as a 'fact' or a 'convention' but was part of a system of representation which perhaps had to be clearly articulated, and explicitly produced because of the contradictions of the poetic and satiric traditions on which it drew. The signs which connected clothes and sex and gender were shifting and ambiguous: writers for the theatre exploited that ambiguity for witty and comic and often disconcerting effect.

From Kathleen McLuskie, *Renaissance Dramatists* (Hemel Hempstead, 1989), pp. 100–22.

NOTES

[The status and significance of the boy players who took on the female roles on the Renaissance stage have been the subject of sustained, highly charged, and still inconclusive debate during the past few decades. In this chapter of her study of gender representation in the plays of Shakespeare and his contemporaries Kathleen McLuskie reads the convention as a shifting and ambiguous phenomenon which was being constantly, and provisionally, renegotiated according to the genre and theatrical context of the play in question, reflecting broader cultural anxieties about the changing roles and status of women in Elizabethan and Jacobean society. All Shakespearean quotations are from *The Complete Works*, ed. Peter Alexander (London, 1951). Ed.]

1. E. J. Jensen, 'The Boy Players: Plays and Playing', *Research Opportunities in Renaissance Drama*, 18 (1975), 6.
2. Lisa Jardine, *Still Harping on Daughters: Women and Drama in the Age of Shakespeare* (Brighton, 1983), pp. 9–36.
3. See Jonas Barish, *The Antitheatrical Prejudice* (Berkeley, CA, 1981), ch. 4.
4. Thomas Heywood, *An Apology for Actors* (London, 1610), sig. C3v.
5. See Henslowe's inventories of costume in R. A. Foakes and R. T. Rickert, *Henslowe's Diary* (Cambridge, 1961), pp. 291–4, 319–20, 321–3. A suggestive modern reconstruction of the role of the boy player is provided by David Gentleman's cartoon showing the transformation of a boy into a woman by the addition of petticoat, corset, bumroll, dress, ruff, wig, fan and jewels in John Russell Brown, *Shakespeare and His Theatre* (Harmondsworth, 1982), pp. 26–7.

6. R. A. Foakes, *Illustrations of the English Stage 1580–1642* (London, 1985), p. 88.

7. The Shakespearean *locus classicus* in *As You Like It*, II.vii. 139–66, 'All the world's a stage', is a case in point. The Seven Ages of Man is a literary construction, listing types much as Heywood's poem does. The evident discrepancy between that conventional representation and the characters of Orlando and Adam validates the greater 'realishness' of the fictional characters.

8. William Dunbar's widow is equipped with 'a watter spunge ... within my wyde clokis / Than wring I it full wylely and wetis my chekis'. See *The Poems of William Dunbar*, ed. W. Mackay Mackenzie (London, 1932), p. 95.

9. William Hazlitt, *Remnants of the Early Popular Poetry of England* (London, 1866), p. 93.

10. Examples include Beaumont and Fletcher, *Philaster*; John Ford, *The Lover's Melancholy*; Ben Jonson, *Epicoene*; Anon., *The Maid's Metamorphosis*.

11. This charge was brought most explicitly by Stubbes and Prynne. For a full discussion of the evidence see W. Robertson Davies, *Shakespeare's Boy Actors* (London, 1932), pp. 10–15, and Lisa Jardine, *Still Harping on Daughters*, ch. 2.

12. See G. E. Bentley, *The Jacobean and Caroline Stage*, vol. 2 (Oxford, 1941), pp. 43–5.

13. On attempts to control the theatre see Glynne Wickham, *Early English Stages*, vol. 3 (London, 1963), chs 3 and 4.

14. Stuart Clark, 'Inversion, Misrule and the Meaning of Witchcraft', *Past and Present*, 87 (1970), 99.

15. Philip Stubbes, *The Anatomy of Abuses* (London, 1583), p. 38.

16. Ibid., p. 39.

17. *Certain Homilies Appointed to be read in the Churches in the time of Queen Elizabeth* (London, 1908), p. 325.

18 Ibid., p. 330.

19 Ibid., p. 328.

20. Ibid., pp. 334–5.

21. Henry Fitzgeffrey, *Satires and Satyricall Epigrams* (London, 1617), sigs B4v, C2.

22. Anon, *Hic Mulier: or the Man Woman* (London, 1620), sig. Cv.

23. Anon., *Haec Vir: or the Womanish Man* (London, 1620), sig. B3.

24. *The Maid's Metamorphosis*, in *The Complete Works of John Lyly*, ed. R. W. Bond (Oxford, 1902).

25. See, for example, the case of the French transexual Marin de Merci, discussed in Stephen Greenblatt, *Shakespearean Negotiations: The Circulation of Social Energy in Renaissance England* (Oxford, 1988), ch. 3.

26. David Seville, 'Political Criticism and Caricature in Selected Jacobean Plays' (M. Phil. Thesis, University of Sheffield, 1986).

27. See R. A. Foakes, 'Tragedy of the Children's Theatres after 1600: A Challenge to the Adult Stage', in *Elizabethan Theatre*, ed. David Galloway (London, 1970).

28. Quoted in Jonathan Goldberg, *James I and the Politics of Literature* (Baltimore, MD, 1983), p. 143.

6

Text and Performance: *The Taming of the Shrew*

GRAHAM HOLDERNESS

TWO SHREWS

Anyone present at a performance of Shakespeare's *The Taming of the Shrew* in Britain at any time since 1913 is quite likely to have witnessed a hybrid amalgamation of two discrete play-texts: the text contained in the First Folio of 1623, which we accept as Shakespeare's play *The Taming of the Shrew*; and the anonymous play known as *The Taming of a Shrew*, printed in 1594, which was once held to be a source of Shakespeare's play, but is now regarded by most scholars as a 'memorial reconstruction' of a Shakespearean original.[1]

Shakespeare's play in the form we have inherited it contains of Christopher Sly only the two opening scenes known as the 'Induction': from the opening of the *Shrew* action, nothing more is seen or heard of the dreaming, drunken tinker. In *The Taming of a Shrew*, by contrast, the Sly-narrative is not a prologue but an extended dramatic framework: Sly and his attendants are kept on stage more or less throughout, and are given several further comments on and interventions in the action of the play. This sustained presence of the choric observer is more in keeping with contemporary stage practice, as exemplified in plays such as Kyd's *The Spanish Tragedy*, Greene and Lodge's *A Looking Glass for London and England*, and Greene's *James IV*.[2] Even a short introductory chorus like that of Marlowe's *Dr Faustus* would be expected at least to reappear as an epilogue: and the 'induction' to *The Taming of the Shrew* seems far too elaborate and promising a theatrical invention to be simply abandoned or dropped out of sight.

Even the two-scene 'Induction' disappeared from the play for centuries while Garrick's *Catherine and Petruchio* and other adaptations held the stage: in 1900 Frank Benson was still producing the play with no trace of Christopher Sly. Subsequent directors such as Oscar Asche (1904), W. Bridges Adams (1933) and F. Owen Chambers (1936) restored the 'Induction', but often in a cut form. It was Martin Harvey, acting under the advice and influence of William Poel, who in a 1913 production at the Prince of Wales Theatre, decided to supplement Shakespeare's text by interpolating the Christopher Sly scenes from *A Shrew*: and to develop the Sly-framework into a constitutive element of the drama. In this and many subsequent productions, Sly and his attendants were kept on stage, where they functioned as a surrogate audience: in accordance with the Lord's directions, the actors involved in the *Shrew* narrative constantly referred and deferred to them as the privileged audience of their presentation. Directors would give Sly lines which belong in the Shakespearean text to other characters: e.g. Tranio's observation (I.i.169) 'That wench is stark mad, or wonderful forward' became, in Theodore Komisarjevsky's 1939 Stratford production, a spectator's observation from outside the dramatic event. In the same production Sly made several abortive attempts to intervene in the action in the manner of Beaumont's intrusive grocer in *The Knight of the Burning Pestle*: at several points he tried to join the actors in the *Shrew* narrative, and had to be forcibly restrained by the Page.[3]

Since Martin Harvey's pioneering production, the Christopher Sly framework has been embraced by the modern theatre with particular enthusiasm: to such an extent that it became commonplace to augment the play in performance with the Sly interventions and epilogue preserved in the 1594 Quarto text.[4] Traditionally, modern edited texts of Shakespeare's plays have been constructed by collating the various available early texts, amalgamating and synthesising, or discriminating between different 'readings'. 'Good' Quarto texts (those thought to have been published with some kind of authorisation from Shakespeare and his company) are judged as reliable, as records of Shakespeare's intentions, as the texts printed in the Folio. Even 'bad' Quarto texts are regarded by modern textual scholars as useful sources of information about the plays in performance. Nonetheless, within the dominant discourses of literary criticism and textual scholarship, the relationship between, on the one hand, a 'good' text like that of the Folio, or that of a 'good' Quarto, and on the other, that of a so-called 'bad' Quarto, is clear: the latter is an inferior, garbled version of the authorial intention faithfully preserved in the former.

Once *The Taming of a Shrew* was acknowledged by editors as a corrupted version of Shakespeare's play, that, as a 'bad' Quarto, rather than as a source-play or an early draft, then it came within the orbit of editorial interest, and could be referred to in the composition of a scholarly edition of *The Taming of the Shrew*. Although the play's authorship, or at least its ancestry, could therefore be traced ultimately to Shakespeare, the actual writing of the text is believed to have been accomplished by other hands, and without the playwright's knowledge or authority. *A Shrew* can thus be recognised as evidence about theatrical production in Elizabethan times, when there was no effective copyright and plays could easily be 'pirated'; but it is not recognised as a play written by Shakespeare. An editor may believe (as does Ann Thompson, editor of the New Cambridge edition of *The Taming of the Shrew*), that *A Shrew*'s complete Sly-framework probably indicates the existence of a similar theatrical structure in performed versions of Shakespeare's play; but no editor has yet thought it appropriate to amalgamate the two texts to the extent of incorporating as a whole the theatrical device preserved in an unauthorised, non-Shakespearean text.

The approach of theatrical practitioners has been quite different. In the case of *The Taming of the Shrew*, theatrical practice began many years ago to prefer the dramatic opportunities offered by the text of *A Shrew* to considerations of textual purity and authorial ascription. Initially this strategy of theatrical appropriation was quite at odds with the views of the literary-critical and scholarly establishment, which was in search of textual and authorial authenticity: for not only was the incompleteness, the insufficiency of Shakespeare's play acknowledged; in addition elements of a text generally regarded as inadequate and self-evidently unShakespearean were being incorporated to satisfy the requirements of theatrical practice.

The science of textual scholarship as applied to Shakespeare has seen considerable change in recent years, though not everyone would agree that the discipline has accomplished the revolution that some of its practitioners claim. Certainly contemporary scholarly editions now aim to acknowledge these plays as dramatic scripts as well as written texts, and to take into account a play's theatrical history when attempting to produce an authoritative text. Most scholarship remains nonetheless committed to discovering or inferring the author's original intentions, and to producing a text which a reincarnated Shakespeare would be able to recognise and approve. In the theatre, the presence of that forbidding and ghostly mythological creature, the absent author, does not always bear with quite the same gravity on the activities of those who work on and reproduce the plays in performance. Hence in the theatre history of *The Taming of the Shrew* we can witness a bold opportunism that can be regarded either as iconoclastic or as pioneering: the amalgamation of 'good' and 'bad' texts is taken to an extreme that more conservative scholars may disapprove, while their more progressive colleagues may look for ways of pursuing the theatre's natural dramatic instincts.

It is possible to attempt some distinctions between the two texts of the *Shrew* by looking at the evidence of their respective stage directions. The Folio text of *The Taming of the Shrew* certainly bears more traces of the Shakespearean 'hand' than does *The Taming of a Shrew*:[5] but while the latter is certainly an acting version, and may be some kind of transcript of an actual performance, it has been observed that the former, on account of inaccuracy and confusion in stage directions and speech headings, 'could not have been used in the theatre'.[6]

A radical divergence of staging between the two texts occurs at the end of the first scene. The opening of Shakespeare's second 'Induction' scene gives:

> *Enter aloft the drunkard with attendants, some with apparel, Bason and Ewer, and other appurtenances, and Lord*

The parallel stage direction in *The Taming of a Shrew* reads:

> *Enter two with a table and a banquet on it, and two other, with Slie asleepe in a chaire, richlie apparelled, and the musick playing*

The Folio stage direction assumes that the rest of Act I, scene i and the whole of Act I, scene ii could have been played 'aloft': that is, we can with some confidence assume, in the gallery or balcony which overlooked the stage in a typical Elizabethan playhouse at the time of this play's original production. No other part of the play (and no part at all of *The Taming of a Shrew*) requires any space other than the bare platform stage available in all public theatres, and conjecturally in inn-yards and other non-purpose-built theatrical venues. Unless there are some hitherto undiscovered facts of Elizabethan stage history, this indicates that an important and elaborate episode would have been played in a confined space out of sight of some members of the audience: and in an excellent discussion Ann Thompson has shown that it is highly unlikely that this could conveniently have been done – too many actors are involved, there is too much detailed business with props, and the temporal extent of an episode sustained in the acting area 'aloft' is too long for normal Elizabethan stage practice. The Quarto stipulates that all the Sly-scenes take place on the main stage, which is much more probable: '... by far the major part of any play was enacted upon the projecting platform, with episode following episode in swift succession, and with shifts of time and place signalled to the audience only by the momentary clearing of the stage between episodes.'[7]

In addition, the Quarto stage direction specifies the number of actors to enter, where the Folio is vague ('with attendants'); props such as table, banquet and chair are listed (Folio's 'other appurtenances' is of little use to someone charged with the responsibilities of stage management: whereas the table brought on at this point in the Quarto evidently remains, and is used to considerable effect at a later point in the action), Sly's costume is defined, and the cue for atmospheric music supplied. This then is either a detailed description of what actually happened in performance, or a practicable set of directions to the actors. The stage direction in the Folio is, in short, not a stage direction proper but a bundle of hints and tentative suggestions from the author as to how the scene might be done: it has the imprecision and generality of the study rather than the practical imperatives of the tiring-room. The instruction for the actors to move 'aloft' was probably tried and rejected in rehearsal.

The stage directions in *A Shrew* display throughout a detailed, particularising quality by comparison with *The Shrew*: Shakespeare's '*Enter Petruchio and Grumio*' (III.ii.76) compares with the Quarto's '*Enter Ferando [Petruchio] baselie attired, and a red cap on his head*'; '*Enter servants with supper*' (IV.i.113) reads in *A Shrew* as '*They cover the board and fetch in the meat ... He throws down the table and meat and all, and beats them*'. Whether we think of the Quarto as a script *for* performance or a transcript *of* performance, it is clear that its incidental instructions bring us closer to contemporary Elizabethan theatrical practice than the vague suggestions of the Folio.

I am not arguing that we can distinguish in any evaluative way between a more strictly 'literary' mode of production traceable to the cloistered creativity of the 'author', and a 'theatrical' mode deriving from the rough practicalities of the playhouse. Since the author in question was no poet hidden in the light of thought, but a species of theatrical entrepreneur – actor, writer and speculative businessman – his role in the process of production is likely to have been a more consistent and sustained involvement than the transmission of a complete text to a distinct group of actors. It is now widely recognised by scholars that the discrete texts of a Renaissance play represent a cultural activity in process, glimpsed at different stages of a productive working in which the 'text' was primarily regarded not as a finished commodity but as a script for performance, remarkably alterable and subject to the conditions governing theatrical presentation at any given time. The rudimentary stage directions of the Folio thus represent not naïve gesturings towards an absent performance, but specific proposals to be attempted, improvised, modified or rejected by a collaborative team of theatrical practitioners at work. Such teams of practitioners have made an amalgamation of two texts a theatrical norm: whereas textual scholars continue to reproduce the apparently incomplete Folio text. The modern descendants of those Elizabethan actors have focused, not with the critics and scholars on the internal organisation, formal coherence and imaginative unity of individual texts; but on the lost but recoverable theatrical practice still visible in the interstices of a text, eloquent in the lacunae between one text and another, and implicit in the material conditions of a theatre eternally restless to interrogate and reopen the closures of written fiction, perpetually resistant to the notion of a sealed and finished form.

Where much criticism and scholarship presupposes Philip Edwards's dictum that 'the nearer we get to the stage, the further we are getting from Shakespeare',[8] this study is based on the alternative premise that 'Shakespeare' is no metaphysical subject of individual authorship, but a collaborative medium of theatrical presentation: 'Shakespeare' is not prior or superior to 'Shakespeare-in-performance'. The one is inextricably involved with the other, and both are components of a larger process: constituent elements in a perpetually contemporary cultural enterprise.

PLAY AND DECEPTION

The decision as to whether to include or exclude Christopher Sly is not a matter of an ordinary playhouse cut: without Christopher Sly the *Shrew* becomes a different play. [...] the excision of the Sly-frame converts the play into a naturalistic comedy (with varying degrees of farce) in which issues of marriage and sexual politics are dramatised (with more or less seriousness) by actors presenting themselves as real characters within a convincingly realistic social and domestic setting. Retention of the Sly-frame creates an entirely different dramatic medium: for the 'inner play' is designated by that frame as an elaborate hoax – part of a series of tricks calculated to fool a poor man into a temporary illusion of riches and power; a contrived fantasy designed (unsuccessfully, as it proves) to keep a drowsy itinerant awake. The 'Induction' of the Folio text alone establishes a theatrical perspective in which the action of the play is illuminated, by stimulating in the audience an invigorated sceptical consciousness, as an enacted artifice: while the entire Sly-frame confronts the audience with a continual, *unforgettable* reminder that the actors of the *Shrew* play are a fortuitously-gathered bunch of travelling players capriciously engaged to enact a whimsical nobleman's practical joke.

The 'Induction' plays with an entire vocabulary of illusion: 'practice', 'flatt'ring dream', 'worthless fancy', 'play', 'usurp' – a discourse which operates implicitly to link the delusion practised on Christopher Sly with the persuasive artifice of the drama itself. In comedy and tragedy illusion is both false and true, as what the theatre represents is both real and artificial. 'If this were played upon a stage now, I could condemn it as an improbable fiction' (*Twelfth Night*, III.iv.140–1). We assent to Fabian's remark: yet although the play is an improbable fiction, we don't for all that 'condemn' it. Viola's story of her sister in the same play (II.iv) is a mere tale improvised to extricate her from an awkward impasse; yet it expresses some deep and moving truth about herself. Othello's epic tales of heroic adventure induct his audience into the realms of fantasy: yet they are a true constitutive element both of his character and of his relationship with Desdemona. His suspicion of Desdemona is a colossal illusion: yet it has reality and power sufficient to shape for both of them a tragic destiny.

In history and farce, illusion has quite a different weight and value. In history it is an evasion or refusal of historical necessity, like the pastoral fantasies of Richard II or Henry VI. In farce it comes close to being mere deception, sharp practice, delusion. In farce the basic facts of life are crudely simple – lust, opportunism, con-artistry: so it is the more extraordinary and the more grotesquely comic that the hoodwinked subject – husband, dupe, fool – is unable to see what is so abundantly plain to the audience. In the *Shrew* plays, the romantic sub-plot derives, through Gascoigne and Ariosto, from Roman comedy, in which farce predominates over comedy, and illusions are 'counterfeit supposes' that cloud the judgement, blear the eye.

The *Shrew* plays were variously categorised as 'comedy' (in the Folio) or, in the words of the Quarto's title-page, 'a pleasant conceited history'. Shakespeare's play contains the tantalising self-definition of comedy as 'a kind of history', a *rapprochement* which invokes expectations of both fact and fiction. Whatever the complex interrelations between these two disparate forms, it can be suggested that the *Shrew* belongs more properly with those genres of 'history' and 'farce' which present illusion principally as deception, trickery or theatrical legerdemain.

The relationship proposed in the 'Induction' between 'illusion' and 'reality' is linked with analogous connections: wealth and poverty, impotence and power. Christopher Sly defines his own poverty in the very act of invoking, like Hardy's John Durbeyfield, a mythical charter of ancestral lineage: 'Look in the Chronicles ... we came in with Richard Conqueror.' The authorising fantasy of noble descent has of course no effective power: whoever he came in with, he is thrown out as plain Christopher Sly of Burton-Heath. The Lord's decision to 'practice on this drunken man' leads to a transformation, by artifice, of the drunken tinker, rapt by fiction into self-oblivion, to an imaginary Lord: 'Would not the beggar then forget himself?' The category of fantasy is tied firmly, as in the Lord's phrase, 'flatt'ring dream', to relationships of authority and subordination: Sly is to be persuaded of the authenticity of his transformation by being offered 'submissive reverence' from ostensibly obsequious servants: 'Look how your servants do attend on you' – I am served, therefore I am whatever my servants tell me I am. The transformation of the page into a woman is identical to that of Sly, except that the page is in on the joke: and again the metamorphosis involves assumption of authority – the page / woman is to serve Sly, 'do him obeisance' in a wish-fulfilment fantasy of female subordination, and thereby persuade Sly of the reality of his own transformation – 'I am your wife, in all obedience.'

'I am your wife, in all obedience.' The charm is wound up: the gulling of Christopher Sly complete. There is, however, a further dimension to the drama beyond this represented action, the deluding of a tinker: the relationship between what is happening within the stage-action, and the theatrical event itself; between the play and the play's own self-consciousness. The transformation of boy into woman was of course standard Elizabethan stage practice: but here the practice has its mechanisms exposed, its devices laid bare. The convention of cross-gender casting which must to an extent have naturalised the boy player within the female role is here subverted, so that the audience can acquire a self-conscious, metadramatic awareness of the illusion. In place of the usual spectacle of boy-actor-impersonating-woman, the Elizabethan spectators saw a boy player, acting the part of a page, directed by specific 'instructions' (Ind.I.126) to 'usurp the grace' (l. 127) of the female sex. The page's maleness is considered to render him inexpert at the voluntary production of those artificial tears, designated by the Lord as peculiarly 'a woman's gift' (l. 120), which might be required for the part. The inadequacy may be remedied, the tears supplied, by the application of an artificial stimulant:

> An onion will do well for such a shift,
> Which in a napkin being close conveyed
> Shall in despite enforce a watery eye.
> (Ind.I.122–4)

Like the references of the Chorus in *Henry V* to the 'four or five most vile and ragged foils' employed in productions of that play to signify the broadswords of Agincourt, such an allusion subverts conventional dramatic practices and properties which an audience would otherwise accept as perfectly adequate representations of reality.[9]

The super-objective of the page's dissimulation is the constitution of Sly, by an inversion of feudal categories, as an ersatz aristocrat – 'When they do *homage* to this simple *peasant*' (Ind.I.131). The group of players which is to perform a comedy within the play, and which thereby has some relationship of analogy with the Elizabethan acting company that performed *The Taming of the Shrew*, is also defined explicitly as a body of servants: 'players /

That offer service' (Ind.I.174) to the Lord: 'so please your Lordship to accept our duty' (l. 78). Like the huntsmen who offer to

> ... play our part
> As he shall think by our true diligence
> He is no less than what we say he is ...
> (Ind.I.65–7)

when the players agree to perform, they contract not only voluntarily to offer a cultural service to an aristocratic patron, but to play a part assigned to them by that patron: their 'part' in the play is a 'part' in the plot to delude Christopher Sly, persuade him that he is 'no less than what [they] say he is' (l. 67).

If the main action of the drama – *Catherine and Petruchio*, as Garrick entitled his Sly-free adaptation – is understood by the audience to be a model of theatrical performance in general, then it is entirely subversive of dramatic illusion and theatrical 'reality', since the 'play' is exposed as a 'flatt'ring dream or worthless fancy' (Ind.I.40), the 'sport' (l. 87) or 'pastime' (l. 63) of an idle nobleman. The players' craftsmanship and professional skills are viewed reductively in the illuminating term 'cunning' (l. 88) which hovers curiously between the older sense of 'knowledge' and the newer meaning of crafty and calculating cleverness.[10] As the servants and players conspire to constitute Christopher Sly's reality – his expulsion at the hands of the hostess – as 'abject lowly dreams', the spectators of *The Taming of the Shrew* may begin to ask themselves if the play is not similarly suppressing and occluding their own reality and replacing it with a persuasive fantasy. The fantasies offered to Sly are all masculine wish-fulfilment dreams of pleasure and power: a luxurious couch equipped for the performance of lust; the aristocratic pleasures of hunting with horse, hawk and hound. The contents of the *Shrew* play are constantly being adumbrated in the 'Induction': in presenting Sly with a collection of paintings, the servants inflame his erotic fantasies and tempt his penchant for dreams of masculine domination, partly by playing with the dangerous equivocations of artistic realism:

> We'll show thee Io ...
> As lively painted as the deed was done ...
> Or Daphne ...
> So workmanlike the blood and tears are drawn ...
> (Ind.II.50–6)

These legends of subdued women, depicted with a wholly convincing appearance of reality, correspond directly to the *Shrew*-play itself, which similarly presents, by realistic *fabliau* techniques, a compelling myth of women subordinated to the reason and power of men.

The moment of Sly's submission to illusion, which in the epilogue to *A Shrew* is paralleled by a corresponding moment of awakening, has more than comic reverberations:

> Am I a lord, and have I such a lady?
> Or did I dream? Or have I dreamed till now?
> I do not sleep: I see, I hear, I speak,
> I smell sweet savours and I feel soft things ...
> Upon my life, I am a lord indeed,
> And not a tinker, nor Christopher Sly.
> (ll. 64–9)

The pathos of these lines derives not only from the elements of guilt and shame that lacerate the pleasures of witnessing innocence beguiled: for the audience this is a moment of theatrical truth. The spectators watch a man wholly absorbed in illusion, entirely convinced by the tangible concreteness of his immediate sensations, that his life has been transformed. But what the spectator sees is similarly capable of being apprehended as an illusion, wherein actors impersonate utterly fictional characters, bring to life a wholly imaginary place and time, and endeavour with persuasive art to bestow truth on falsehood, convert illusion to reality, 'give to airy nothings / A local habitation and a name'. Is the spectator of *The Taming of the Shrew* as much a victim of illusion as the tinker? Is every playgoer an '*hypocrite lecteur*', the '*semblable et frère*' of Christopher Sly?

PRODUCTION VALUES

I want in this section to consider (in so far as it is possible) in a Renaissance historical context, those aspects of the play that have a bearing on stage design and on production 'style': geographical and historical setting, acting methods and costume.

The fact that compared with later conventions of stage-setting, specific geographical and historical locations in plays had relatively few 'stage design' implications for the Elizabethan theatres, is paradoxically a matter of some importance. Although the players in the purpose-built public playhouses could presumably have used illusionistic scenery and elaborate props to localise time and space, they evidently did not: in the style of the popular drama from which the Renaissance theatre evolved, they were content with rudimentary props and made no attempt at scenic illusion. The Elizabethan public theatre maintained some of the unlocalised qualities of the popular drama, a practice to which neo-classical critics like Sir Philip Sidney (in his *Defence of Poesie*, 1595) indignantly objected, in the belief that such dramatic liberty violated the fundamental laws of drama. For a stage without pictorial scenery or any other means of signifying place, location could be signified either verbally or via the language of costume. *The Taming of the Shrew* is set in Padua, *The Taming of a Shrew* in Athens: but when these two plays (if they were two plays) were performed in the Renaissance public playhouse, the stage retained an identical visual appearance: each drama was enacted on that same physical space of bare thrust stage, plain or curtained tiring-house facade, two doors and a gallery above.

Although Renaissance plays are often highly specific in their constructions of the past and of other societies,[11] the representation of place on their stages was thus entirely unlocalised. This does not indicate that 'Athens' and 'Padua' were quite meaningless or relativistic terms: on the contrary, the discourses of classicising romance and of Italianate commercialism so prominent respectively in *A Shrew* and *The Shrew* are thereby located in appropriate historico-geographical contexts. What it does indicate is that the stage could represent 'both many days, and many places' without any recourse to the mechanical construction of scenic illusion. In *The Taming of the Shrew*, the location of the primary dramatic narrative shifts from a rural and provincial English location, linked by place-names to Shakespeare's native Warwickshire, to the Italian commercial and academic city of Padua; but on the Elizabethan stage this shift probably involved nothing of what we consider to be a 'scene-change'.

The material conditions of a play's historical origin, the physical architecture and shape of the originating performance space, exercised a determining influence on its dramatic structure and theatrical rhythm. Since space and time were not represented visually, they remained flexible and relative dimensions of dramatic narrative, which could be realised as objectively present, or estranged into fictional distance, by the verbal and gestic codes of the drama. Just as the Christopher Sly 'Induction' introduces into the play a fundamental indeterminacy about the relations of reality and illusion so the unlocalised theatrical practice of the Elizabethan public stage constructed within these dramatic narratives an indeterminate relationship between present and past, the exotic and the immediate, here and now and there and then. The implications of these facts for modern theatrical practice are profound: since they indicate that, in so far as productions are incorporated into nineteenth-century traditions of pictorial realism and illusionistic staging, they will operate to fix time and place in a manner entirely foreign to the indeterminacy and flexibility of the Renaissance theatre. Discussion of the consequences of that introduced constraint necessarily involves value-judgements which are better canvassed in relation to specific productions than theoretically; and since the two most widely-seen and influential productions discussed here – a film and a television version – operate within the nineteenth-century conventions of pictorial realism, some sharp distinctions and discriminations will have to be made.

The other principal ingredient of Elizabethan stagecraft, acting method, is again difficult to discuss: since there is little surviving concrete information and in the space of that absent evidence flourishes a plenitude of myths. Hamlet's advice to the travelling players who arrive in Elsinore as opportunely as their counterparts turn up in *The Shrew* has been accepted almost universally[12] as a record of Shakespeare's personal observations on principles of acting. Yet an adherence to the kinds of naturalism and neo-classical decorum there advocated would render the role of Hamlet (which involves assuming the melodramatic rant of the revenge hero) unplayable; and that play itself could scarcely be contained, as Sidney's critique would suggest, within the Aristotelian principles of the Prince's expressed dramatic theory.[13]

There is little doubt that during the period of Shakespeare's professional career the drama became more realistic: though it is highly questionable, and to me extremely improbable, that any kind of naturalism was ever a dominant method. The internal evidence of the plays points rather to a considerable range and variety of acting methods, consistent with certain constitutive features of the Elizabethan theatre: the flexibility of the unlocalised acting area; the heterogeneity of its theatrical influences and antecedents; and the generic variety of the dramatic medium. A theatrical space without specific location does not call for any particular style of acting, by contrast with an illusionistic set which requires naturalism of speech and behaviour: if space and time are relative and iterable, so is the vehicle by means of which actors occupy that imaginative dimension. Acting can be naturalistic, expressionistic, emblematic, metadramatic, alienatory at different points in a single play.

There is, again, hardly enough external evidence about the uses of costume on the early Elizabethan stage to form the basis for a serious historical discussion: we only know that plays were performed in some combination of contemporary dress, historical costume, and gestural probably emblematic signs of cultural context. It is necessary, in the absence of more contextual evidence, to examine the internal details of the play-texts for information about costume: and certainly in *The Taming of the Shrew* we soon discover that costume is one of the principal theatrical languages of the stage narrative. The language of clothes begins to speak with Christopher Sly:

> Ne'er ask me what raiment I'll wear, for I have no more doublets than backs, no more stockings than legs, nor no more shoes than feet – nay, sometimes more feet than shoes, or such shoes as my toes look through the overleather.
>
> (Ind.II.7–10)

This sartorial self-portrait is so specific in its depiction of Elizabethan costume – doublets, stockings – that it will raise problems for a naturalistic 'modern-dress' production, or for one set in any other period. Furthermore it is a description of a condition of poverty and deprivation signified by dress, which a stage production will have to express in one way or another, and which would presumably have been directly represented on the Elizabethan stage. The very notion of transformation, if it is to be visually enacted, depends on clear and sharp distinctions between one costume and another: and for the audience immediate recognition of the meanings attached to particular styles of dress.

In the case of the tinker's metamorphosis the passage from poverty to affluence presents no difficulty; but the next transformation encountered in the play is far less clear-cut for a modern audience than it would have been for the Elizabethans –

> **Lucentio** Tranio, at once
> Uncase thee; take my coloured hat and cloak.
>
> (I.i.197–8)

The exchange of outer garments would be quite meaningless to an audience unless the two characters were immediately recognisable by the codes of their dress as fashionable master and liveried servant. As a process of exchanging meaning, transformation by dress discloses a deeply interesting relationship between ideology and theatrical art. The meanings expressed by clothes in Tudor society were not regarded as arbitrary socially-constructed distinctions of function, but as inherent differences of rank, natural, even biological in origin. Yet these meanings were invested in signs external to the body, easy to remove or change. The theatre specialised in the inversion, substitution and transgression of these sartorial codes, which bore some of society's fundamental political meanings: this is doubtless one of the many reasons why an institution which has often been evaluated in historical criticism as an ideological state apparatus was frequently suspected in its own time of subversive and seditious influence. Counter to the ideological assumption that distinctions of rank were natural, the play seems to draw attention to fashion's arbitrary system of signs, to the biological similarity of people across divisions of family, kin and class:

> Nor can we be distinguished by our faces
> For man or master.
>
> (I.i.191–2)

In the play's medium of comic transformation a mere switch of clothes alters distinctions traditionally held immutable. The language of clothes is clearly recognised here as an eloquent but unstable discursive system.

Further inversion of the visual codes of fashion occurs at the wedding of Katherina and Petruchio, where the bridegroom denies the expectation of conventional nuptial apparel, and is described as an apparition of the grotesque:

> Petruchio is coming in a new hat and old jerkin; a pair of old breeches thrice turned; a pair of boots that have been candle-cases, one buckled, another laced; an old rusty sword tane out of the town armoury, with a broken hilt and chapless; with two broken points ... his lackey ... with a linen stock on one leg and a kersey boot-hose on the other, gartered with a red and blue list; an old hat and the humour of forty fancies pricked in't for a feather; a monster, a very monster in apparel, and not like a Christian footboy or a gentleman's lackey.

The bravura rhetoric of this reported description excites in an audience expectations which the stagecraft of the production must endeavour to fulfil: Petruchio and Grumio must look at least as ludicrous as Biondello's farcical portrayal, and the distance in visual impression between a 'gentleman's lackey' and a 'monster in apparel' must be clearly and unmistakably demarcated.

Baptista explicitly endorses the conventional relationship between clothes and social meanings, criticising Petruchio's 'unreverent robes' as a 'shame to (his) estate' and 'an eye-sore to our solemn festival'. Petruchio denies that there is any such stable relationship between clothes and the wearer: the relationship he claims between himself and Kate is much more direct, body to body, dispensing with the signifying systems of dress – 'To me she's married, not unto my clothes.' The visual grotesque of Petruchio's stipulated costume is a necessary context for this puritanical affirmation of unclothed morality, which in turn enters into contradiction with Petruchio's very obvious use of his own eccentric but nonetheless authoritarian signifying code. Petruchio imposes the same ethic of counter-fashion on Kate herself in the 'tailor-scene' (IV.iii.3) which decisively foregrounds the play's self-conscious interrogation of the language of dress. Petruchio's denunciation of the fashionable Italian cap and elaborate designer gown supplied for his wife, incorporating as it does the details of a dressmaker's inventory, could hardly be more specific as instructions to a costume designer, and faces the modern producer with clear-cut choices: between adherence to Renaissance costume, the cutting or rewriting of the lines, or the adoption of a non-naturalistic technique which refuses any direct relationship between verbal and visual languages. The comic energy of the scene contains a curious ambivalence between the avowed puritan distaste for extravagances of dress, and an obsessively literal preoccupation with the physical appearance and texture of clothes. When at the end of the play Petruchio wishes to demonstrate Kate's spontaneous obedience, he does so via this pervasive language of costume: 'Doff thy cap ...'. 'Costume' is not by any means an optional addition to the substantive meaning of a Renaissance play: together with other constituent dialects of the language of performance, it is a primary signifier, an indispensable bearer of theatrical meaning.

All histories of Renaissance drama in interpretation or production may be said to reside between two polarised positions. At one extreme lies the traditional historicist and literary-critical assumption that a play is a stable, immanent, 'authored' entity, which in turn authorises and polices the boundaries of its own system of reproduction; at the other lies the theatrical or 'deconstructionist' premise that a play exists only in its productions, as a book exists only in its readings. The former position would deduce from the above discussion that *The Taming of the Shrew* would be performed [...] in 'traditional' costume: that is, the reconstructed Renaissance costume which began to appear on the stage in the course of the nineteenth century. The latter position would infer that the originating moment of a text's production exercises no control over its subsequent reproduction in criticism and performance: that the text is raw material for the construction of contemporary meaning. Both traditional literary criticism and a powerful body of opinion within dramatic criticism, associated particularly with the name of John Barton,[14] would argue that a body of 'intentions' or 'directions' inscribed into the text by its author can be elicited from it in the practices of textual criticism and theatrical experiment; while many theatrical practitioners would insist, together with deconstructionist critics, on the necessary independence and autonomy of their creative efforts. It seems to me that an exploration of the internalised language of costume demonstrates that a distinct level of meaning *is* inscribed within and *can* be disclosed from, the text; but that it would be mere conformism and abject submission to the power of bardolatry to regard that inscription as prescriptive rather than indicative, as historically determining rather than historically determined. Theoretically then, decisions about stage and costume design and acting methods in any given production are essentially voluntary; provided only that the production recognises the extent to which within the text meaning is habitually encoded in a language of space, dress and mimetic art.

From Graham Holderness, *Shakespeare in Performance: 'The Taming of the Shrew'* (Manchester, 1988), pp. 1–17.

NOTES

[Taken from Graham Holderness's study of the stage history of *The Taming of the Shrew*, for which it forms the introductory chapter, this discussion brings together questions of performance and of textual history. Taking issue with the traditional critical view that the anonymous 1594 Quarto *Taming of a Shrew* is an inferior derivative of Shakespeare's play as represented by the Folio text, Holderness points out the disparity between stage practice and editorial tradition as regards the use of the Christopher Sly framework. Holderness argues that the completion of the frame in *A Shrew* creates a sophisticated metadramatic structure which problematises both the gender and class politics of the play, and the spectator's response to the theatrical pleasures it offers. Like Robert Weimann, Holderness describes the Elizabethan popular stage in terms of a flexible, dialectical and interrogative dramaturgy, placing a particular emphasis upon the collaborative and provisional nature of theatrical work. Ed.]

1. The Folio is the basis of all modern editions of *The Taming of the Shrew. The Taming of a Shrew* can be found in an old-spelling edition in Geoffrey Bullough, *Narrative and Dramatic Sources of Shakespeare*, vol. 1 (London, 1957); and in facsimile reproduction in Charles Praetorius's edition for the Shakspere Society in 1886, from which my quotations are drawn [it is also available in an edition edited by Graham Holderness and Bryan Loughrey in the 'Shakespeare Originals' series (Hemel Hempstead, 1992). Ed.] A 'memorial reconstruction' is a play-text put together by spectators and/or actors recalling a script from its stage performance.
2. See Thomas Kyd, *The Spanish Tragedy*, ed. Philip Edwards (Manchester, 1977); Robert Greene (with Thomas Lodge), *A Looking-Glass for London and England*, ed. G. A. Clugston (New York, 1980); and Robert Greene, *The Scottish History of James IV*, ed. Norman Sanders (London, 1970).
3. The information used here derives from prompt-books in the records of the Shakespeare Memorial Theatre and Royal Shakespeare Company, held in the Shakespeare Centre Library, Stratford-upon-Avon. Martin Harvey's production is discussed in Tori Haring-Smith's invaluable stage-history, *From Farce to Metadrama: a stage history of 'The Taming of the Shrew', 1594–1983* (Westport, CT, 1985), pp. 98–103, which also gives a full account of eighteenth-century adaptations.
4. Stratford productions in this category include: Robert Atkins (1946); Michael Benthall (1948); George Devine (1953); John Barton (1960); Trevor Nunn (1967); Barry Kyle (1982).
5. See Brian Morris (ed.), The New Arden Shakespeare *The Taming of the Shrew* (London, 1982), pp. 8–9.
6. See Ann Thompson (ed.), The New Cambridge Shakespeare *The Taming of the Shrew* (Cambridge, 1984).
7. Richard Hosley (ed.), The Pelican Shakespeare *The Taming of the Shrew* (Harmondsworth, 1964, rev. edn 1970), p. 11.

8. Philip Edwards (ed.), The New Cambridge Shakespeare *Hamlet* (Cambridge, 1985), p. 32.
9. For further discussion of *Henry V* in this context see Graham Holderness, Nick Potter and John Turner, *Shakespeare: The Play of History* (Basingstoke, 1988), pp. 72–5.
10. Baptista's use of the world at I.i.97 contains, unintentionally on his part, both meanings of 'cunning'.
11. See Holderness, Potter and Turner, *The Play of History*, *passim.*
12. For an honourable exception see Robert Weimann, 'Mimesis in *Hamlet*', in Patricia Parker and Geoffrey Hartman (eds), *Shakespeare and the Question of Theory* (London, 1986).
13. For further discussion see Graham Holderness, *Hamlet* (Milton Keynes, 1987).
14. See John Barton, *Playing Shakespeare* (London, 1984).

7

Race and the Comedy of Abjection in *Othello*

MICHAEL D. BRISTOL

GUILTY CREATURES SEATED AT A PLAY

Ritual and theatre have a long history of strained and sometimes openly hostile relations. This conflict between hieratic ceremonies and the meretricious performances of actors is, however, deeply equivocal. The manifest antagonism between the liturgical forms of religion and the dramatic spectacles of the theatre are continually haunted by the trace of a hidden complicity. The integrity of religious practice depends to a considerable extent, therefore, on the control of access to redemptive media and to places of sanctity within a given community. Such integrity is, of course, of decisive importance for maintaining the collective life of the believers.

For Emile Durkheim, every rite, both in its ceremonial formality and in the transgression that accompanies it, is a process by which a community reproduces modes of consciousness and social interaction that maintain its solidarity over time.[1] Durkheim argues that ritual depends on misrecognition. A community reaffirms its own well-established social hierarchies which are experienced by the believers as a manifestation of the sacred. The divine presences evoked in ritual may be non-existent; however, contact with the sacred is not, for that reason, some kind of delusionary fantasy, since the communal life so richly experienced in ritual has a concrete and sensuous actuality that does support and sustain the members of the community. Ritual misrecognition always has some element of objective cogency, no matter how fantastical its overt manifestations may be and no matter how fallacious the interpretations of the participants. Moreover, the anomie that appears at the time of the festival is a functional undifferentiation that strengthens the resolution and closure that concludes the rite. Misrecognition is a special kind of mistake, one that somehow seems a necessary condition for the possibility of social continuity.

Those responsible for the management of liturgical practice must always ensure that ritual, despite its spectacular accoutrements, is never linked openly to theatre. The ontological claims on which ritual depends are not always easy to sustain, for the very good reason that the practical exigencies of any liturgy are not very different from those of a theatrical performance. The distinction between a priest's vestments and an actor's costume is never an easy one to maintain, and this is especially so in a historical setting such as Elizabethan and Jacobean England, where some theatrical costumes are in fact expropriated vestments transferred from the altar to the *mise-en-scène*.

Contamination of religious authority by illicit contact with theatre was a condition that occasioned chronic anxiety during the early modern period and this anxiety has been examined in a number of recent studies.[2] Stephen Greenblatt's important essay on 'Shakespeare and the Exorcists', for example, shows that the scandal of exorcism is precisely its character as a theatre that dissembles its own theatricality.[3] The evacuation of religious significance from exorcism, the chastisement of its practitioners, and the instruction of the public in the correct allocation of charismatic and juridical authority are all accomplished by means of a thoroughgoing theatricalisation of exorcism. This is done in part by the exposure of various theatrical techniques and special effects used by the exorcists on an unsuspecting audience, and in part by the re-staging of the exorcists' performances in a juridical setting. As Greenblatt's essay shows, however, the use of theatre as the primary instrument for this evacuation of a vitiated or unauthentic ritual is extremely dangerous. By openly asserting its capacity for dissimulation, theatre addresses the element of misrecognition necessary to any liturgical enactment of the sacred. Theatre thus has the capacity to theorise all redemptive media and even to make visible the links between ritual, repression, and social contradiction. The strategy of evacuation through the use of a theatrical pedagogy, though carefully focused on specific unauthentic practices, is paradoxically self-condemnatory in the way it foregrounds the element of collective misrecognition on which charismatic and juridical authority depends.

Despite its capacity to theorise ritual practices, theatre is not simply the logical 'opposite' of liturgy. There are important isomorphisms between these two symbolic protocols. Ritual and theatre are based on formalities, on conventional social etiquette, and on the use of selected artifacts or symbols within a well-defined spatial frame. In addition, theatre resembles ritual in that it requires its own particular brand of 'misrecognition' in the form of a temporary and contractual make-believe. However, a fiction does not require the unselfconscious and unreflective misrecognition necessary for ritual.[4] Fictions may, however, inspire powerful feelings of acute discomfort experienced, for example, at performances of *Othello*. The apparent dilemma between a classic sociology of religion that interprets ritual as a necessary though wholly unselfconscious misrecognition and a classic sociology of theatrical reception that interprets performance in light of the necessarily lucid recognition of make-believe may be resolved in part by an appeal to Mikhail Bakhtin's category of the carnivalesque. Carnival is an ensemble of practices that seems to be both 'full' of positive social content, like a ritual, and 'empty' of any substantive social meaning, like a theatrical performance. This theory can help to make sense of the apparently paradoxical notion of a knowledgeable misrecognition that seems to be the condition of the possibility of a proper response to a theatrical performance. One of the salient features of carnival is its capacity to open up an alternative space for social action.[5] Within the spatio-temporal boundaries of a carnivalesque event, the individual subject is authorised to renegotiate identity and to redefine social position *vis-à-vis* others. In Bakhtin's reading of carnival, the social effervescence and the energy generated by a radical popular will to otherness is not simply recaptured for the purposes of the official culture. In its capacity for excess and derangement, carnival empowers the popular element to voice its opposition to the imperatives of official culture.

The theory of carnival distinguishes between the affirmative character of ritual consciousness as such, and the negative and corrosive force of popular festive form. This distinction corresponds to the distinction between official culture – the legitimated stories and interpretations of social hierarchy reproduced in the ideological apparatus – and popular culture – the alternative values and interpretations of the social life-world sedimented in the symbolic practices of various excluded or partially excluded groups. Carnival analyses and dismantles the official order of things, not in a spirit of pure negation, but rather as the expression of an alternative understanding of the social world as an ensemble of material practices.[6] To be sure, this alternative understanding may be profoundly conservative in its thematic content and in its evaluation of various social practices. However, such a conservatism by no means implies a blanket endorsement of all decisions taken by individuals and groups with access to mechanisms of political power, or an indiscriminate willingness to submit to authority. In fact, the knowledge sedimented in the artifacts and the symbolic vocabularies of carnival is a reaffirmation of practical consciousness that may be significantly at odds with the ideologies officially sanctioned by ruling elites. This practical consciousness is best thought of as the outlook of social agents sufficiently knowledgeable to 'get on' within the constraints of economic and institutional reality.[7] Such knowledgeability is not always equivalent to the self-understanding of a particular social agent but is instead sedimented within certain institutional practices, including but not limited to the conventions of theatre and theatre-going.

Bakhtin's view of carnival is in some sense a development of what appears to be the contrasting position articulated in Durkheim's sociology of religion. It is important to realise, however, that Bakhtin's anthropology preserves the central insight of Durkheim's sociology of religion and of the view that both official ritual and its popular cognates, as moments of greatly intensified social life, tend powerfully towards the reaffirmation of a deeply felt 'way-of-being-together-in-the-world'.[8] The notion of the carnivalesque, however, adds an element to the sociology of religion which helps to account for the possibility of social change, and for the presence of differentiated interests that have to participate in the negotiation of that change. The carnivalesque would thus be a mode of authentic cognition, a kind of para-scientific and pre-theoretical understanding of social forms that would disclose whatever is hidden by ritual misrecognition.

The following analysis outlines a hypothesis that would interpret *Othello* as a carnivalesque text in the Bakhtinian sense. Carnival is operative here as something considerably more than a novel decor for the *mise-en-scène* or an alternative thematics for interpretation. The play is read here as the carnivalesque derangement of marriage as a social institution and of the contradictory role of heterosexual desire within that institution. As a serio-comic or carnivalesque masquerade, the play makes visible the normative horizons against which sexual partners must be selected, and the latent social violence that marriage attempts to prevent, often unsuccessfully, from becoming manifest. More specifically, I want to draw attention to the play as an adaptation of the social custom, common throughout early modern Europe, of charivari.[9] This was a practice of noisy festive abuse in which a community enacted its objection to inappropriate marriages and more generally exercised a general surveillance of sexuality. As Natalie Davis has pointed out, this 'community' actually consists of young men, typically the unmarried ones, who represent a social principle of male solidarity which is in some respects deeply hostile to precisely that form of institutionally sanctioned sexuality whose standards they are empowered to oversee.[10]

CHARIVARI

The abusive language, the noisy clamour under Brabantio's window, and the menace of violence of the opening scene of *Othello* link the improvisations of Iago with the codes of a carnivalesque disturbance or charivari organised in protest over the marriage of the play's central characters. Charivari does not figure as an isolated episode here, however, nor has it been completed when the initial on-stage commotion ends.[11] Despite the sympathy that Othello and Desdemona seem to be intended to arouse in the audience, the play as a whole is organised around the abjection and violent punishment of its central figures. If certain history plays can be read as rites of 'uncrowning' then this play might be read as a rite of 'un-marrying'.[12] In staging the play as a ceremony of broken nuptials, Iago assumes the function of a popular festive ringleader whose task is the unmaking of a transgressive marriage.

As the action of *Othello* unfolds, the audience is constrained to witness a protracted and diabolical parody of courtship leading to a final, grotesquely distorted consummation in the marriage bed. To stage this action as the carnivalesque thrashing of the play's central characters is, of course, a risky choice for a director to make, since it can easily transform the complex equilibrium of the play from tragedy to *opera buffo*. Although the play is grouped with the tragedies in the first folio and has always been viewed as properly belonging to this genre, commentators have recognised for a long time the precarious balance of this play at the very boundaries of farce.[13] *Othello* is a text that evidently lends itself very well to parody, burlesque and caricature.[14] Alteration of the play's formal characteristics, however, would not be the most serious problem encountered in contemplating a carnivalised performance. Since the basis for the charivari is an interracial marriage, many of the strongest effects of this ritual practice would be realised here through use of derisory and stereoptypical images of 'The Moor'.

It is important to remember that Othello does not have to be a black African for this story to work itself out. Racial difference is not absolutely required to motivate any of the play's fundamental plot moves. The feelings expressed by the various characters that prompt each of the turns in the action could just as well be tied to some other difference between the two romantic protagonists and in fact the difference in age seems as important if not more important than the fact of Othello's blackness in the concrete unfolding of the story.[15] The image of racial otherness is thus tangential to the primary narrative interest here. At the time of the play's earliest performances, the supplementary character of Othello's blackness would be apparent in the white actor's use of black-face makeup to represent the conventionalised form of 'The Moor'. In the initial context of its reception, it seems unlikely that the play's appeal to invidious stereotypes would have troubled the conscience of anyone in the audience. Since what we now call racial prejudice did not fall outside prevailing social norms in Shakespeare's society, no one in the early audience would have felt sympathy for Othello simply on grounds that he was the victim of a racist society.[16] It is far more probable that 'The Moor' would have been seen as comically monstrous. Under these conditions the aspects of charivari and of the comical abjection of the protagonists would have been entirely visible to an audience for whom a racist sensibility was entirely normal.

At the end of the sixteenth century racism was not yet organised as a large-scale system of oppressive social and economic arrangements, though it certainly existed as a widely shared set of feelings and attitudes. Racism in this early, prototypical form entails a specific physical repugnance for the skin colour and other typical features of black Africans. The physical aversion of the English towards the racial other was rationalised through an elaborate mythology, supported in part by scriptural authority and reinforced by a body of popular narrative.[17] Within this context, the image of the racial other is immediately available as a way of encoding deformity or the monstrous.

For Shakespeare and for his audience, the sensibilities of racial difference are for all practical purposes abstract and virtually disembodied, since the mythology of African racial inferiority is not yet a fully implemented social practice within the social landscape of early modern Europe. Even at this early stage, however, it had already occurred to some people that the racial other was providentially pre-ordained for the role of the slave, an idea that was fully achieved in the eighteenth- and nineteenth-century institutions of plantation slavery and in such successor institutions as segregation and apartheid. The large-scale forms of institutional racism that continue to be a chronic and intractable problem in modern societies are, of course, already latent within the abstract racial mythologies of the sixteenth century, since these mythologies enter into the construction of the social and sexual imaginary both of the dominant and of the popular culture. In more recent contexts of reception the farcical and carnivalesque potentiality of the play is usually not allowed to manifest itself openly. To foreground the elements of charivari and comic abjection would disclose in threatening and unacceptable ways the text's ominous relationship to the historical formation of racism as a massive social fact in contemporary Europe, and in the successor cultures of North and South America as well as in parts of the African homeland itself. Against this background the text of *Othello* has to be construed as a highly significant document in the historical constitution both of racist sensibility and of racist political ideology.

The relationship of marriage is established through forms of collective representation, ceremonial and public enactments that articulate the private ethos of conjugal existence and which mark out the communal responsibilities of the couple to implement and sustain socially approved relations of reproduction. In the early modern period the ceremonial forms of marriage are accompanied (and opposed) by parodic doubling of the wedding feast in the forms of charivari.[18] This parodic doubling is organised by a carnivalesque wardrobe corresponding to a triad of dramatic agents – the clown (who represents the bridegroom), the transvestite (who represents the bride) and the 'scourge of marriage', often assigned a suit of black (who represents the community of unattached males or 'young men'). Iago of course is neither unattached nor young, but part of his success with his various dupes is his ability to present himself as 'one of the boys'. Iago's misogyny is expressed as the married man's resentment against marriage, against wives in general, and against his own wife in particular. But this resentment is only one form of the more diffuse and pervasive misogyny typically expressed in the charivari. And of course Iago's more sinister function is his ability to encourage a kind of complicity within the audience. In a performance he makes his perspective the perspective of the text and thus solicits from the audience a participatory endorsement of the action.

The three primary characters in charivari each has a normative function in the allocation of marriage partners and in the regulation of sexual behaviour. These three figures parody the three characters of the wedding ceremony – bride, groom, and priest. It is the last of these three figures who confers both social and sacred authority on the marriage. The ensemble as a whole, however, is a travesty of the wedding ceremony itself. The counter-festive vocabulary of charivari provides the community with a system of critical resources through which marriage as a social arrangement and as a private form of sexuality may be either negated or reaffirmed.

Charivari features the three primary figures mentioned above; that is, a bride, a groom, and a ringleader who may in some instances assist the partners in outwitting parental opposition, but who may also function as a nemesis of erotic desire itself and attempt to disrupt and to destroy the intended bond. In the actual practice of charivari, the married couple are forced to submit to public ridicule and sometimes to violent punishment. In its milder forms, a charivari allows the husband and wife to be represented by parodic doubles who are then symbolically thrashed by the ringleader and his followers. This triad of social agents is common to many of Shakespeare's tragedies of erotic life and it even appears in the comedies. Hamlet stages 'The Murder of Gonzago' partly as a public rebuke to the unseemly marriage of Claudius and Gertrude.[19] This is later escalated to a fantasy of the general abolition of the institution of monogamy, 'I say we will have no more marriages'. Hamlet's situation here expresses the powerful ambivalence of the unattached male towards marriage as the institutional format in which heterosexual desire and its satisfaction are legitimated. His objection to the aberrant and offensive union of mother and uncle is predicated on the idealisation of marriage and in this case on the specific marriage of mother and father. This idealisation is, however, accompanied by the fantasy of a general dissolution of the institution of monogamy back into a dispensation of erotic promiscuity and the free circulation of sexual partners. A similar agenda, motivated by a similar ambivalence, is pursued by Don John in *Much Ado About Nothing*, and by Iachimo in *Cymbeline*.

The argument I hope to outline out here requires that readers or viewers of *Othello* efface their response to the existence of Othello, Desdemona, and Iago as individual subjects endowed with personalities and with some mode of autonomous interiorised life. The reason for such selective or wilful ignorance of some of the most compelling features of this text is to make the determinate theatrical surfaces visible. To the extent that the surface coding of this play is openly manifested, the analysis presented here will do violence to the existence of the characters in depth. Instead of striving to understand the grandeur and the sublime dignity of the play's hero and heroine, this argument seeks to stop at the surface in order to focus attention on the carnivalesque scenario or charivari that governs the dramatic action.

In order to grasp the primary characters of *Othello* at this level of representation, it is necessary to withdraw from the position of empathy for the characters as subjects constituted in the way we are constituted and to seek out an appropriate mode of counter-identification. I believe that the withdrawal of empathy and identification from the play's main characters is difficult, not least because the experience of individual subjectivity as we have come to know it *is* objectively operative in the text. The constellation of interests and goal values most characteristic of the institutional processing of literary texts has given rise to an extremely rich critical discourse on the question of the subject; it is precisely the power and the vitality of this discourse that makes the withdrawal of empathy from the characters so difficult. I have discussed elsewhere the claim that the pathos of individual subjectivity was actually invented by Shakespeare, and that this experience appears for the first time in the history of Western representation in his plays. Whether or not arguments of this kind are historically accurate, however, there is the more immediate difficulty that modern readers and viewers naturally desire to reflect on and identify with the complex pathos of individual subjectivity as it is represented in Shakespeare's *oeuvre*. This is especially so, perhaps, for professional readers and viewers, who are likely to have strong interests in the experience of the speaking/writing subject and in the problematic of autonomy and expressive unity. Nevertheless, for Shakespeare's characters to exist as Othello, Desdemona, and Iago, they have to use the carnivalesque 'wardrobe' inscribed within this text, and this wardrobe assigns them the roles of clown, transvestite, and 'scourge of marriage' in a charivari.

The clown is a type of public figure who embodies the 'right to be other', as Bakhtin would have it, since the clown rejects the categories available in routine institutional life.[20] The clown is therefore both criminal and monster, although such alien and malevolent aspects are more often than not disguised. Etymologically, clown is related to *colonus* – a farmer or settler, someone not from Rome but from the agricultural hinterland. As a rustic or hayseed the clown's relationship to social reality is best expressed through such contemporary idioms as 'He's out of it!' 'He doesn't know where it's at!' or simply 'Mars!' In the drama of the early modern period a clown is often by convention a kind of country bumpkin, but he is also a 'professional outsider' of extremely flexible social provenance. Bakhtin has stressed the emancipatory capacity of the clown function, arguing that the clown mask embodies the 'right to be other' or *refus d'identité*. However, there is a pathos of clowning as well, and the clown mask may represent everything that is social and sexually maladroit, credulous, easily victimised. And just as there is a certain satisfaction in observing an assertive clown get the better of his superiors, so there is also satisfaction in seeing an inept clown abused and stripped of his dignity. This abuse or 'thrashing' of the doltish outsider provides the audience with a comedy of abjection, a social genre in which the experience of exclusion and impotence can be displaced on to an even more helpless caste within society.

To think of Othello as a kind of black-faced clown is perhaps distasteful, although the role must have been written not for a black actor, but with the idea of black makeup or a false face of some kind. Othello is a Moor, but only in quotation marks, and his blackness is not even skin-deep but rather a transitory and superficial theatrical integument. Othello's Moorish origins are the mark of his exclusion; as a cultural stranger he is, of course, 'out of it' in the most compelling and literal sense. As a foreigner he is unable to grasp and make effective use of other Venetian codes of social and sexual conduct. He is thus a grotesque embodiment of the bridegroom – an exotic, monstrous, and funny substitute who transgresses the norms associated with the idea of a husband.

To link Othello to the theatrical function of a clown is not necessarily to be committed to an interpretation of his character as a fool. Othello's folly, like his nobility and personal grandeur, are specific interpretations of the character's motivation and of his competence to actualise those motives. The argument here, however, is that the role of Othello is already formatted in terms of the abject clown function and that any interpretation of the character's 'nature' therefore has to be achieved within that format. The eloquence of Othello's language and the magnanimity of his character may in fact intensify the grotesque element here. His poetic self-articulation is not so much the *expression* of a self-possessed subject but is instead a form of discursive indecorum that strains against the social meanings objectified in Othello's counter-festive *persona*. Stephen Greenblatt identifies the joke here as one of the 'master plots of comedy', in which a beautiful young woman outwits an 'old and outlandish' husband.[21] Greenblatt reminds us here that Othello is functionally equivalent to the gull or butt of an abusive comic action, but he passes over the most salient feature of Othello's outlandishness, which is actualised in the black face makeup essential to the depiction of this character. This discretion is no doubt a political judgement rather than an expression of a delicacy of taste. To present Othello with a black face, as opposed to presenting him as a black man, would confront the audience with a comic spectacle of abjection rather than with the grand opera of misdirected passion. Such a comedy of abjection has not found much welcome in the history of the play's reception.

The original audience of this play in Jacobean England may have had relatively little inhibition in its expression of invidious racial sentiments, and so might have seen the derisory implications of the situation more easily. During the nineteenth century, when institutional racism was naturalised by recourse to a 'scientific' discourse on racial difference, the problem of Othello's outlandishness and the unsympathetic laughter it might evoke is 'solved' by making him a Caucasoid Moor, instead of a 'Veritable Negro'.[22] Without such a fine discrimination, a performance of *Othello* would have been not so much tragic as simply unbearable, part farce and part lynch mob. In the present social climate, when racism, though still very widespread, has been officially anathematised, the possibility of a black-faced Othello would still be an embarrassment and a scandal, though presumably for a different set of reasons. Either way, the element of burlesque inscribed in this text is clearly too destabilising to escape repression.

If Othello can be recognised as an abject clown in a charivari, then the scenario of a such a charivari would require a transvestite to play the part of the wife. In the context of popular culture in the early modern period, female disguise and female impersonation were common to charivari and to a variety of other festive observances.[23] This practice was, among other things, the expression of a widespread 'fear' of women as both the embodiment of and the provocation to social transgression. Within the pervasive misogyny of the early modern period, women and their desires seemed to project the threat of a radical social undifferentiation.[24] The young men and boys who appeared in female dress at the time of carnival seem to have been engaged in 'putting women in their place' through an exaggerated pantomime of everything feminine. And yet this very practice required the emphatic foregrounding of the artifice required for any stable coding of gender difference. Was this festive transvestism legitimated by means of a general misrecognition of the social constitution of gender? Or did the participants understand at some level that the association of social badness with women was nothing more than a patriarchal social fiction that could only be sustained in and through continuous ritual affirmation?

Female impersonation is, of course, one of the distinctive and extremely salient features of Elizabethan and Jacobean dramaturgy and yet surprisingly little is known of how this mode of representation actually worked.[25] The practice of using boy actors to play the parts of women is derivative of the more diffuse social practice of female impersonation in the popular festive milieu. Were the boy actors in Shakespeare's company engaging in a conventional form of ridicule of the feminine? Or were they engaged in a general parody of the artifice of gender coding itself? A transvestite presents the category of woman in quotation marks, and reveals that both 'man' and 'woman' are socially produced categories. In the drama of Shakespeare and his contemporaries, gender is at times an extremely mobile and shifting phenomenon without any solid anchor in sexual identity. To a considerable degree gender is a 'flag of convenience' prompted by contingent social circumstances, and at times gender identity is negotiated with considerable grace and dexterity. The convention of the actor 'boying' the woman's part is thus doubly parodic, a camp put-down of femininity and, at another level, a way to theorise the social misrecognition on which all gender allocations depend.

Desdemona's 'femininity' is bracketed by the theatrical 'boying' of her or his part. This renders her or his sexuality as a kind of sustained gestural equivocation and this corresponds to the exaggerated and equivocal rhetorical aspect of Desdemona's self-presentation. As Desdemona puts it, 'I saw Othello's visage in his mind'; in other words, her initial attraction to him was not provoked by his physical appearance. The play thus stipulates that Desdemona herself accepts the social prohibition against miscegenation as the normative horizon within which she must act. On the face of it she cannot be physically attracted to Othello, and critics have usually celebrated this as the sign of her ability to transcend the limited horizons of her acculturation. These interpretations thus accept the premise of Othello as physically undesirable and thus insinuate that Desdemona's faith is predicated on her blindness to the highly visible 'monstrosity' of her 'husband'. In other words, her love is a misrecognition of her husband's manifestly undesirable qualities. Or is it a misrecognition of her own socially prohibited desire? Stanley Cavell interprets her lines as meaning that she saw his appearance in the way that he saw it: that she is able to enter into and to share Othello's self-acceptance and self-possession.[26] According to this view Desdemona is a kind of idealisation of the social category of 'wife', who can adopt the husband's own narrative fiction of self as her own imaginary object. Desdemona is thus both a fantasy of a sexually desirable woman and a fantasy of absolute sexual compliance. This figure of unconditional erotic submission is the obverse of the rebellious woman or shrew, but, as the play shows us, this is also a socially prohibited *métier* for a woman. In fact, as Stephen Greenblatt has shown in his very influential essay, the idea that Desdemona might feel an ardent sexual desire for him makes Othello perceive Iago's insinuations of infidelity as plausible and even probable.[27] The masculine fantasy projected in the figure of Desdemona cannot recognise itself as the object of another's desire.

Like all of Shakespeare's woman characters, Desdemona is an impossible sexual object, a female artifact created by a male imagination and objectified in a boy actor's body. This is, in its own way, just as artificial and grotesque a theatrical manifestation as the black-faced Othello who stands in for the category of the husband. What is distinctive about Desdemona is the way she embodies the category of an 'ideal wife' in its full contradictoriness. She has been described as chaste or even as still a virgin and also as sexually aggressive, even though very little unambiguous textual support for either of these readings actually exists.[28] Her elopement, with a Moor no less, signals more unequivocally than a properly arranged marriage ever could that the biblical injunction to leave mother and father has been fulfilled. It is probably even harder to accept the idea of Desdemona as part of a comedy of abjection than it is to accept Othello in such a context. It is, however, only in such a theatrical context that the hyperbolic and exacerbated misrecognition on which marriage is founded can be theorised.

At the level of surface representation then, the play enacts a marriage between two complementary symbols of the erotic grotesque. This is a marriage between what is *ipso facto* hideous and repellent with what is most beautiful and desirable. The incongruity of this match is objectified in the theatrical hyper-embodiment of the primary categories of man and woman or husband and wife. It is not known to what extent Elizabethan and Jacobean theatre practice deliberately foregrounded its own artifice. However, the symbolic practice of grotesque hyper-embodiment was well known in popular festive forms such as charivari. The theatrical coding of gender in the early modern period is thus still contaminated by the residue of these forms of social representation.

The marriage of grotesque opposites is no more a private affair or erotic dyad than a real marriage. Marriage in the early modern period, among many important social classes, is primarily a dynastic or economic alliance negotiated by a third party who represents the complex of social sanctions in which the heterosexual couple is inscribed. The elopement of Desdemona and Othello as well as their reliance on Cassio as a broker or clandestine go-between already signals their intention deliberately to evade and thwart the will of family interests. To the extent that readers or viewers are conditioned by the normative horizons that interpret heterosexual love as mutual sexual initiative and the transcendence of all social obstacles, this elopement will be read as a romantic confirmation of the spiritual and disinterested character of their love. However, it can also be construed as a flagrant sexual and social blunder. Private heterosexual felicity of the kind sought by Othello and Desdemona attracts the evil eye of erotic nemesis.

The figure of erotic nemesis and the necessary third party to this union is Othello's faithful lieutenant, Iago. It is Iago's task to show both his captain and his audience just how defenceless the heterosexual couple is against the resources of sexual surveillance. The romantic lovers, represented here through a series of grotesque distortions, do not enjoy an erotic autonomy, though such autonomy is a misrecognition of the socially inscribed character of 'private' sexuality. His abusive and derisory characterisations of the couple, together with his debasement of their sexuality, are a type of social commentary on the nature of erotic romance. The notion of mutual and autonomous self-selection of partners is impugned as a kind of mutual delusion that can only appear under the sign of monstrosity. In other words, the romantic couple can only 'know' that their union is based on mutual love *and on nothing else* when they have 'transcended' or violated the social codes and prohibitions that determine the allocation of sexual partners.

Iago is a Bakhtinian 'agelast'; that is, one who does not laugh. He is, of course, very witty, but his aim is always to provoke a degrading laughter at the follies of others rather than to enjoy the social experience of laughter *with* others. He is a demythologiser whose function is to reduce all expressivity to the minimalism of the *quid pro quo*. The process represented here is the reduction of quality to quantity, a radical undifferentiation of persons predicated on a strictly mechanistic, universalised calculus of desire. Characters identified with this persona appear throughout Shakespeare's *oeuvre*, usually in the guise of a nemesis of hypocrisy and dissimulation. Hamlet's 'I know not seems' and Don John's 'it cannot be denied I am a plain dealing villain' are important variants of a social/cognitive process that proclaims itself to be a critique of equivocation and the will to deception. It is ironic, of course, that these claims of honesty and plain dealing are so often made in the interests of malicious dissimulation. What appears to be consistent, however, in all the variants of this character type is the disavowal of erotic attachment and the contemptuous manipulation of the erotic imagination.

The supposedly 'unmotivated' malice enacted by this figure is puzzling, I believe, only when read individualistically. Is Iago envious of the pleasure Othello enjoys with Desdemona, or is he jealous of Othello's sexual enjoyment of Emilia? Of course, both these ideas are purely conjectural hypotheses that have no apparent bearing on Iago's actions. In any case there is no sustained commitment to either of these ideas, as numerous commentators have pointed out. Nevertheless, there is an important clue to understanding Iago as a social agent in these transitory ruminations. Iago seems to understand that the complex of envy and jealousy is not an aberration within the socially distributed erotic economy, but rather the fundamental pre-condition of desire itself. Erotic desire is not founded in a qualitative economy or in a rational market, but rather in a mimetic and histrionic dispensation that Iago projects as the envy–jealousy system. In this system men are the social agents and women the objects of exchange. Iago's actions are thus socially motivated by a diffuse and pervasive misogyny that slides between fantasies of the complete abjection of all women and fantasies of an exclusively masculine world.

Iago's success in achieving these fantasies is made manifest in the unbearably hideous tableau of the play's final scene. If the play as a whole is to be read as a ritual of unmarrying, then this ending is the monstrous equivalent of a sexual consummation. What makes the play unendurable is the suspicion that this climax expresses all too accurately an element present in the structure of every marriage. This is an exemplary action in which the ideal of companionate marriage as a socially sanctioned erotic union is dissolved back into the chronic violence of the envy–jealousy system. Iago theorises erotic desire and thus marriage, primarily by a technique of emptying out Othello's character, so that nothing is left at the end except the pathetic theatrical integument, the madly deluded and murderous black-faced clown. Desdemona, the perfect wife, remains submissive to the end. And Iago, with his theoretical or pedagogical tasks completed, accepts in silence his allocation to the function of sacrificial victim and is sent off to face unnamed 'brave punishments'.

The cultural text of charivari has had a durable life of its own, especially in rural settings where it has from time to time been used to police interracial marriages. Such events can have grim consequences. In *Roughing it in the Bush*, a journal of her life in upper Canada in the 1830s, Susanna Moodie has devoted an entire chapter to the custom of charivari, which was evidently common throughout the region during this period. Moodie herself is unfamiliar with the practices of charivari, but her neighbour explains that the Canadians 'got it from the French' in the Lower Province.[29] After explaining the purposes of charivari and the various functions of disguise, the neighbour recounts the following example.

> There was a runaway nigger from the States came to the village, and set up a barber's poll, and settled among us. I am no friend to the

> blacks; but really Tom Smith was such a quiet, good-natured fellow, and so civil and obliging that he soon got a good business. ... Well, after a time he persuaded a white girl to marry him. She was not a bad-looking Irishwoman, and I can't think what bewitched the creature to take him. The girl's marriage to the black man created a great sensation in the town. All the young fellows were indignant at his presumption and her folly, and they determined to give them the charivari in fine style, and punish them both for the insult they had put upon the place. Some of the young gentlemen in the town joined in the frolic. They went so far as to enter the house, drag the poor nigger from his bed, and in spite of his shrieks for mercy, they hurried him out into the cold air – for it was winter – and almost naked as he was, rode him upon a rail, and so ill-treated him that he died under their hands.[30]

I am not suggesting here that the murder of 'Tom Smith' was in any sense scripted from the text of *Othello*, though the insinuation that the young Irishwoman must have been 'bewitched' is a suggestive detail. What I do insist upon, however, is that both Moodie's anecdote and any given performance of *Othello* necessarily express the historical exigencies of race within the successor cultures of Western modernity. The fate of Tom Smith's Irish wife is unknown. It is nevertheless clear that the aim of the ringleaders was not only to punish her, but also in a sense to rescue her from the consequences of her own folly. The fantasy of rescue has also figured prominently throughout the reception history of *Othello*.

RESCUING DESDEMONA

Othello is a text which severely tests the willingness of an audience to suspend its disbelief, although the problem is not necessarily that the situation can degenerate into farce. For many commentators it is not the potentially ludicrous character of the action, but the exacerbated pathos of the ending that have provoked discomfort amounting to revulsion with this play. Horace Howard Furness found the play horribly painful, and wished that Shakespeare had never written it.[31] The problem was not simply that an innocent woman is murdered by her husband, though Furness was clearly very sensitive to the play's candid suggestions of erotic intimacy. His discomfiture is aggravated by the even more candid spectacle of miscegenation. Furness' *Variorum* edition of *Othello* was published in 1885, just twenty years after the end of the American Civil War.

Although plantation slavery had been officially ended by the defeat of the South, race relations scarcely improved. This is the period of the rise of the Ku Klux Klan, and of other institutions that aimed to enforce racial separateness. In this context it is not altogether surprising that Furness would find the play unbearably difficult, or that he would yearn for some way to rescue Desdemona from her intolerable predicament.

One way to rescue Desdemona of course is simply to rewrite the story, so that Othello's stark blackness is modulated to a more acceptable and less threatening skin colour. Edmund Kean was evidently the crucial innovator in this respect, repudiating the venerable tradition maintained by Betterton, Garrick, and Kemble, all of whom played Othello with black faces, in favour of a light brown that preserves a desirable exoticism without troubling the racial sensibilities of a white audience. By changing the makeup used to portray Othello's Moorishness, Kean solved the problem first hinted at in Rymer's critique and later articulated more emphatically by Charles Lamb.

> [Desdemona] sees Othello's colour in his mind. But ... I appeal to every one that has seen *Othello* played, whether he did not ... sink Othello's mind in his colour; whether he did not find something extremely revolting in the courtship and wedded caresses of Othello and Desdemona.[32]

Lamb's solution to this insuperable difficulty is simply not to attend theatrical productions, which can only coarsen the response of the imagination to Shakespeare's works. It is much better to read the texts, and to permit the mind to 'overpower and reconcile the first and obvious prejudice'.[33]

For Lamb, 'the Moors are now well enough known to be by many shades the less unworthy of white woman's fancy'.[34] Changing Othello's skin colour and his racial identity does nothing, of course, to save Desdemona's life. It does, however, permit her to suffer death with her dignity intact, a thought that many readers have found consoling. Coleridge's assessment of Shakespeare's achievement in conceiving *Othello* depends on maintaining a sharp distinction between 'negro' and 'Moor'. 'It would be something monstrous to conceive this beautiful Venetian girl falling in love with a veritable negro.'[35] As a 'negro', Othello must be read as a savage and a slave, and his murder of Desdemona is thus the expression of brutal passion. As a 'Moor', Othello is a warrior, and the murder, though tragically misguided, is nevertheless transmuted into a sacrifice made in the name of honour.

The amendment of Othello's colour from black, to light brown, and finally to 'tawny' becomes the orthodox solution to the play's racial difficulties throughout the nineteenth and well into the twentieth century. The compromise settlement allows the play to be accommodated to the sensibilities of a white audience. It even makes possible a way to teach the play to young, southern women. In the volume of *Shakespeariana* for 1884, Professor William Taylor Thom arranges to publish the 'prize examination on the play of *Othello*' written by Miss Fanny E. Ragland, his pupil at Hollins Institute in Roanoke, Virginia. Among the many questions posed, Thom asks his students the following question: 'Do you agree with Schlegel's view, that Othello is of the African type?' Miss Ragland's response to this question is admirable for its clarity and directness.

> Othello is not of the African type, I think, either mentally and morally or physically. He is distinctly spoken of all through the play as a 'Moor', and the Moors differed widely from the mere negroes in both intellect and colour. Roderigo calls Othello '*Thick lips*', but we must remember that he speaks as an unsuccessful rival. Othello is several times spoken of as 'black', but then, as now, 'black' was often used of a dark complexion in contradistinction to a fair one. ... Besides, there is something repulsive to my mind in the idea of a beautiful Venetian girl falling in love with an African prince, and Shakespeare would hardly have made Othello a prince if he had intended him for a negro.[36]

Miss Ragland, closely following Coleridge, rescues Desdemona's honour by carefully distinguishing Moors from 'mere negroes'. Her use of this precise 'physical anthropology' opens up the possibility for much fuller interpretive response. Othello is 'a type of moral grandeur'; the killing of Desdemona is prompted not by jealousy, but by honour.[37] The 'final scene of agony' is the consequence of injured moral laws.[38] Ragland was well acquainted with the important critical literature on the play; she refers not only to Schlegel and to Coleridge, but to Johnson, Macauley, Wordsworth, and several times to Hudson. It's clear however, that the examination is something more than a purely academic exercise. Behind the always tactful and confident language of the examination it is easy to sense a deeper uneasiness occasioned by the politics of racial difference in the American South.

The critical revisions of Lamb and Coleridge, along with the theatrical innovations introduced by Kean, rescue Desdemona from the crude spectacle of miscegenation and vulgar domestic violence. At the same time they eradicate the comedy of abjection from the play, and thus absolve audiences of any need to confront their own racial attitudes. The motives that prompt this revisionary strategy are very complex. On one level it simply expresses commonly held racist beliefs in the naturally abject and servile nature of black Africans. At the same time, however, the bleaching of Othello's skin is a powerfully effective way to hide the truth of white racism. The slave trade was abolished in England and her colonies in 1807, though slavery persisted in the United States until Emancipation in 1865. In this context an honest production of *Othello* would be just as intolerable as an honest production of *The Merchant of Venice* in the post-Holocaust context. The rescue of Desdemona through the resources of nineteenth-century physical anthropology is a kind of misrecognition for a collective guilty conscience.

The transformation of Othello from a 'mere negro' into a caucasoid Moor saves Desdemona by suppressing the play's comedy of abjection and thus permitting a less difficult imaginative compromise. A more direct and violent form of rescue is described in the following anecdote recounted by Stendhal.

> *L'année dernière (août 1822), le soldat qui était en faction dans l'intérieur du théâtre de Baltimore, voyant Othello qui, au cinquième acte de la tragédie de ce nom, allait tuer Desdemona, s'écria: 'Il ne sera jamais dit qu'en ma présence un maudit nègre aura tué une femme blanche.' Au même moment le soldat tire son coup de fusil, et casse un bras à l' acteur qui faisait Othello. Il ne se passe pas d'années sans que les journaux ne rapportent des faits semblables.*[39]
>
> [Last year (August of 1822), the soldier standing guard at the interior of the theatre in Baltimore, seeing Othello who, in the fifth act of the tragedy of that name, was going to kill Desdemona, cried out 'It will never be said that in my presence a damned black would kill a white woman'. At that moment the soldier fired his gun, and broke the arm of the actor who played Othello. Not a year goes by without newspapers reporting similar facts.]
>
> (My translation)

The moral that Stendhal wants to draw from the story of the soldier in Baltimore is that only someone who is extremely ignorant or stupid – i.e. an American – fails to distinguish an actual murder from a dramatic representation of one. In the perhaps more definitive variant of the anecdote the performance takes place in a barn, and the unlucky actor playing Othello is not merely wounded but killed outright. In this version the soldier's behaviour is less a matter of the 'perfect illusion' described by Stendhal than a militant defence of white women notwithstanding the fictional status of Desdemona's 'murder'.

It is difficult to confirm whether the Baltimore incident described by Stendahl in such circumstantial detail actually took place. There was, however, a theatrical riot in Paris at about the same time. A group of young French liberals hounded a troop of English performers off the stage with the cry *A bas Shakespeare, c'est un aide-de-camp du duc de Wellington!* The play scheduled for the night in question was almost certainly *Othello*. Conservatives at the time were appalled by the rioters' lack of civility, but the liberal press defended the protesters for their spirited defence of the national honour of France. Stendahl, who was otherwise sympathetic to the liberal position, none the less defended Shakespeare as the author of *chef-d'oeuvres de l'esprit humain* that transcend the lively but ephemeral conflicts inspired by nationalist feeling. Still, the nativist and chauvinistic strain of the protests should not be allowed to obscure the real sense of threatened group consciousness that inspired the protesters.

Stendahl's editor claims that the story of Othello's wounding by an outraged security guard in Baltimore is repeated in *l'Almanach des spectacles* for 1823, but there is no local corroboration for the story in any Maryland newspapers of this period. There is, however, an item in the *Maryland Republican and Political and Agricultural Museum* for 27 August 1822, concerning a violent attack on the 'African theatre'.

> *Unmanly Outrage*. – Saturday night a gang of fifteen or twenty ruffians, among whom was arrested and recognised one or more of the Circus riders, made an attack upon the *African Theatre*, in Mercer-street, with full intent, as is understood, to break it up root and branch ... entering the house by regular tickets, they proceeded, at quick time, to extinguish all the light in the house, and then to destroy every thing in the shape of furniture, scenery &c. ... The actors and actresses, it is said, were fairly striped like so many squirrels, and their glittering apparel torn in pieces over their heads.

The reasons for the attack remain obscure, except for the tantalising reference to 'Circus riders'. Was the incident prompted only by commercial rivalry and carried out by a group of itinerant performers? Or was it the expression of local sentiment, enforced by the actions of local thugs? The item reports only that several of the perpetrators were arrested, and that the public prosecutor would attempt to seek a compromise.

Stendahl may have conflated information about these two actual incidents to create the philosophically more interesting story about shooting Othello. The ideas of summary popular censorship and violent racial antagonism are related as crucial elements in the level of public tolerance of fictional provocations. Although the actual tale about the misguided soldier and the luckless actor in Baltimore may in all likelihood be itself a fiction, the *fantasy* of rescuing the beautiful Venetian girl from the clutches of a murderous black man has probably occurred more than once to various spectators in the history of the play's many performances. Such a fantasy has also been realised in a range of derivative forms.

Perhaps the most stirring and influential re-enactment of Desdemona's rescue is the ride of the Ku Klux Klan to save young Elsie Stoneman from a menacing black rapist in D. W. Griffith's *Birth of a Nation*. Here the story is re-told, as if from the point of view of Brabantio, as a forcible abduction rather than an elopement. Unless she were a completely abandoned whore, Desdemona/Elsie has no business 'seeing Othello's visage in his mind'. There is in principle no possibility for mutual attraction of any kind between racial opposites. And there is no question here of wishy-washy compromises with Othello's blackness. This is a much more severe rewrite of the play than the traditional nineteenth-century compromise that preserves the dignity of the characters by making Othello a 'tawny Moor'. Instead the film heightens and intensifies the radically antipathetic valences of black man and white woman in a sexual context. Elsie is virginal and completely defenceless. Her abductor represents the menace of black sexual aggression in the most crudely stereotypical way, without the extenuation of exotic origins and certainly without any trace of heroic dignity.[40] Her rescue must therefore take the form of virile and direct action, as Elsie's captor is summarily punished by the outraged Klansmen.

Later films return more directly to *Othello* and to the way in which the story tends to breach the fragile boundary between actuality and make-believe. In George Cukor's *A Double Life* (1947), Ronald Coleman plays an actor who becomes obsessively preoccupied with his wife's infidelity as he rehearses the role of Othello.

Here the iterative recitation of the dramatic text becomes internalised as the character becomes more fully identified with his theatrical role. The actor is literally possessed by Othello. André Forcier's *Une Histoire Inventée* (1990) develops the more farcical possibilities of the situation. In this film the roles of Othello and Desdemona are played by a young couple who are initially lovers in their off-stage existence. When she discovers her boy-friend with another woman she immediately ends the relationship, though they continue to work together in their theatrical capacity. In the meantime the play's chief financial backer becomes increasingly anguished over the suffering and death of 'beautiful Desdemona'. Each rehearsal is more painful than the last, until finally on opening night, during the final scene, he takes out a pistol and kills not only the murderous 'Othello', but 'Desdemona's' new lover as well. The recurring wish to prevent the catastrophe, to rewrite the play by disrupting its performance, has its partial basis in the equivocal ontological and social status of theatre as a form of representation. The tension and uneasiness provoked by the ambiguous 'reality' of every theatrical performance is, however, greatly heightened in the case of *Othello*.

In his discussion of the ontological status of the theatrical representations, Stanley Cavell identifies *Othello* as the exemplary instance where acute theatrical discomfort may provoke an outright refusal of the *mise-en-scène*.

> What is the state of mind in which we find the events in a theatre neither credible nor incredible? The usual joke is about the Southern yokel who rushes to the stage to save Desdemona from the black man. What is the joke?[41]

Cavell's willingness to take this joke seriously suggests that the impulse to rescue Desdemona is not some sort of fantastical aberration, but is in fact a response common to a great many (male?) viewers. Something real is at stake for the audience of *Othello*, even though the actual performance of the play depends on recognition of its status as a fiction.

> At the opening of the play it is fully true that I neither believe nor disbelieve. But I am something, perplexed, anxious. ... Much later, the warrior asks his wife if she has said her prayers. Do I believe he will go through with it? I know he will; it is a certainty fixed forever; but I hope against hope he will come to his senses; I appeal to him, in

> silent shouts. Then he puts his hands on her throat. The question is: What, if anything, do I do? I do nothing; that is a certainty fixed forever. And it has its consequences. *Why* do I do nothing? Because they are only pretending? ... Othello is not pretending.[42]

Does Cavell want to suggest that the Southern yokel is somehow doing the right thing, and that performances of *Othello* should henceforth be disrupted? Such disruption is not actually recommended here, but Cavell is willing to take such a possibility seriously in order to point out that such a violation of theatrical etiquette has substantive moral content. But if this is true, then behaving properly in a theatre also has a moral content *vis-à-vis* the action represented.

Cavell does not push the argument to the point of suggesting that knowing how to make-believe and agreeing to acquiesce in the social conventions of performance here is the moral equivalent of complicity in a murder. On the contrary, the disruption of the *mise-en-scène* would really be a trivial gesture, since the murder will take place no matter what anyone does at any given theatrical performance. For, as Cavell puts it, 'Quiet the house, pick up the thread again, and Othello will reappear, as near and as deaf to us as ever. – The transcendental and the empirical crossing; possibilities shudder from it.'[43] Cavell does want to make himself and his readers accountable for their response as moral agents to what the play discloses, and therefore he must insist on the element of consent and affirmation that theatre demands from the members of an audience.

Given the painful nature of the story, the history of both the interpretation and the performance of *Othello* has been characterised by a search for explanations that allow the show to go on. These consoling interpretations usually work to prevent disruptions of the play in performance. Nevertheless, the history of anguished responses to this play signals a chronic unwillingness amounting at times to outright refusal to participate in the performance of a play as the ritual or quasi-ritual affirmation of certain social practices. *Othello* occupies a problematic situation at the boundary between ritually sanctioned reality and theatrically consensual fiction. Does the play simply depict an inverted ritual of courtship and marriage, or does its performance before an audience that accepts its status as a fiction also invite complicity in a social ritual of comic abjection, humiliation, and victimisation? At a time when large-scale social consequences of racist sensibilities had not yet become visible, it may well have been easy to accept the formal codes of charivari as the expression of legitimate social norms. In later contexts of reception it is not so easy to accept *Othello* in the form of a derisory ritual of racial persecution, because the social experience of racial difference has become such a massive scandal.

Finita la commedia. What does it mean to accept the *mise-en-scène* of this play? And what does it mean to know that we wish it could be otherwise? To the extent that we want to see a man and a woman defying social conventions in order to fulfil mutual erotic initiatives, the play will appear as a thwarted comedy and our response will be dominated by its pathos. But the play also shows us what such mutual erotic initiatives look like from the outside, as a comedy of abjection or charivari. The best commentators on this play have recognised the degree to which it prompts a desire to prevent the impending débâcle and the sense in which it is itself a kind of theatrical punishment for the observers.[44] This helpless and agonised refusal of the *mise-en-scène* should suggest something about the corrosive effect on socially inscribed rituals of a radical or 'cruel' theatricality.

The idea of theatrical cruelty is linked to the radical aesthetics of Antonin Artaud. However, the English term 'cruelty' fails to capture an important inflection that runs through all of Artaud's discussion of theatre. The concept is derived from words that mean 'raw' or 'unprocessed'. In French, '*cruauté*' expresses with even greater candour this relationship with 'le cru' and its opposition to 'le cuit'. Cruelty here has the sense of something uncooked, or something prior to the process of a conventional social transformation or adoption into the category of the meaningful.[45] *Othello*, perhaps more than any other Shakespeare play, raises fundamental questions about the institutional position and aesthetic character of Shakespearean dramaturgy. Is Shakespeare raw – or is he cooked? Is it possible that our present institutional protocol for interpreting his work is a way of 'cooking' the 'raw' material to make it more palatable, more fit for consumption?

The history of the reception of *Othello* is the history of attempts to articulate ideologically correct, that is, palatable interpretations. By screening off the comedy of abjection it is possible to engage more affirmatively with the play's romantic *Liebestod*. Within these strategies, critics may find an abundance of meanings for the tragic dimension of the play. In this orientation the semantic fullness of the text is suggested as a kind of aesthetic compensation for the cruelty of its final scenes. Rosalie Colie, for example, summarises her interpretation with an account of the play's edifying power.

> In criticising the artificiality he at the same time exploits in his play, Shakespeare manages in *Othello* to reassess and to reanimate the moral system and the psychological truths at the core of the literary love-tradition, to reveal its problematics and to reaffirm in a fresh and momentous context the beauty of its impossible ideals.[46]

This is recognisably the language of the ritual misrecognition of what the play as a comedy of abjection is capable of theorising. The fullness of the play, of course, is what makes it possible for viewers and readers to participate, however unwillingly, in the charivari or ritual victimisation of the imaginary heterosexual couple represented here. Such consensual participation is morally disquieting in the way it appears to solicit at least passive consent to violence against women and against outsiders, but at least we are not howling with unsympathetic laughter at their suffering and humiliation.

Colie's description of the play's semantic fullness is based in part on her concept of 'un-metaphoring' – that is, the literalisation of a metaphorical relationship or conventional figuration. This is a moderate version of the notion of theatrical cruelty or the unmaking of convention that does not radically threaten existing social norms. In other words, the fate of Desdemona and Othello, or Romeo and Juliet, is a cautionary fable about what happens if a system of conventional figurations of desire is taken literally. But the more powerful 'un-metaphoring' of this play is related not to its fullness as a tragedy, but to its emptiness as a comedy of abjection. The violent interposing of the charivari here would indeed make visible the *political* choice between aestheticised ritual affirmation and a genuine refusal of the sexual *mise-en-scène* or relations of reproduction in which this text is inscribed.

From Michael D. Bristol, *Big-time Shakespeare* (London and New York, 1996), pp. 176–202.

NOTES

[Employing a methodology which is strongly influenced by the sociological thought of Emile Durkheim and Mikhail Bakhtin's account of the carnivalesque, Michael Bristol sets Othello in the context of the popular ritual practice of charivari. Proposing that it is an anachronistic misreading of the text to play Othello as a noble or sympathetic character, he interprets the match with Desdemona as a grotesque inversion of legitimate marriage, and the subsequent events of the play as an exposure and punishment of miscegnation and disordered sexuality. If an honest production of the play would necessarily bring its implicit racism into unacceptable visibility, attempts to ameliorate the text throughout its history of performance have been only partially successful in assuaging the guilt and anxiety this provokes. Ed.]

1. Emile Durkheim, *The Elementary Forms of the Religious Life* (London, 1915), p. 39.

2. See Steven Mullaney, *The Place of the Stage: License, Play, and Power in Renaissance England* (Chicago, 1988); Richard Schechner, *Performance Theory*, revised edn (New York, 1988); Victor Turner, *From Ritual to Theatre: The Human Seriousness of Play* (New York, 1982).

3. Stephen Greenblatt, *Shakespearean Negotiations: The Circulation of Social Energy in Renaissance England* (Berkeley: CA,1988), pp. 94–128.

4. Ibid., p. 106.

5. Mikhail Bakhtin, *Speech Genres and Other Late Essays*, ed. Caryl Emerson and Michael Holquist, trans. Vern McGee (Austin, TX, 1968), pp. 145–96.

6. Michael D. Bristol, *Carnival and Theater: Plebeian Culture and the Structure of Authority in Renaissance England* (London and New York, 1985), pp. 59–111.

7. Anthony Giddens, *The Constitution of Society: Outline of a Theory of Structuration* (Cambridge, 1984), pp. 3–4.

8. Bristol, *Carnival and Theater*, pp. 26–59.

9. David Underdown, *Revel, Riot and Rebellion: Popular Politics and Culture in England 1603–1660* (Oxford, 1985), pp. 99–103. See also Jacques LeGoff and Jean-Claude Schmitt (eds), *Le Charivari: Actes de la table ronde organisée à Paris (25–27 April 1977) par l'Ecole des Hautes Etudes en Sciences Sociales et le Centre National de la Recherche Scientifique* (Paris, 1977); Henri Rey-Flaud, *Le Charivari; Les rituels fondamentaux de la sexualité* (Paris, 1985); E. P. Thompson, 'Rough Music: Le Charivari Anglais', *Annales: Economies, Sociétés, Civilisations*, 27 (1972), 285–312.

10. See Natalie Z. Davis, 'The Reasons of Misrule: Youth Groups and Charivaris in Sixteenth Century France', *Past and Present*, 50 (1981), 49–75.

11. François Laroque, 'An Archaeology of the Dramatic Text: *Othello* and Popular Traditions', *Cahiers Elisabethains*: 32 (1987), 13–16.

12. See Carol Thomas Neely, 'Women and Men in *Othello*: "What Should such a Fool / Do with so Good a Woman?"', in *The Woman's Part: Feminist Criticism of Shakespeare*, ed. Carolyn S. Lenz, Gayle Greene and Carol Thomas Neely (Urbana, IL, 1985).

13. Susan Snyder, *The Comic Matrix of Shakespeare's Tragedies* (Princeton, NJ, 1979), pp. 70–4.

14. Lawrence Levine, *Highbrow/Lowbrow: The Emergence of Cultural Hierarchy in America* (Cambridge, MA, 1988), pp. 14–20; Michael Neill, 'Unproper Beds: Adultery and the Hideous in *Othello*', *Shakespeare Quarterly*, 40 (1989), 391–3.

15. Janet Stavropoulos, 'Love and Age in *Othello*', *Shakespeare Studies*, 19 (1987), 125–41.

16. See G. K. Hunter, 'Elizabethans and Foreigners', *Shakespeare Survey*, 17 (1964), 37–52, and '*Othello* and Colour Prejudice', *Proceedings of the British Academy*, 53 (1967), 139–63; Martin Orkin, 'Othello and the Plain Face of Racism', *Shakespeare Quarterly*, 38 (1987), 166–88.

17. See Winthrop Jordan, *White Over Black* (Chapel Hill, NC, 1968); Elliot Tokson, *The Popular Image of the Black Man in English Drama 1550–1688* (Boston, MA, 1982).

18. Violet Alford, 'Rough Music or Charivari', *Folklore*, 70 (1959), 505–18.

19. Davis, 'The Reasons of Misrule', p. 75.

20. Mikhail Bakhtin, *The Dialogic Imagination*, trans. Caryl Emerson and Michael Holquist (Austin, TX, 1981), pp. 158–67.

21. Stephen Greenblatt, *Renaissance Self-Fashioning: From More to Shakespeare* (Chicago, 1980), p. 234.

22. Karen Newman, '"And Wash the Ethiop White": Femininity and the Monstrous in *Othello*', in *Shakespeare Reproduced: The Text in History and Ideology*, ed. Jean Howard and Marion O'Connor (London, 1987), p. 144.

23. Natalie Z. Davis, '"Women on Top": Symbolic Sexual Inversion and Political Disorder in Early Modern Europe', in *The Reversible World: Symbolic Inversion in Art and Society*, ed. Barbara Babcock (Ithaca, NY, 1974), pp. 147ff.

24. Linda Woodbridge, *Women and the English Renaissance: Literature and the Nature of Womankind, 1540–1620* (Urbana, IL, 1984).

25. Phyllis Rackin, 'Androgyny, Mimesis and the Marriage of the Boy Heroine on the English Renaissance Stage', *PMLA*, 102 (1987), 29–42.

26. Stanley Cavell, *Disowning Knowledge in Six Plays of Shakespeare* (Cambridge, MA, 1987), p. 129.

27. Greenblatt, *Renaissance Self-Fashioning*, pp. 237–52.

28. T. G. A. Nelson and Charles Haines, 'Othello's Unconsummated Marriage', *Essays in Criticism*, 33 (1981), 1–18; Stephen Booth, 'The Best *Othello* I Ever Saw', *Shakespeare Quarterly*, 40 (1989), 332–6.

29. Susanna Moodie, *Roughing It in the Bush* (Toronto, 1989), p. 208.

30. Ibid., p. 210.

31. Horace Howard Furness, *The Letters of Horace Howard Furness* (Boston, MA, 1922), vol. 2, p. 149.

32. Charles Lamb, *Plays and Dramatic Essays*, ed. R. Dircks (London, 1893), p. 191.

33. Ibid.

34. Ibid.

35. Samuel Taylor Coleridge, *Notes and Lectures Upon Shakespeare and Some of the Old Poets and Dramatists With Other Literary Remains of S. T. Coleridge*, ed. Mrs H. N. Coleridge (London, 1849), vol. 1, p. 42.

36. Fanny E. Ragland, 'Prize Examination on the Play of *Othello*', *Shakespeariana*, I (1884), 252.

37. Ibid.

38. Ibid., p. 254.

39. Stendahl, *Racine et Shakespeare*, vol. 18 in *Ouvres Complètes*, ed. Pierre Martino (Paris, 1925).

40. Michael Rogin, 'The Sword became a Flashing Vision', *Representations*, 9 (1985), 161ff.

41. Cavell, *Disowning Knowledge*, 1987, pp. 98ff.

42. Ibid., p. 100.

43. Ibid., p. 103.

44.. See Kenneth Burke, 'Othello: An Essay to Illustrate a Method', *The Hudson Review*, 4 (1951), 165–203; Neely, 'Women and Men in *Othello*'; Patricia Parker, 'Shakespeare and Rhetoric: "Dilation" and "Delation" in *Othello*', in *Shakespeare and the Question of Theory*, ed. Patricia Parker and Geoffrey Hartman (London, 1985); Peter Stallybrass, 'Patriarchal Territories: The Body Enclosed', in *Rewriting the Renaissance: The Discourses of Sexual Difference in Early Modern Europe*, ed. Margaret W. Ferguson, Maureen Quilligan and Nancy Vickers (Chicago, 1986).

45. See Antoinin Artaud, *The Theatre and its Double*, trans. Mary Caroline Richards (New York, 1958), p. 42 *et passim*.

46 Rosalie Colie, *Shakespeare's Living Art* (Princeton, NJ, 1974), p. 167.

8

Royal Shakespeare: Theatre and the Making of Ideology

ALAN SINFIELD

> a theatrical backwater, an adjunct to the tourist industry which was largely ignored by critics and stars ...
>
> (Richard Findlater)[1]

> every conceivable value was buried in deadly sentimentality and complacent worthiness – a traditionalism approved largely by town, scholar and Press ...
>
> (Peter Brook)[2]

> Certainty of financial support from the tourist public would have been every excuse for a *laissez faire* policy of artistic standard – and, indeed, this was the policy ...
>
> (Charles Landstone)[3]

A critic, a director and an officer of the Arts Council agree that what we now call the Royal Shakespeare Company was, at the end of the Second World War, artistically, culturally and politically insignificant. Since that time this has become one of the most prestigious companies in the world, the repeated winner of major international awards. In the 1950s the company broke even or made a small profit from box office receipts; in 1984–5 its Arts Council grant totalled nearly five million pounds. [...] The rapid and convincing development of the RSC has been both a cause and an effect of the construction of Shakespeare which has become dominant in modern British society. It intersects fundamentally with our ways of thinking about the plays and about 'the arts' and political change within welfare capitalism.

The crucial structural changes in the RSC were made by Peter Hall when he became director in 1960 at the age of 29. He leased a London theatre, the Aldwych, thus making it possible to keep a permanent company together and to perform modern plays, and he pressured the Arts Council into subsidising the consequent deficit. The prevailing Stratford image was conservative – 'It was acknowledged that each year there should be some celebration of the bard, and audiences arrived in Stratford very much as if they were on a pilgrimage'.[4] Hall's innovations signalled a new direction, they seemed politically progressive. The idea of a permanent company was egalitarian and was associated with Brecht's Berliner Ensemble; modern playwrighting meant the new wave which was challenging the establishment at the Royal Court and Theatre Workshop (and, indeed, it led the RSC into disagreements with the censor and a dispute in the press in 1964 about dirty plays); and State subsidy was widely regarded as necessary to protect innovative work from commercial pressures.

'I am a radical, and I could not work in the theatre if I were not. The theatre must question everything and disturb its audience' – so said Peter Hall in 1966.[5] This became the image of the RSC: 'The company was developing a radical identity which could be seen in every aspect of its existence'; 'While there was no question of the theatre promulgating an ideology, it was generally understood that the beliefs and ideals of the RSC were left of centre.'[6] And this image has persisted, broadly, through the replacement of Hall by Trevor Nunn in 1968 to the present; in 1974 Nunn declared, 'I want a socially concerned theatre. A politically aware theatre.' This radical RSC identity is so well known that it may be taken for granted, but it is composed, surely, of paradoxes and surprises which suggest a more complicated and confused relationship between innovation and establishment. 'The Royal Shakespeare Company': as someone remarked, 'It's got everything in it except God'.[7] National subsidy for the company devoted to Shakespeare seems obvious and the royal epithet goes with that. But how did it get mixed in with radicalism? – to the point, apparently, where the chairman of the Arts Council 'questioned whether it was the duty of the state actually to subsidise those who were working to overthrow it'.[8] And given this anxiety, why did the Arts Council maintain and increase its support?

Trevor Nunn reports that Hall 'insisted upon one simple rule: that whenever the Company did a play by Shakespeare, they should do it because the play was relevant, because the play made some demand upon our current attention'. Nunn said that he himself produced the Roman plays in 1972 because they seemed 'to me to have the most meaning and the most point and the most relevance'.[9] Shakespeare-plus-relevance: this is the combination of traditional authority and urgent contemporaneity which proved so effective. We shall consider, in the changing political context of the time, what kind of authority this has been, what kinds of relevance and radicalism have been developed, and why the combination has been so necessary and powerful.

The Wars of the Roses (1963) was important in establishing the radical image of the RSC, and the conception was certainly adventurous. The three *Henry VI* plays and *Richard III* were rewritten by John Barton as three plays, titled *Henry VI, Edward IV* and *Richard III*. The playing text contained just over half the lines of the original four plays, and to those were added 1400 lines written by Barton, so that he was responsible for almost a tenth of what was said; also, many lines and scenes were moved around. One reason was that the company could not sustain, in box-office terms, three lesser-known plays in one season. Also, the rewriting was designed to substantiate a particular view of the political relevance of the plays.

Hall said that his direction of *The Wars of the Roses* was guided by two convictions about Shakespeare. One is that he believed in the 'Elizabethan World Picture' as described by Tillyard: 'All Shakespeare's thinking, whether religious, political or moral, is based on a complete acceptance of this concept of order. There is a just proportion in all things: man is above beast, king is above man, and God above king.' This, of course, is an extremely conservative idea (it was even conservative in theatrical terms, for Anthony Quayle had drawn upon Tillyard for his conception of *Richard II, Henry IV* and *Henry V* at Stratford in 1951). An ordered and harmonious society may be a good thing, but to base it upon such hierarchisation is to build in all the oppression which liberals, let alone socialists, have resisted. Hall, like Tillyard, seemed to justify such a vision with an extreme and partial idea of the alternative: 'Revolution, whether in the individual's temperament, in the family, or in the state or the heavens destroys the order and leads to destructive anarchy.' In a classic conservative move, every possibility which is not the status quo is stigmatised as 'anarchy' – no other idea of order and harmony is admitted. Moreover, the hierarchy is reinforced, Hall said, by the claim that it is both natural and the concern of a retributive deity: 'punishment will follow the violation of natural laws. Bolingbroke ... and his family, suffer retribution for generations.' Such a threat is plainly designed to induce docility, and moreover, by projecting violent retribution on to a deity it legitimates punitive institutions and habits of mind in society. Hall said, amazingly, that he saw all this as 'humanitarian in its philosophy and modern and liberal in its application'.

Most of the rewriting of the text was in the service of this conservative viewpoint. In particular, the death of the Bishop of Winchester (*2 Henry VI*, III.iii) was moved to follow the death of Suffolk (IV.i) and made to conclude the first play. The idea was that Winchester's 'death-bed confession' of responsibility for the death of Gloucester would make 'the main moral point that self-seeking and wickedness breed guilt in the doer, and rejection by other people'. But Winchester does not, in the received text, make such a confession: Hall and Barton therefore added a question from Warwick about it and a response in which Winchester implicitly admits the murder. It was also thought a good idea, to enforce the same moral in this concluding scene, to 'make Henry guiltily aware that his weakness has been responsible for the death of Gloucester'.[10] For this purpose, King Henry was given a speech made up of three lines from another character in *3 Henry VI*, an invented line, and six lines spoken by Henry elsewhere. Thus the scene was adjusted in three ways (including its move to a climactic position) to yield a coherence of event and ideology which, it might be thought, the received text assiduously eschews.

The radical reputation of the RSC did not derive from a commitment to the propaganda of the Elizabethan State, however, but from Hall's other conviction: that the rhetoric of the plays' characters was 'really' 'an ironic revelation of the time-honoured practices of politicians. I realised that the mechanism of power had not changed in centuries. We also were in the middle of a blood-soaked century. I was convinced that a presentation of one of the bloodiest and most hypocritical periods in history would teach many lessons about the present.'[11] Hall found support for this in Jan Kott's book *Shakespeare Our Contemporary*, which he had read in proof. Kott argues that twentieth-century history has re-equipped us for the political violence of Shakespeare – he invites us to see in Gloucester's seduction of the Lady Anne 'the night of nazi occupation, concentration camps, mass-murders. One must see in it the cruel time when all moral standards are broken, when the victim becomes the executioner, and vice versa.' This analogy (or perhaps continuity) is presented by Kott partly in political terms, as 'a cruel social order in which the vassals and superiors are in conflict with each other, the kingdom is ruled like a farm, and falls prey to the strongest'; but also as something like the human condition, an unalterable given which political action cannot affect, offered as a pessimistic revision of the Marxist emphasis on history – 'The implacable roller of history crushes everybody and everything'.[12]

Kott's scepticism about any positive possibilities in politics is comprehensible enough, especially in relation to his native Poland, but whether it was constructive in England in 1963 is doubtful. However this is the aspect which Hall seized upon: 'Shakespeare always knew that man in action is basically an animal. Before man developed religion or philosophy, he had an instinctive will to dominate. This lust may be excused as self-defence, or the need to obtain food – but it is as basic to an animal as the desire to eat, to sleep or to procreate.'[13] The combination of this notion that people are 'basically' animals (a common motif in the post-war period[14]) with the World Picture idea of divinely instituted order is most powerfully conservative. It offers no hope for humanity and no analysis of the sources and structures of injustice, whilst siphoning any residual idealism into deference towards the magnates who perpetrate oppression and reverence for the social system which sustains them. Kott at least repudiated the World Picture; he finds satisfaction in the idea that the kings also (and Hitler and Stalin) are the ridiculous victims of history. This is applied even to Richmond at the end of *Richard III*: Kott says he 'suddenly gives a crowing sound like Richard's, and, for a second, the same sort of grimace twists his face. The bars are being lowered. The face of the new king is radiant again.'[15] This is, of course, an interpretation not explicitly suggested by the text; Kott represents the accession of the king who in Tillyard's view is the divinely appointed answer to political violence as just another cruel trick of history. Hall and Barton, contrariwise, were eager to exempt Richmond from the discredit attaching generally to politicians. Therefore they elaborated upon the received text by writing in a part for the Princess Elizabeth so as to 'bring out the historical and thematic point that her marriage with Richmond defined the reconciliation of York and Lancaster, and brought the Wars of the Roses to an end'.[16] Thus the arrival (in Elizabethan terms) at the status quo is made to seem even more satisfying than in the received text – the one miraculous exception to the otherwise universal human bestiality.

Such, then, is the conservative slant of *The Wars of the Roses*; how it appeared to be and perhaps was radical in the social context of 1963 will be considered later on. The other great influence on the RSC was Peter Brook. From the beginning, Brook's orientation was Modernist – in 1960 he asked: 'is there nothing in the revolution that took place in painting fifty years ago that applies to our own crisis today? Do we know where we stand in relation to the real and the unreal, the face of life and its hidden streams, the abstract and the concrete, the story and the ritual?'[17] This kind of concern, though a challenge to the complacency of west-end theatre in 1960 – a challenge cognate with attention to Beckett, Ionesco, Pinter and Artaud – neglects as external and trivial the realities of political power and political action. In 1963 Brook explained his opposition to a Shakespeare of 'outer splendour' – of romance, fantasy and decoration, declaring; 'on the inside lie themes and issues, rituals and conflicts which are as valid as ever'.[18] He allowed no space for a historical reality which is neither superficial nor subjective. In 1977 his basic position had not changed: 'I don't have any sense of or interest in history as a reality. ... What interests me is that there are channels through which we can come into contact for a limited time with a more intense reality, with heightened perceptions.'[19]

Brook's *King Lear* (1962) was perceived, with *The Wars of the Roses*, as setting the tone and policy of the company. The production was a determined realisation of Kott's chapter '*King Lear* or Endgame' – the idea that Shakespeare's vision in this play is like Beckett's. Charles Marowitz said of the rehearsals: 'our frame of reference was always Beckettian. The world of this Lear, like Beckett's, is in a constant state of decomposition. The set consists of geometrical sheets of metal which are ginger with rust and corrosion. The costumes, dominantly leather, have been textured to suggest long and hard wear. ... Apart from the rust, the leather and the old wood, there is nothing but space – giant white flats opening on to a blank cyclorama.'[20] The politics of this is nihilist; Brook made sure that his *Lear* could not be construed as offering any positive possibilities for humanity by making the servants hostile instead of sympathetic to the blinded Gloucester, deleting Edmund's final repentance, and introducing as a last gesture a renewed rumbling of thunder, suggesting the storm still to come.

Brook's work on modern plays for the RSC in the 1960s developed the radical image of the company, though its political imprecision was gradually perceived.[21] His presentation of *A Midsummer Night's Dream* in 1970 was praised in England and the United States as an astonishing vision of the play. 'Tittuping fairies and fat jolly avuncular actors wearing loveable asses' heads' were replaced by

> the rougher magic of the circus, of the puppet theatre and of the music hall. Thus Bottom sports a clown's nose when under the influence of the potion, love in idleness; thus we have Titania floating down from the flies in a crimson bower of ostrich feathers straight out of a folies bergères revue; thus we have Puck in yellow pantaloons trailing with him memories of the sturdy accomplishments of the *commedia dell'arte* troupers; thus we have Oberon nonchalantly spinning a saucer on the end of a stick whilst airborne on a trapeze. To say all this proved exhilarating would be the understatement of the year.[22]

Few people asked what it all meant; Brook said it was 'a work of pure celebration ... a celebration of the arts of the theatre' and that 'The play is about something very mysterious, and only to be understood by the complexity of human love'.[23]

Brook's distrust of political relevance set him in principle at odds with Hall, but in effect Brook's anguished Modernist disdain for history, politics and material reality approximated to Hall's despondent argument that nothing can be done because we are animals and unable to live up to the Elizabethan World Picture. Between them they implied a sense of general violent destruction, proceeding both from uncontrollable political systems and from mysterious inner compulsions. This Hall–Brook convergence amounted to the political stance of the RSC in the 1960s. That it helped to channel initially at least a certain radical impetus may be attributed to Kott, whose criticism was certainly more political than the main western academic tradition (though not in the Lear–Beckett chapter); to the intermittent invocation and influence of Brecht; and above all to the confused political awareness of the time.

The purposes and success of the RSC in the 1960s, and the imprecision of its radical gesture, should be perceived in terms of its situation at the focus of diverse cultural assumptions: the ineluctable status of Shakespeare, the feeling that the main impetus in English society demanded radicalism and relevance, and the idea that the State had a responsibility to support such work. This conjuncture must be analysed in its wider significance. The ruling concept I shall call *culturism*: the belief that a wider distribution of high culture through society is desirable and that it is to be secured through public expenditure. Culturism is an aspect of the theory of welfare capitalism, within which the market is accepted as the necessary agency for the production of wealth, and its tendency to produce unacceptable inequality is to be tempered by State intervention. Anthony Crosland in his seminal book *The Future of Socialism* (1956) envisaged this happening in two ways: 'first, by removing the greater handicap which poorer families suffer as compared with richer, during sickness, old age and the period of heaviest family responsibility, and secondly by creating standards of public health, education and housing which are comparable in scope and quality with the best available for private purchase.'[24]

The subsidisation of high culture fits precisely into this wider pattern of social policy: there is the same assumption that the market, left to itself, will produce inadequacies of quality and distribution, the same insistence upon State responsibility to extend to all classes the kind of provision which the middle classes have historically made for themselves. And from the vantage point of the present the outcome of culturism is unsurprising: the subsidised product has been appreciated and used overwhelmingly by middle-class audiences – one study suggests that in 1976 the top twenty per cent of households received over forty per cent of public expenditure on theatres, sporting events and other entertainments while the bottom twenty-five per cent received just four per cent. Thus the pattern I have been pursuing is completed, for recent work has shown that 'Almost all public expenditure on the social services in Britain benefits the better off to a greater extent than the poor'.[25]

The location of culturism within welfare capitalism helps to explain the attention to Shakespeare and the assumption of State responsibility. The further factor – the accompanying radical identity – derives from the particular orientation of the left in England in the late 1950s and early 1960s. This we may call 'left culturism': the belief that socialists must now concern themselves with 'the quality of life' in the society. [...]

Frank Parkin in an analysis of the Campaign for Nuclear Disarmament published in 1965 found a commitment to some left causes (those more individually oriented) and not others (trades unions, for instance).[26] This was 'middle-class radicalism', but with the stimulus of the Vietnam War it became clearer and more purposeful. I have argued elsewhere that the theatre, from the opening of the English Stage Company in 1956, was a cultural site where a new, youthful, left-liberal intelligentsia identified itself.[27] Parkin found a link between his subjects and the theatre, and Williams had already noted that the new life in the English theatre was based on 'an important growth of middle-class dissidence'.[28] The major matrix in which this dissidence developed was higher education, which expanded rapidly in the period. It afforded the institutional bonding in which a culture of critical discourse, respect for high culture, and left culturism could cohere. Here the youthful left-liberal intellectuals found their structural role and their sense of validity. State support for 'the arts', and for Shakespeare especially, seemed an obvious extension of their experience, their concerns and, indeed, their political commitment.

The RSC can be observed feeling its way towards this class fraction. Hall realised that he needed a differently-constituted audience if he was to dispense with the conservative middle-class theatre tradition of Shakespeare which he regarded as moribund. In January 1963 he said: 'We want to run a popular theatre. We don't want to be an institution supported by middle-class expense accounts. We want to be socially as well as artistically open. We want to get people who have never been to the theatre – and particularly the young – to see our plays.' By March 1965 the 'popular' and the 'open' had been refocused entirely in terms of the 'the young' and particularly those in higher education: Hall saw that this was a growth area in English society and that it was creating the RSC's obvious new reference point:

> There is now an extraordinary and dangerous division in our audience – between what (roughly speaking) those over 45 and those under 45 want. ... There is a new generation who do not think of the theatre as a high-brow, intellectual and difficult institution. They only object when it is middlebrow, safe and intellectually specious. ... it is an audience that is growing and growing fast – as fast as our new universities, as fast as the large sale of LP records and paperback books.[29]

Of course, 'those over 45' had to be catered for while the new audience was constituting itself, and this no doubt accounts for much of the vagueness in stance of the RSC. But the crucial convergence was with the other audience, which was perceived by Hall in the image of the RSC: involved in high culture, concerned with the radical and relevant, prepared to demand State support.

'They only object when it is middlebrow, safe and intellectually specious', Hall said: that 'only' indicates the problem with the radicalism of the mid 1960s youthful intelligentsia. The state of England in general and the theatre in particular seemed so desperately stultified that any challenge to customary pieties seemed to be going in the right direction. It was difficult to envisage, let alone expect, specifically socialist policies. This was the feeling which Harold Wilson's rhetoric picked up and amplified: 'We are living in the jet-age but we are governed by an Edwardian establishment mentality. Over the British people lies the chill frost of Tory leadership. They freeze initiative and petrify imagination. ... We want the youth of Britain to storm the new frontiers of knowledge, to bring back to Britain that surging adventurous self-confidence and sturdy self-respect which the Tories have almost submerged by their apathy and cynicism.'[30] When Labour came into government in 1964 (and boosted Arts Council and RSC grants) the inadequacies of this programme quickly appeared and, together with the Vietnam War, this helped to focus a more strenuous interrogation of the ills of modern society.

Hall's direction of David Warner as Hamlet in 1965 affords access to the complexity of this cultural formation. Warner (rather like Jimmy Porter before him) invaded one cultural milieu with the lifestyle of another: 'his lank blond hair ruffled, a rust-red scarf looped about his neck, and his cloak rucked up like a belted grey mackintosh, reminds us of a drama student, or an inconspicuous undergraduate, or a worried young man leaving a coffee-bar in the King's Road.'[31] This was something with which to disturb the A level teacher! For Hall, the production evoked a scepticism about political action which, we have seen, was his own – but he attributed it to young people: 'the young of the West, and particularly the intellectuals, have by and large lost the ordinary, predictable radical impulses which the young in all generations have had.' But the effects of cultural production are always negotiated in the particular conditions of reception. The young in the audience found in the performance something they could use more positively: they showed, wrote J. C. Trewin, 'by their overwhelming cheers at the close that David Warner was the Hamlet of their imagination and their heart'. They saw Warner's Hamlet not as a figure of apathy but as one of rebellion or, at least, refusal: he refused the corrupt world of Claudius and Polonius. True, he had little but style with which to resist, but this might contribute a necessary initial independence of stance; as Warner observed, 'This was a young man who made his own rules and did not mind appearing ridiculous or eccentric'.[32] There was a stronger radical impulse in his young intellectuals than Hall had realised. By 1968, when he yielded the directorate of the RSC to Trevor Nunn, the conditions of political radicalism in society and in the theatre were changing rapidly.

The eruption of extraparliamentary political activism which we associate with 1968 (but which of course was a more gradual and uneven process) had a major impact on theatre, for it involved especially the youthful intelligentsia who had supported theatrical innovations in the 1960s and it manifested itself partly through the growth, almost from nothing in 1966, of fringe groups, venues and plays.[33] The wider breakdown of consensus politics, initially in the move to the right of the Heath Conservative administration of 1970 and then in the Tory leadership of Margaret Thatcher, placed in question RSC hopes of taking its conservative and radical audiences along together. The opening by the company of its own 'fringe' venues – with notable successes at The Place, the Other Place and the Warehouse with both Shakespeare and new work[34] – signals this split.

The response to Warner's Hamlet had already suggested that the radicalism of a part of the audience might outrun Hall's; in 1970 he deplored 'a new generation who want to shout down all opposing opinions' – he wanted to direct *The Tempest* 'because it's about wisdom, understanding and also resignation'.[35] Trevor Nunn's initial stance was a refusal of politics. In *Plays and Players* in September 1970 – with the nude review *Oh Calcutta!* pictured on the front cover – Nunn said he was 'not a political animal': 'In most of our work now we are concerned with the human personalities of a king or queen rather than with their public roles.'[36] In 1969 he produced the late plays in a 'chamber' setting designed 'to work within the scale of the individual actor – to make his words, thoughts, fantasies and language seem important'; his *Hamlet* of 1970 sought 'to focus upon that man's predicament in a very domestic and familiar way'. A 'white box' set and schematic contrasts of customer suggested both a landscape of the mind and current fashion in decor, and there were explicitly religious motifs.

Nunn moved back towards the Hall–Barton mode with his production in 1972 of Roman plays (*Coriolanus, Julius Caesar, Antony and Cleopatra* and *Titus Andronicus*). He believed that Shakespeare used Roman settings 'to conduct a less inhibited examination of political motives and social organisation than was possible when he was dealing with English history' and that these plays 'are speaking directly to us now'. But Nunn's reading of the current political situation manifested the same generalised nihilism that we saw previously – in the programme for *Titus Andronicus* he suggested: 'Shakespeare's Elizabethan nightmare has become ours ... are we already in the convulsion which heralds a fall greater than Rome's?' Despite the explicitness of some of the modern political parallels – Rome in *Julius Caesar* was a police State controlled through black-shirted soldiers – Nunn laid himself open to charges that his main concern was with stage effect, style and spectacle (he had installed lighting and stage machinery of unprecedented sophistication). In 1974 Nunn restated the original RSC programme: 'I want to be concerned with a theatre that is determined to reach beyond the barriers of income, I want an avowed and committed popular theatre. I want a socially concerned theatre. A politically aware theatre.'[37]

In fact RSC policy swung to and fro in the 1970s and early 1980s. In 1974 John Barton produced a doctored 'relevant' *King John*: 'Our world of outward order and inner instability, of shifting ideologies and self-destructive pragmatism, is also the world of King John.'[38] In 1977 Terry Hands' *Coriolanus* was remarkable for the extent to which the production diminished the political implications of the play. The main theatre responded intermittently to the Women's Movement: after Barton's 1970 production of *Measure for Measure* it became common for Isabella to indicate a lack of enthusiasm for the Duke's final proposal of marriage. Michael Bogdanov in 1978 even managed a feminist interpretation of *The Taming of the Shrew*. He turned the play as it has traditionally been understood on its head, simply by making it clear that what the men say and do is morally repugnant; in a brilliant and moving conclusion he made Petruchio and the other men flinch in horror from the destruction of Katherine which they have achieved. Yet very many productions seemed mainly opportunist – deploying the battery of staging devices developed during the 1960s for merely immediate effect.

The Hall–Brook convergence of the 1960s, confused as it was, grew up in direct dialogue with the political conditions of that decade. But since then it has seemed that the mannerisms of radical relevance are being reused without even that initial purchase in social change, and without even the original analysis, limited as that was, of how they were supposed to signify. The strongest evidence of this tendency is productions which are intended to address political and historical matters, and which in some respects do that, but which at the same time make contradictory gestures towards a purportedly transcendent reality. In such cases Hall and Brook don't just converge, they jostle and hamper each other. In 1974 Barton, with Barry Kyle and Clifford Williams, directed *Cymbeline*. On the one hand, they suggested 'that the play, so far from being a fairy-tale to its Jacobean audience, dealt seriously with the political issues of empire and internationalism', and to this end the Roman scenes were elaborated. But on the other hand they gave major characters symbolic attributes which implied a Brookian vision of an interior experience which is also some kind of ultimate reality: 'the Queen was a practising sorceress whose spell-working filled the stage with smoke; while the King wore a cloak of senility from which, on the news of the Queen's death, he burst, like a butterfly.'[39] The powerful *King Lear* of 1982, to take another instance, was meant, according to its director Adrian Noble, to be relevant in the political climate produced by the Falklands War and to show 'the potential for violence which you get within an absolute state'.[40] In some respects the production demystified conventional notions of transcendence – 'Ripeness is all' was shouted, desperately, over the drum of the preparing army in turbulent lighting; when Lear woke at Dover he was wearing pyjamas rather than the flowing robes of an Old Testament prophet/penitent; an emphasis on touching inhibited the blind/sight imagery from setting up a dichotomy between mundane and transcendent vision. But at the same time, contradictorily, the storm and the Fool were offered as projections of Lear's state of mind and the analysis of a society in dissolution was transformed into the universe in apocalypse. The 1960s proclamation and abrogation of the political persists, and apparently without much attempt to develop a new analysis – Noble actually invoked Jan Kott.

The political confusion of the RSC since 1970 has been, finally, a confusion about its audiences and roles. As a liberal, consensual institution in a society which was polarising, it received criticism from both left and right. For the left, it was a victim of its own success: it seemed part of a new establishment – liberal, but an establishment nevertheless (like the BBC, parts of the churches and much of the education system). It employed between five-hundred and six-hundred people and if it was not quite, as Hall had feared, the ICI of the theatre, it had many features of a medium-sized business. One might say it was like a family, but perhaps that was not a good thing: 'the traditional implications hold true. The Company remains a male-dominated hierarchy, with those who are definitely parents and those who are definitely children (and if they happen to be secretaries and women, which is most often the case, they will be servicing their wise, humanist "fathers" with cups of tea or coffee).'[41] This kind of critique developed alongside a more theoretical kind of socialism, which denied that the State could protect culture or anything else from the impact of capitalism – seeing the State rather as the essential instrument of capitalism. From his position as director of the National Theatre Peter Hall perceived in all this criticism of the RSC 'a perfect metaphor of how the radical dreams of yesterday become the institutions of today, to be fought and despised'.

At the same time, the waning of governmental commitment to the welfare-capitalist principle of State support for the arts increased the company's economic difficulties and forced it to listen to criticism from the right. In 1975, when Britain in general and the RSC in particular were thought to be in great danger from inflation (attributed to the OPEC increase in oil prices – the external threat to the kingdom is relevant), it seemed a good idea to start the season with *Henry V*. The Duke of Edinburgh expressed his hope that the 'marvellous spirit of the play' would inspire courage 'to overcome the menace of rising costs and inflation in the years ahead'. The struggle which Terry Hands faced as director was to give a positive reading of the play which was not so clumsily patriotic as to violate the company's political identity. The war was offered, to me shockingly, as an opportunity for individuals to become 'aware of their responsibilities, both to themselves and to each other, voluntarily accepting some abdication of that individuality in a final non-hierarchic interdependence – a real brotherhood'.

The theme of brotherhood was difficult to square with the text and it was not picked up by the critics. They either heralded 'a gutsy, reviving production at a time of national adversity. And, boy, do we need it' (*Daily Express*) or accepted the idea of 'troops driven to the limit to enable the king to achieve self-realisation' (*The Times*). That the RSC was being forced back on to the audience which Peter Hall had tried to resist is indicated by the letter of a company director who had bought six tickets for a gala performance 'but was horrified to learn from a friend that the performance of *Henry V* is to be given with the actors dressed in boiler suits or similar garb. I cannot believe this is true for such a performance, especially with royalty present ...'[42] [...]

We have surveyed a whole period of cultural change, a complex institution, and a range of productions by different people working from different theories. What is constant, as we follow it all through, is the importance of being Shakespeare. It is that name which has made so much of it possible, let alone important. Hence the insistence by all the directors that what they are presenting is *really Shakespeare*. Even Bogdanov's feminist *Taming of the Shrew* was offered by him as a rediscovery of Shakespeare's true intentions: 'In this world where bodies are sold to the highest bidder Kate's attempt to establish independence challenges the regime and the preconceived ideas of a woman's role in society. Does Shakespeare *really* believe that this is the way that society should behave or is he asking for an egalitarian society of equal rights and opportunity? I believe the latter.'[43]

Despite the frank acknowledgement of Hall and Barton that their rewriting in *The Wars of the Roses* must be considered dubious in principle, Hall announced their belief that 'there are important – and, we think, Shakespearean – values embedded in' the plays; both his Tillyard and Kott convictions are given, always, as discoveries about Shakespeare ('Shakespeare believed ... I realised that Shakespeare's history plays were full of ... Shakespeare always knew ... Shakespeare recognises ...'). And Barton writes of the introduction of Princess Elizabeth in *Richard III* as if it were something Shakespeare unaccountably overlooked: 'We tried as economically as possible to *stress* and *clarify* the importance of the young Princess Elizabeth in *Richard III* (Shakespeare leaves her out of the play). To present her and explain her function seemed essential if we were to *bring out* the historical and thematic point.'[44] Brook's position is only apparently more complex. In an interview published in 1977 he denied '"serving" Shakespeare', insisting instead that 'there is only one service, which is to the reality which Shakespeare is serving'. But this comes to rather the same thing, because 'you've got the greatest channel to it (i.e. reality), through the greatest creator in this form, which is Shakespeare'.[45]

My point is *not* that the RSC should have stayed closer to a true idea of Shakespeare. It is that the whole business of producing Shakespeare in our society, and all the cultural authority which goes with that, depends upon the assumption that through all the metamorphoses to which the plays are subjected we still have the real presence of Shakespeare. He justifies public and private expenditure of resources and ensures the scope and quality of attention; he is the cultural token which gives significance to the interpretations which are derived from him. Rival productions are, in effect, contests for the authority of Shakespeare, rival attempts to establish that he speaks his position rather than (or, at least, as well as) that.

The range of existing interpretations might seem to embarrass the notion of Shakespeare's essential presence in them all, but there is an answer to this: it is characteristic of his genius that he is endlessly interpretable. Peter Hall declared: 'He has everything: he is domestic as well as tragic, lyrical *and* dirty; as tricky as a circus and as bawdy as a music hall. He is realistic *and* surrealistic. All these and many other elements jostle each other in rich contradictions, making him human, not formal. That is why you can now read Samuel Beckett in *Lear*, or the Cuban crisis in *Troilus*.'[46] Peter Brook proclaims: 'The history of the plays shows them constantly being re-interpreted and re-interpreted, and yet remaining untouched and intact.'[47]

The other strategy which maintains the essential Shakespeare through all interpretations is an appeal to the unevenness of the received text. Michel Foucault in his paper 'What Is an Author?' exposes the dubiousness of the whole concept of the author, which he sees in part as 'a principle of unity' serving to neutralise contradictions, a construct through which 'any unevenness of production is ascribed to changes caused by evolution, maturation, or outside influence'.[48] The case of Shakespeare is more subtle, for the unevenness of the received text (attributable to early work, collaboration, the conditions of the Elizabethan and Jacobean theatre, unsatisfactory copy texts and printers' eccentricities) is emphasised and used to justify directorial inventiveness which claims, always, to retrieve the real Shakespeare from behind the unevenness. For his production of *Henry V* in 1975 Terry Hands cut the speeches in which the Archbishop of Canterbury elaborates upon the sudden and total reformation of Henry V upon his father's death (I.i.25–59) – they conflicted with Hands's wish to stress 'the doubts and uncertainties inherent in the role of Henry'. Hands's explanation complains about the thematic and dramatic implications of the passage and concludes: 'Furthermore it is not well written. It is over written. Shakespeare could write badly, especially for special occasions. This may be one of them. Accordingly we treated it as a later insertion and cut it.' Two arguments for the imperfection of the text are run together – that Shakespeare was writing below his best and that the speeches are later insertions (for the latter there is no scholarly warrant). And, of course, Hands believes that in the rejection of the 'saintly' king he is recovering the true Shakespeare, 'the specific unity explored in the play itself'.[49] The central idea of Shakespeare, so far from affording some control over what it is that the plays might represent, is actually used to justify at least sufficient interpretive scope to secure relevance. Then, conversely, the relevance of any particular production is guaranteed by the fact that it is Shakespeare, who is always relevant. The circle seems unbreakable.

The RSC has, from the start, fostered this potent combination of relevance and the real Shakespeare by announcing its respect for the scholarship which seems to authenticate the process. John Barton's academic credentials are often mentioned. Hall declared: 'you should approach a classic with the maximum of scholarship you can muster – and then you honestly try to interpret what you think it means to a person living now'.[50] The outcome has been a convergence of the academic and theatre Shakespeares which is without precedent – and which corresponds neatly to the concerns of the higher-educated audience. The company's programmes characteristically sustain this effect: they consist of a collage of scholarly materials – bits from Shakespeare's sources, original contextual gobbets, even discussion of the provenance of the text – spliced in with modern material, especially quotations of political significance and commentary from modern critics (the main device is quotation, which seems to guarantee authenticity). John Elsom walks right into the trap when he remarks: 'The search for social relevance could obviously get out of hand, but at the RSC it was tempered by a concern for textual accuracy and scholarship.'[51] Precisely: this is the combination which cannot be faulted.

Not *any* interpretation will pass as Shakespeare, of course. A major role of theatre criticism is to police the boundaries of the permissible (which is perceived as the consistent or the credible), judging whether or not particular productions fall within the scope of Shakespeare as currently recognised. All the productions discussed in this chapter provoked dispute about their legitimacy, and several points about this preoccupation may be made quite quickly.

First, the discourse of the acceptably Shakespearean shifts, and interpretations which initially seem too adventurous become acceptable with time (this is excellently shown by Ralph Berry in his book *Changing Styles in Shakespeare*). Second, the main outcome which this kind of commentary secures is the continuance of criticism: it is its function to engage in such discussions. Third, such controversy does not necessarily damage audience figures – people like to join in and make their own assessment of the limits of Shakespearean production. Fourth, dispute about a particular interpretation does not undermine the principle of interpretation, for it assumes that there are limits within which interpretation is good; and fifth, what is certainly not brought into question is Shakespeare, for he is the given against which particular instances are measured.

For all these reasons, disputes about the scope of interpretation are finally unimportant – part of the conditions for the continuance of the game. But there is a persistent note of deep anxiety about productions which diverge too far from conventional understanding of the plays, and the reason for it is this: if you push the Shakespeare-plus-relevance combination too hard, it begins to turn into a contradiction. Then its force is lost, and questions about the whole enterprise start to formulate themselves. This became more likely and more disturbing with the break up of consensus from 1968, as some directors attempted a more purposeful and precise radicalism. Jonathan Miller provoked disputes with his production of *The Tempest* (Mermaid Theatre, 1970) and *Merchant of Venice* (National Theatre, 1970) by presenting Ariel, Caliban and Shylock as members of oppressed racial minorities (Miller held nevertheless that he was producing Shakespeare: 'The mystery of Shakespeare's genius lies in the fact that innumerable performances of his plays can be rendered, few of which are closely compatible with one another'[52]).

Benedict Nightingale, among others, took on the critic's supervisory role, disallowing Miller's interpretations: 'his view seems to be that Shakespeare's plays are fair game for the vivisectionist. It is, he thinks, interesting to see what can be done with them; how far the daring director-surgeon is able to go without the experimental animal expiring'; yet 'Shakespeare must be at least nominally responsible for everything we hear'. Nightingale seems to be anticipating my point, but in fact he is not prepared to question the underlying structure of Shakespeare-plus-relevance, as we can see from the care with which he proceeds. He declares that Miller's *Tempest* is a savage reduction ('Caliban, a tattered field nigger, incapable of progress; Ariel, the educated black, preparing to take over the country after independence', and responds with his own idea of the play: 'a celebration of youth and spring, an unsentimental declaration of faith in the future, a marvellously mellow confession of love and charity for men'. Nightingale does not push this particular reading at all dogmatically: he does not need to, he has offered an acceptable enough 'relevant' theme, and so can safely repudiate Miller's. But the *Merchant* does seem to be anti-semitic, and that is not the kind of relevance that is required; Nightingale observes: 'it is pro-Christian and, though it offers him a certain, paradoxical sympathy, anti-Shylock – while Miller is anti-Christian and pro-Shylock. This is, of course, an emphasis any good contemporary radical would prefer. Just now, it looks like the play Shakespeare ought to have written. The only trouble is that he didn't.' In the present climate of opinion anti-semitism cannot be brushed aside, although 'Just now' almost permits that, so Nightingale allows: 'It could be that Miller made a better and bigger play of the *Merchant*'. This is a very unusual move: faced with a discrepancy between the production and the usual understanding of Shakespeare, Nightingale suggests that Shakespeare had not in every respect the superior wisdom. But the *Merchant* is not a central play (how could it be, when it so resists the dominant ways of producing Shakespeare?) and anti-semitism is very tricky. So rather than stretch intolerably the scope of interpretation – which could bring into disrepute the whole strategy of Shakespeare-plus-relevance – Nightingale is prepared to withhold from this play the full authority of Shakespeare. The main enterprise is rescued at the expense of one relatively insignificant part. Even then, Nightingale still has a formula which could be used to retrieve the *Merchant*: 'It could be that the relevance he [the modern director] is rightly trying to achieve is of too limited a kind. It could be that it is too merely social. It could be that he is forgetting that the reason Shakespeare has survived is that he speaks to generation after generation, not merely or mainly about the public issues that happen to preoccupy them, but about the elemental, lasting problems of human nature.'[53] Nightingale does not say whether he would prefer to regard anti-semitism as a 'merely social' preoccupation. What is clear is that if we read the *Merchant* for some 'elemental, lasting problems' we will get the anti-semitism as well. Neither Nightingale nor Miller can obscure totally the contradictions in the dominant construction of Shakespeare.

The reason for adjusting Shakespeare to radical ends is that he is an established cultural token [...] But it is precisely that establishment status which proves, always, a hindrance. In the work of the RSC we may perceive a strain of opportunism, or at least a wish to sustain the company itself, but there has also, no doubt, been a great deal of genuine radical purpose. But within the culturalist ethos of 'Royal Shakespeare', one either makes an acceptable compromise with received ideas of the play and the radical purpose is ineffectual, or, like Bogdanov with the *Shrew*, one goes for political explicitness which is easily set aside as 'not Shakespeare'. The problem, of course, is *Shakespeare* – the whole aura of elusive genius and institutionalised profundity. For even when the resistances set up by received notions of the plays are overcome and a genuinely radical interpretation is rendered persuasive (and it is not clear that this has occurred), the idea of the real Shakespeare from which it all emanates nevertheless registers cultural authority, and implies that every innovation has been anticipated. The underlying pressure is towards deference and inertia.

It is the cultural, and therefore political authority of Shakespeare which must be challenged – and especially the assumption that because human nature is always the same the plays can be presented as direct sources of wisdom. One way of doing this is to take aspects of the plays and reconstitute them explicitly so that they become the vehicles of other values. Brecht in *Coriolanus*, Edward Bond in *Lear* (1971), Arnold Wesker in *The Merchant* (1976), Tom Stoppard in *Rosencrantz and Guildenstern Are Dead* (1966) and Charles Marowitz in a series of adaptations[54] have appropriated aspects of the plays for a different politics (not always a progressive politics). Even here, it is possible that the new play will still, by its self-conscious irreverence, point back towards Shakespeare as the profound and inclusive originator in whose margins we can doodle only parasitic follies.

The other way is proposed by Michael Billington in an interview with Bogdanov about the *Shrew*: 'To us, it may seem repugnantly chauvinist: treat it as an Elizabethan play and it reveals a lot about social attitudes to women.'[55] This proposal is repudiated by all the directors whose work has been discussed here: it amounts to treating Shakespeare as a historical phenomenon, implicated in values which are not ours but which can in production be made to reveal themselves, can become contestable. The relevance then develops through our critical response to that representation, the questions about modes of human relationships which it provokes. Productions designed to do this would seek explicitly to share cultural authority with Shakespeare; they would be instructive, and, at the least, they would stimulate awareness of change instead of submerging the range of historical and future possibilities into a permanent human wisdom author-ised, allegedly, by Shakespeare.

From *Political Shakespeare: Essays in Cultural Materialism*, ed. Jonathan Dollimore and Alan Sinfield, second edn (Manchester, 1994), pp. 182–205.

NOTES

[Alan Sinfield's essay investigates the cultural politics of the mode of Shakespearean production that has been dominant within the state-subsidised theatre in Britain during the postwar period, paying particular attention to the role of the Royal Shakespeare Company. Sinfield traces the ways in which the RSC's persuasively youth-oriented formula of 'Shakespeare-plus-relevance' reflects the company's cultural base within the new university-educated middle classes. Sinfield argues that the contradictory pressures within the formula mean that the RSC's ostensible radicalism masks a more fundamental conservatism, and proposes that a more productive way of staging a radical Shakespeare would be not to attempt to endorse or appropriate traditional Shakespearean authority, but to contest it. Ed.]

1. Richard Findlater, *The Unholy Trade* (London, 1952), p. 57.
2. Peter Brook, *The Empty Space* (Harmondsworth, 1972), p. 51.
3. Charles Landstone, *Off-Stage* (London, 1953), p. 180.
4. Trevor Nunn in Ralph Berry, *On Directing Shakespeare* (London, 1977), p. 56.
5. David Addenbrooke, *The Royal Shakespeare Company* (London, 1974), p. 66.
6. Sally Beaumann, *The Royal Shakespeare Company* (Oxford, 1982), p. 273; Ralph Berry, *Changing Styles in Shakespeare* (London, 1981), p. 7.
7. Addenbrooke, *Royal Shakespeare Company*, pp. 182, 63.
8. Beaumann, *Royal Shakespeare Company*, p. 284.
9. Berry, *Directing Shakespeare*, p. 56; Addenbrooke, *Royal Shakespeare Company*, p. 174.

10. John Barton and Peter Hall, *The Wars of the Roses* (London, 1970), pp. x, xix.
11. Ibid., p. xi.
12. Jan Kott, *Shakespeare Our Contemporary*, second edn (London, 1967), pp. 37, 25, 39.
13. Barton and Hall, *Wars of the Roses*, p. xii.
14. See Alan Sinfield (ed.), *Society and Literature 1945–1970* (London, 1983), pp. 97–100.
15. Kott, *Shakespeare Our Contemporary*, p. 46.
16. Barton and Hall, *Wars of the Roses*, p. xxii.
17. Charles Marowitz, Tome Milne and Owen Hale (eds), *The Encore Reader* (London, 1965), p. 251.
18. Royal Shakespeare Company, *Crucial Years* (London, 1963), p. 22.
19. Berry, *Directing Shakespeare*, p. 129.
20. Charles Marowitz and Simon Trussler (eds), *Theatre at Work* (London, 1967), p. 134.
21. See Sinfield, *Society and Literature 1945–1970*, pp. 186–7.
22. John Roberts, *Plays and Players*, October 1970.
23. Interview in *Plays and Players*, October 1970. See further David Selbourne, *The Making of A Midsummer Night's Dream* (London, 1982).
24. C. A. R. Crosland, *The Future of Socialism* (London, 1956), p. 519.
25. Julien Le Grand, *The Strategy of Equality* (London, 1982), p. 158. See also Sinfield, *Society and Literature 1945–1970*, p. 180.
26. Frank Parkin, *Middle Class Radicalism* (Manchester, 1968), chs 2, 7 and 8. See also Michael W. Miles, 'The Student Movement and Industrialisation of Higher Education', in *Power and Ideology in Education*, ed. Jerome Karobel and A. H. Halsey (New York, 1977).
27. See Sinfield, *Society and Literature 1945–1970*, ch. 6.
28. Raymond Williams, *The Long Revolution* (Harmondsworth, 1965), p. 293.
29. Addenbrooke, *Royal Shakespeare Company*, pp. 63, 112.
30. Harold Wilson, *The New Britain: Labour's Plan* (Harmondsworth, 1964), pp. 9–10.
31. Quoted in Berry, *Changing Styles*, p. 97.
32. Stanley Wells, *Royal Shakespeare* (Manchester, 1977), p. 25, 36, 34.

33. See Catherine Itzin, *Stages in the Revolution* (London, 1980).

34. See Beaumann, *Royal Shakespeare Company*, pp. 308–14, 319–21, 329–30, 333–7; Colin Chambers, *Other Spaces* (London, 1980).

35. Addenbrooke, *Royal Shakespeare Company*, p. 310.

36. 'Director in Interview: Trevor Nunn talks to Peter Ansorge', *Plays and Players*, September 1970. See also Addenbrooke, *Royal Shakespeare Company*, pp. 170–2.

37. Addenbrooke, *Royal Shakespeare Company*, pp. 317, 174, 182.

38. Quoted in John Elsom, *Post-War British Theatre*, second edn (London, 1979), p. 171.

39. Richard David, *Shakespeare in the Theatre* (Cambridge, 1978), p. 187.

40. Alan Sinfield, '*King Lear* versus *Lear* at Stratford', *Critical Quarterly*, 24 (1982), 7–8, 10–11.

41. Chambers, *Other Spaces*, p. 17.

42. Sally Beaumann (ed.), *The Royal Shakespeare Company's Production of Henry V* (Oxford, 1976), Foreword, pp. 15, 253, 250, 262.

43. Michael Bogdanov and Joss Buckley, *Shakespeare Lives!* (London, 1983), p. 5.

44. Barton and Hall, *Wars of the Roses*, pp. ix, x, xii, xiii, xxii.

45. Berry, *Directing Shakespeare*, p. 123.

46. Royal Shakespeare Company, *Crucial Years*, p. 14.

47. Berry, *Directing Shakespeare*, p. 117.

48. Michel Foucault, *Language, Counter-Memory, Practice* (Oxford, 1977), p. 128.

49. Beaumann, *RSC Henry V*, pp. 103, 15.

50. Addenbrooke, *Royal Shakespeare Company*, p. 129.

51. Elsom, *Post-War British Theatre*, p. 171.

52. Berry, *Directing Shakespeare*, p. 9 and *passim*.

53. Benedict Nightingale, 'Shakespeare Is as Shakespeare's Done', in *Theatre 71*, ed. Sheridan Morley (London, 1971), pp. 159, 157, 161.

54. Charles Marowitz, *The Marowitz Shakespeare* (London, 1978) – *Hamlet, Macbeth, The Taming of the Shrew, Measure for Measure, The Merchant of Venice*. On Bond, see Sinfield, '*King Lear* versus *Lear*'.

55. Michael Billington, 'Why Old Bill needs rejuvenating', *Guardian*, 30 December 1982, rpt. In Bogdanov, *Shakespeare Lives!*, p. 4.

9

Robert Lepage's Intercultural *Dream* Machine

BARBARA HODGDON

> At bottom, dreams are nothing other than a particular *form* of thinking.
>
> (Sigmund Freud, *The Interpretation of Dreams*)

Waking from his 'most rare vision', Bottom is at a loss to 'say what dream it was' or even to 'expound' it until he seizes on the idea of having Peter Quince write a ballad that will make his dream readable or, more accurately, sing-able. Characteristically, however, Bottom desires authorial control over Quince's interpretation: he provides a title – 'Bottom's Dream' – and a gloss – 'because it hath no bottom' – simultaneously naming and (uncharacteristically) disavowing himself as the ballad's subject. As an early modern interpreter of dreams, Bottom tropes a relation between dreamers, dreams, and their discursive representation that figures the concerns of twentieth-century reception studies, which seek to map the relations among a text and its readers in order to understand how distinct affective and interpretive experiences, produced historically in specific social formations, shape the cultural destinies of a text.

I will not attempt to expound Bottom's dream but to explore how similar instances of naming and disavowal figure in the discourses surrounding Robert Lepage's production of Shakespeare's *A Midsummer Night's Dream*, which ran in repertory at London's

Royal National Theatre from 9 July 1992 through 6 January 1993. Drawing on contemporary critical and cultural studies, such work moves beyond text-centred analyses to situate spectators and their reading strategies as the primary objects of investigation. Consequently, I offer neither a self-referential thick description nor a performance-driven account of the theatrical aesthetics or semiotics of either 'Shakespeare's' or 'Lepage's' *Dream*, except insofar as to note what textual and/or theatrical signs might prompt a particular reading. To do so can, to be sure, offer a certain notion of culture and of intercultural performance, but almost invariably such accounts tend to locate codes and the production of meaning in relation to the collaborative efforts of the writer-director-actor-designer and so privilege the creative processes at work within an exclusively enclosed world of theatrical culture. Rather than assuming that the performance text itself contains or produces immanent meanings or focusing on the marks of its making and its makers, I want to consider how this *Dream* was (re)constituted by the concrete conditions of its spectators. For it is, after all, in the 'discursively saturated materiality' of its historical circumstances that a performance makes its demands for narrative intelligibility. What I shall be pursuing, then, is how spectators' first-night encounters with Lepage's production marked a particular *event*: the emergence of Shakespeare's *Dream* as a national cultural property, an instance in which theatre, to appropriate Herbert Blau's phrase, 'becomes like ideology itself, ... something other than what it appeared to be'.[1] Traces of that event appear in various print materials – including some twenty-three reviews, primarily from the British press; interviews with Lepage and with his actors; and the souvenir programme for the production, containing both images and quoted excerpts. To analyse these traces, textually as well as culturally, is to write a history that not only characterises the social significance of that event in relation to a particular interpretive community but also reveals how what might be called a cultural logic of the postcolonial circulates equally in Lepage's performance text and its attendant discourses.

I will return to the question of how that logic operates, but first I want to call attention to my own position as an historically mediated reader who is imbricated within the analytical results. Because I saw Lepage's *Dream* on press night, I occasionally interweave my own observations with those of the reviewers I cite. However, it is important to bracket the distinctions between their politics of location and my own, for I am neither a native informant nor a participant observer privy to insider narratives or backstage gossip, but a traveller and collector of sorts who speaks from an appropriately problematic intercultural space – appropriate not simply because situating myself on a border or margin marks a fashionable place to be, but also because, as an American academic in London, I watched a *Dream* staged by a Québecois (until recently, the artistic director of the French theatre of the Canadian National Arts Centre) which featured a multicultural cast made up of British, Québecoise, Anglo-Indian, Anglo-West Indian, and Anglo-African performers. Unlike those of the critics, however, my account has neither been constrained by a late-night deadline nor offered up for immediate, widespread public consumption; rather, it is a product of recollection and is addressed to a fairly specialised readership. In addition to privileging my own viewing position, I wish to make two further points. First, that because the discursive formation surrounding any historical event (and theatrical performances are no exception) is contradictory and heterogeneous, no reading of that event is unified; and second, that my analyses avoid categorising reviewers' responses, Lepage's comments, or my own observations into preferred, negotiated, or resistant readings. What follows, then, represents field-work – a 'story of the night told over' which does not, as Hippolyta would have it, '[grow] to something of great constancy' but rather aims to illuminate the cultural meanings of Lepage's *Dream* to particular spectators in a specific sociohistorical moment and so to contribute to discussions about the spectatorial effects of performed Shakespeare.

The use value of such a study lies in its ability to clarify how sociologies of taste and value and contextual protocols for reading determine frameworks for making meaning from materially inscribed theatrical data. Here, Tony Bennett's concept, reading formation, by which he means a set of intersecting discourses that productively activate a text, is especially useful, for not only are theatrical representations always produced within cultural limits and theoretical borders, but clearly spectators 'read' performed Shakespeare (perhaps more so than other dramatic texts) through knowledges drawn from literary as well as theatrical cultures, knowledges which are necessarily implicated in particular economies of truth, value, and power, serving to mark one performance as a more acceptable interpretation than another. Also important to a study which dissolves a performance text into its reading relations is what Janet Staiger calls 'historically constructed "imaginary selves", the subject positions taken up by individual spectators'; tracking these provides insight into how individuals as well as social groups use cultural forms in the process of defining themselves.[2] As will become apparent, certain shared contexts of reading and theatrical formations and constructed identities of the self in relation to historical conditions which undergird the interpretive strategies for, and affective responses to, Lepage's *Dream* make it possible to read these discourses not only as a struggle over the meaning of theatrical signs but as symptomatic of current cultural anxieties about gender, race, and nationality.

Across the range of materials on Lepage's *Dream*, one particular reading strategy consistently emerges: the construction of binary oppositions indicative of categories linked in a hierarchic relation that is fundamental to mechanisms of ordering and sense-making in Western – especially European – cultures. Peter Stallybrass and Allon White argue that cultures '"think themselves" in the most immediate and affective ways' through such oppositions, which are often duplicated across various discursive realms and symbolic systems, especially psychic forms, the human body, geographical spaces, and the social order. Repeatedly, one symbolic system evokes another to justify its ordering; within such figurations, the categories of high and low bear an especially powerful symbolic charge which structures all other elaborations: 'the top *includes* the low symbolically, as a primary eroticised constituent of its own fantasy life'. The result, they claim, is 'a mobile, conflictual fusion of power, fear and desire in the construction of subjectivity: a psychological dependence upon precisely those Others which are being rigorously opposed and excluded at the social level. It is for this reason that what is *socially* peripheral is so frequently *symbolically* central.'[3] Using precisely similar hierarchical relations, the review discourse maps Lepage's *Dream* as a transgressive domain where intersecting points of antagonism between high and low, between 'Shakespeare' and his 'Other', signal powerful dissonances within British culture. In that discourse, figurations of place, body, national as well as ethnic identities, and gendered subjectivity interconnect and are used to shore up commonly held cultural codes, values and norms and to reassert literary, theatrical, social, and political boundaries; moreover, such figurations are further marked out by the use of metaphor and analogy.

Perhaps the most overriding opposition articulated by reviewers can be expressed as a fort-da game played with two structuring absences: what Nicholas de Jongh called 'Shakespeare's old *Dream*, as we have come to know it',[4] complete with Athenian palace and Mendelssohn's wood, and Peter Brook's 1970 Royal Shakespeare Company white-box production, widely acclaimed as *the* theatrical event of the decade and subsequently mythologised (by John Styan) as the culminating moment of a 'Shakespeare revolution', ensuring its canonical status. This binary not only marks out a history of *Dream*'s theatrical formations but tropes a nexus of its supposed cultural functions in constructing a perfected national community. On the one hand, it evokes a geography that no longer exists and an imaginative space riddled with desire. As Angela Carter writes:

> The English wood offers us a glimpse of a green, unfallen world a little closer to Paradise than we are. ... This is the true Shakespearian wood – but it is not the wood of Shakespeare's time, which did not know itself to be Shakespearian, and therefore felt no need to keep up appearances. No. The wood we have just described is that of nineteenth-century nostalgia, which disinfected the wood, cleansing it of the grave, hideous and elemental beings with which the superstition of an earlier age had filled it. Or, rather, denaturing, castrating these beings until they came to look just as they do in those photographs of fairy folk that so enraptured Conan Doyle. It is Mendelssohn's wood. ... However, as it turns out, the Victorians did not leave the woods in quite the state they might have wished to find them.[5]

Nonetheless, both this magical, enraptured, and quintessentially *English* wood and the Athenian patriarchy offer locales where a late twentieth-century spectator (even one who has read Jan Kott) may still come away refreshed, having been offered the promise of correctly channelled desire, of accessing anxiety over destabilising identities or positionalities – those of sex, gender, ethnicity, and class – only to have it brought to rest. On the other, situating Brook as the cultural presence who lurks in the margins of Lepage's *Dream* opens onto a discourse that hailed him into the space of genius to legitimate him as Shakespeare's 'true' heir, the maestro who had reinvented non-illusionistic theatre. Moreover, reviewers constructed him in terms of his own work: the only quotation in the souvenir programme for Brook's production, frequently cited in whole or in part by reviewers, came from his own manifesto, *The Empty Space*: 'Once the theatre could begin as magic: magic at the sacred festival, or magic as the footlights came up. Today it is the other way round. ... We must open our empty hands and show that really there is nothing up our sleeves. Only then can we begin.'[6] At least two review headlines – 'Peter Brook's Creative *Dream*' and 'Peter Brook's Most Original Shakespeare Play' – conflated author with director-auteur, a move that, in positing dual (or synonymous) personalities as the origins for the performance text, has ideological import for humanist social formations. The *Times*, seeking to discern the relationship between his 'bizarre ... delight' and 'the original', even evoked Plato's doctrine of forms to argue the congruence of 'Mr Brook' and 'William Shakespeare': 'for all the trapezes, juggling, helical wire trees, and general non-Elizabethanism, the Stratford production is not just good theatre but a *true production* of the *Dream*' (my emphases).[7] That such 'truth' had emerged at the site of Shakespeare's birth touched off a myth of origins in which *Dream* could be reclaimed as a kind of foundational centre for British culture.

Just as, in Louis Montrose's reading of *Dream* as an early modern cultural production, the Amazonian space of gendered otherness operates as a mythological formation against which dominant heterosexuality is tested and eventually reinstalled, Brook's production serves a similar mythic function for Lepage, and he both extends and interrupts the process of filiation that positions him as Brook's heir:[8] For in the 1990s, it is no longer the 'author' alone whose presence determines meanings; rather, as Blau maintains, the symbolic economy of previous theatrical productions activates a constant self-reflexivity whereby performance gets constructed against itself. Although Irving Wardle claimed to have been the first to 'lumber Lepage with a comparison to Peter Brook which has been clanking along behind him ever since' and on reviewing his *Dream* was 'glad to have the chance to strike off this ball and chain', Lyn Gardner's comments on Lepage's previous work clearly framed it through Brook's 1970 *Dream*: 'highly visual but not afraid of the literary, ... combining the lushness of opera with the spectacle of circus, the excitement of carnival, and the fluidity of film'.[9] When Lepage had first staged *Dream* in 1988 at Québec's Théâtre du Nouveau Monde, his design – three vertical staircases that represented the hierarchical levels of textual reality (spirits, noble Athenians, worker-comedians) and were mounted on a turning platform in the shape of England – prompted Micheline Cambron to recall Brook's equally forthright critique of *Dream's* traditional theatrical display of gauze-winged fairies, muslin mists, and painted trees.[10] Yet, in writing of how one theatrical sign (or production) can evoke another so that both, simultaneously 'present', reverberate in memory, Cambron could not efface her desire for the glacial purity of Brook's *Dream*, which for her, as for many, had become a theatrical fetish.

Indeed, my own initial reaction to Lepage's *mise-en-scène* – Michael Levine's black upstage screens surrounding a stage covered with gray mud, a watery pool at its centre, over which hangs a light bulb suspended on a long flex – was that it engaged Brook's production through a process of negative quotation. As a chronotope of theatrical culture – that is, an organising, historicising image – Levine's environment signalled Lepage's impudent raid on Brook, a deconstructive move that turned his dazzling white-walled 'empty space', where Shakespeare's spoken text became a squash ball bouncing off its pristine surfaces, topsy-turvy down. And when Angela Laurier's Puck, costumed in a red leather bodysuit which bared one breast, scuttled slowly into the centre of the pool, reached up, and took out the single point of light, it was also apparent that Lepage's much darker *Dream*, like his precursor's, was committed to forcing a confrontation between spectator and the materiality of actors' bodies that, unlike Brook's, would eventually displace character in favour of the self-validating presence of the performer.

Positioning Brook as the model for *Dream*'s cultural capital spawned further binaries: 'earth-shattering' versus 'mud-spattering'; 'fantastically airborne' versus 'stubbornly earthbound'; 'authentic magic, comic joy, and rigorous attention to the verse' versus 'pervers[ity], humourless[ness] and vile [speech]' – 'a lugubriously eccentric vision that reduces even the best performers ... to mud-caked puppets'. Those critics who could not discover 'Shakespeare's jokes ... submerged beneath the splashing games' either wrote joke titles – 'Dreaming in the goo'; 'Mudsummer Night's Dream'; 'Puck in Muck' – or, by performing their own comic moments, mapped out fissures between high and low culture, as in Ian Shuttleworth's 'Peter Brook wrestles Ken Russell in a dark, bonkers circus version of *Chariots of Fire*'.[11]

Voicing the minority opinion, Benedict Nightingale thought it 'the most original *Dream* since Peter Brook's version two decades ago, and the most strange and disturbing since – but there I have no memory to match it'.[12] Yet Nightingale's memory seems to have its own empty space, for twenty years before, titling his review 'Dream 2001 AD', he labelled Brook's production 'Shakespeare as he might be conceived by a science fiction addict or, indeed, performed by enthusiastic Vegans', adding, 'Big British Peter ... has laboured and brought forth, among other things, Mickey Mouse' – a reference to Brook's Bottom, whose black bulb nose, black leather ears, and huge black clogs had translated the traditional, and dearly beloved, ass's head. Singling out 'gabbling, writhing lovers', 'fairies in baggy pyjamas, like Japanese wrestlers', and a Puck in 'billowing yellow silks and a blue skullcap' like some 'fantastical Chinese rabbi', Nightingale complained that both plot and characterisation suffered and stacked up associations with Disneyland, Billy Smart's Circus, International Wrestling on ITV, August Bank Holiday, Isle of Wight, and 'the grind and clank of the industrial Midlands' to cheapen it further.[13] Since identical objections – especially with regard to character, the perceptual locus of hidden cultural assumptions – trace through much of the review discourse for Lepage's *Dream*, reading Nightingale's past and present reviews as Louis Montrose does Simon Forman's dream[14] might ascertain not only what this particular changeling boy desired from performance but why he found 'brilliantly imaginative' performative signs analogous to those he had once marked off as alien – or, more significantly, Oriental – and marginalised as mass culture entertainment.

If regarding his reviews as dream-texts might explain how Nightingale forgets (or represses) his own previous statements, comparing the two certainly displays the complex interdependence of the categories he evokes and explodes the permanence of such structuring oppositions. Recall Stallybrass and White, 'What is socially peripheral is ... symbolically central. ... The primary site of contradiction, the site of conflicting desires and mutually incompatible representation, is undoubtedly the "low"'.[15] In rejecting what he sees as popular and sentimental, Nightingale reveals, one might argue, his latent desire for the 'low', at least insofar as it represents a non-Shakespearean 'other'. But what also seems to be apparent has to do with how the fantasies of one particular reader are linked to reading formations. For Nightingale's wish to disavow Brook's *Dream* is tied to its lack: 'His manic decoration has deprived it of suffering, fear, horror and, apart from one moment, when Bottom's phallus is crudely mimed by the fairies, even of lust.' These emphases on fear and suffering, together with the notion that in no play is 'eroticism expressed so brutally', emerge from Kott's reading of *Dream*, which he cites. That Lepage's *Dream*, using Shakespeare's text as a machine for performing the body erotic, fulfilled Nightingale's dark Kottian tastes, particularly in its representation of the lovers' nightmare struggles on the production's two stages – the mud and the bed, the primordial ooze and the site of sex and dreams – and in Titania's seduction of Bottom, observed by an Oberon who responds by fondling Puck, suggests that it confirmed a *literary* reading formation which (although he does not mention Kott's name) remained more firmly installed in Nightingale's memory than either his own response to or review of Brook's production.

Rather than pursuing the relationship between Nightingale's dream-reading formations and his psyche, I want to explore two especially crucial oppositions which trace through both Lepage's interviews and the review discourse: seeing versus hearing; body versus voice – interrelated terms that catch up values associated with national theatrical cultures and, more particularly, with 'native' versus 'foreign' Shakespeares. Dennis Kennedy summarises what has become a widely accepted distinction between English and foreign-language Shakespeare: 'unable to place the same emphasis on Shakespeare's verbal resourcefulness, foreign performances have explored scenographic and physical modes more openly than their Anglophone counterparts, often redefining the meaning of the plays in the process.'[16] Although Lepage brought to the National his acknowledged skill as an image maker whose work is grounded in the physical materiality of the performative body,[17] his *Dream* is neither a production mounted in a foreign country nor, strictly speaking, an 'import', even though many reviewers came close to figuring it as a local production from India. And in this case, Shakespeare's 'native' *textual* identity was disturbed not by the problematics of translation, but by several sorts of tensions – between individual performers' acting styles and between idiosyncratic speech patterns marking them as non-native 'others' and the King's English.

As a Québecois performance artist who emerges from a bilingual culture and whose own theatre texts interweave French and English (and, in *Dragons Trilogy*, Chinese), Lepage had foregrounded the traffic between linguistic and cultural identities in his previous work with Shakespeare's texts, most particularly in *Romeo and Juliette* (1989), where distinctions between English-speaking Montagues and French-speaking Capulets were specifically linked to differing sexual identities and both illuminated and critiqued the fragmentation underlying the Canadian myth of bilingual unity.[18] Remarking on his own linguistically situated identity, Lepage quotes one of

Dream's actors: 'In French, you don't speak of an audience, you say "spectateurs", ... in the English culture, the word is important.' This statement, he says, defines the problems non-native speakers of English face with Shakespeare: 'we're really struck by *seeing* how to *do* it instead of trying to *hear* it' (my emphases). Largely through his encounter with Shakespeare's 'authentic' text (as opposed to either Victor Hugo's romanticised nineteenth-century translations or Michel Garneau's more recent 'tradaptations'), Lepage claims to be reconsidering the 'magical power' of words and music to evoke images.[19] Here, he seems to be subscribing to Brook's belief in Shakespeare's *textual* power. Yet in describing himself as 'very caught by the image', he argues less for a doubled signifying system where, as in Brook's 1990 *Tempest*, all that was said or thought was also represented by a visual or tactile materiality of signs, than for the *physical* performative power that drives the present-day theatrical marketplace, predicated more than ever before on an economy of 'physical capital', with representations of the body as the site of exchange value.[20] 'There's a lot of work to be done', he maintains, 'to convince people that you can transmit theatre physically, that the text, even if you don't hear it, is respected in what a spectator sees and feels.'[21]

Once again, the reviewers who acclaimed Brook's *Dream* provide a touchstone for the difficulties the critical community had with discerning 'Shakespeare' in the 'chronic strangeness' of Lepage's 'huge underground swamp'.[22] Even those most cautious about the circus gimmickry could sense Shakespeare's authentic textual presence. Wrote Gavin Millar, 'Brook's images are drawn from the text and constantly refer to it'; J. C. Trewin, summarising the majority opinion, waxed eloquent: 'however Brook illustrates Shakespeare, it is Shakespeare that matters. Brook has simply polished the mirror. ... [He] gets us to listen because he treats the Dream as something none of us has heard or seen before. ... Always he gets the verses to reach us as if it were new, spoken by characters who are never the stereotypes of an hundred revivals. ... We are made to imagine: sight and hearing are sharpened.'[23] By contrast, reviewers of Lepage's *Dream* complained of the actors' carelessness with words, of an inability to hear, and of physical activity distracting attention from the dialogue; even Nightingale acknowledged that 'some good lines are lost in the physical ado'. 'How much', mourned Steve Grant, 'would someone who hadn't seen or read the play learn about its structure, meaning and beauty? Not much.' Michael

Coveney spoke for the majority when, referring to Peter Hall's practice, he wrote, 'actors speak the words, not the lines'.[24] Predicated on Foucault's dictum that seeing punctures time-worn codes of saying, Lepage's striking anatomy lesson – deploying mime, dance, music, and lighting as means of frustrating the linear, the narrative, and the rational – had turned the wor(l)d upside down.

Reviewers' responses to one particular moment aptly illustrate what was at stake in inverting – or, to some, perverting – the relationship between hearing and seeing. Just as in Lepage's *Dragons Trilogy*, where a character delivered a meditation on the importance of the bicycle in China from a moving bicycle, Theseus spoke his lecture on cool reason supplanting the inventions of lunatics, lovers, and poets against an upstage image of the story of the night being replayed as a child's infantile romantic game of musical chairs, mockingly reinstalling the floating subject positions that Theseus would pin down and dismiss to the margins of experience. Here, the remarks of two reviewers point to a tension between dominant and emergent reading formations. Objecting to 'moronic upstaging that wilfully sabotage[s] the speeches', Martin Hoyle lamented Lepage's deliberate demystification of time-honoured themes; Clare Bayley, however, wished 'that some of the speeches could be over more quickly, and the next vision of wonder revealed'.[25] Not surprisingly, critics fantasised a top-down directorial move to erase the word and undermine the authority of Shakespeare's immortal lines. No one associated the image with a likely pop culture analogue, Madonna's 'Keep It Together' (from her 'Blond Ambition Tour'), or thought of the chairs not as signs of themselves but as a quotation of other spectacles, other events – a low-high rip-off by a director who situates his foundational experiences of theatre and theatricality not in Canadian theatrical culture, which he describes as 'not reflecting anybody's identity', but, more globally, in Genesis and Jethro Tull concerts and in Peter Gabriel's highly theatrical rock shows.[26] A long programme note on the gamelan, a Javanese instrument constructed especially for the production and parodied in the mechanics' playlet, suggests the importance Lepage places on music to ground his work and to enhance (or displace) the sound of Shakespeare.

Curiously enough, in this particular nexus of sight and sound, Allan Mitchell's patrician Theseus was the only actor reviewers did not trash for o'ertopping or muffling Shakespeare's language.

Played as blind, he becomes the figure both for the traditionally codified performance techniques of English-speaking theatre that Lepage was accused of debasing and for the reviewer who not only represses all that he sees in favour of hearing but whose ear, attuned to Received Standard pronunciation, invalidates what might be called the sound of the other. As Pierre Bourdieu writes, verbal manners function as valuable cultural currency through which members of the ruling class seek to maintain their social positions: not only are such manners one of the key markers of class, but they are also the ideal weapon in strategies of distinction that seek to mark distance and maintain national as well as cultural boundaries.[27] Erecting as well as policing such boundaries was, after all, a foundational principle of the theatre where Lepage staged *Dream*. At a 28 January 1946 press conference given by the combined Old Vic and Shakespeare Memorial National Theatre committees, Viscount Esher had remarked that 'the National Theatre would reclaim the English language from American vulgarisations'.[28] And in the 1949 British House of Commons debate on the National Theatre, Oliver Lyttelton (a Tory MP and chair of the Shakespeare Memorial National Theatre Trust) asserted that the 'National Theatre would preserve from pollution the language in which the dramatic works are played [and] would help to keep undefiled the purity of the English language'.[29] If such comments reflect an anxious reclamation of what the Second World War had placed in jeopardy, clearly neither Lyttelton nor Esher could have anticipated that the future might bring a French, much less a French-Canadian, assault on the Shakespearean mother tongue.

The ideologies driving the opposition between hearing and seeing – an intellectual conservatism that favours the finite (voice) over the infinite (sign) – became most apparent, however, as they were articulated across the bodies of two central performers, Angela Laurier (Puck) and Timothy Spall (Bottom). Without exception, critics lauded Laurier's 'unforgettably unearthly performance': an 'amazing, jointless, acrobatic and androgynous Puck ... [who] takes on the likeness of any creature from any element' – 'a woman who is nothing less than a two-legged Kama Sutra'. They seemed eager to relive either her initial appearance, angling crablike across the stage, with legs where her arms ought to be; her gravity-defying spin, ten feet off the floor, to put a girdle round the earth; or the moment when she attaches herself to Bottom's back 'like an incubus, waggling feet doing an eloquent job as ass's ears'. But most were also clearly troubled by a presence that grafted together supposedly incompatible categories: high/low culture; male/female; animal/human; 'French Canadian'/Shakespeare. One strategy involved qualifying their amazement by aligning her physical virtuosity with that of a circus performer or contortionist to fashion her either as a mass culture misfit who disordered all expectations of the human body or a freak-show artist performing Indian rope tricks. Another not only was more forthrightly misogynistic but sought, by demonising her marred language, to subordinate and efface her dazzling performance by marking her body as resistant to Shakespeare's lexical authority. Said one, 'She isn't Puck, what with her funny accent and one breast hanging out, but she's a cute act'; carped another, 'she negotiates English verse with all the nimbleness of Inspector Clouseau: "wat 'empern 'omesperns 'ave we swaggereeng 'ere?"'[30]

Somewhat similar anxieties condensed around Timothy Spall's Bottom, driven, it would seem, by more threatening territorial imperatives. As the only mortal who crosses boundaries, Bottom opens up a subject position for (predominantly, though not exclusively male) theatre critics not only to live out their dreams of acting on a real stage rather than writing about it, but also to experience a first-rate sexual fantasy – in this case, with Sally Dexter's 'gorgeously snake-like' Titania who hangs, batlike, suspended upside down in space until, waking to Bottom's song, she ravishes him. Clearly disturbed by the public primordial scene Nightingale had relished, one critic compared it to a rape (which indeed it is), while another, remarking on the voyeuristic spotlight that seeks out Bottom's groaning ecstasy, divorced himself further from the sight by claiming to be alienated. Even more significantly, by coding Spall's body with an impressive list of American stereotypes – 'a Brando-smitten narcissist', 'a reincarnation of ... your seventies macho man with medallion, platform shoes and naff American drawl', 'flaunting his Liberace wig, bare chest and Californian swagger' – reviewers kept Bottom's dark Kottian bestiality at a distance. In a series of transparently xenophobic blocking moves, most disavowed the sight of themselves bouncing orgasmically with Titania on the creaking bedsprings of Lepage's ubiquitous prop by figuring him as a stateside other. But Michael Billington, who saw and heard a 'hopelessly unfunny Bottom impersonating, of all people, Laurence Olivier',[31] suggested an even more profound transgression: to parody Olivier on the stage that bears his name in the theatre he had been partly responsible for founding was to strike deep at the heart of British national theatrical culture.

When it came to the visual spectacle and imagistic prowess that undergirds Lepage's directorial reputation, critics marked out cultural and geographical distinctions in a discourse tangled with nationally naturalised assumptions, as though replaying voices from a nineteenth-century past. Those appalled at the mud-wrestling spectacle overlooked the programme's initial citation – lines taken from that quintessential Edwardian, Rupert Brooke: 'One may not doubt that, somehow, good / Shall come of water and of mud. / And, sure, the reverent eye must see / A purpose in liquidity.' Instead, their eyes seized on the connections to Hades and Dante's dark wood, and turned photographs and excerpts documenting European as well as Asian and African rites of passage to sexual identity into 'adolescent tussles' or 'inter-sex wrestling'; only a few picked out the programme's appeal to a 'Jungian ancestral psyche springing from its root beneath the earth' – and then only to suggest that 'Freudian undercurrents' were somehow more appropriate to *Dream* than Jung's elemental ooziness.[32] Despite Titania's weather report (II.i.81–117) – the 'authenticity' of which Lepage discovered late in the rehearsal period and evoked to shore up his choice of *mise-en-scène* which, he maintained, came out of a preliminary workshop – what critics saw was a *Dream* that floated away from Shakespeare as well as theatrical history on Lepage's sea of mud.

'It is true', writes Freud, 'that we distort dreams in attempting to reproduce them. ... But this distortion is itself no more than a part of the revision to which the dream-thoughts are regularly subjected as a result of the dream censorship.'[33] In attempting to revise what many construed as a disfigured or missed encounter with Shakespeare, reviewers repressed any potentially post-imperial guilt to write Lepage's *Dream* into a discourse that reinvented English history. Titania's Indian boy bore much of the textual brunt for critics, one of whom compared the opening scene, where an Indian Philostrate poled a bed containing the four sleeping lovers – Theseus and Hippolyta posed at its corners – across the muddy pool, to 'some strange ceremony in the upper Ganges'.[34] Here as elsewhere, animalistic metaphors aided the distancing move that pushed images and performers into the space of the primitive, away from 'civilised' First World cultures. Those who had apparently never stood on Waterloo Bridge looking down toward the National Theatre at low tide figured the pool as an 'African salt-lick where animals come to drink' and the 'reptilian sprites' who slithered through it, 'eagerly sniffing stray mortals as if about to sink their teeth in', as 'mud-covered, blue-faced Congolese boys'.[35] Although Angela Laurier's Québecoise Puck was, strictly speaking, the only non-British citizen in the cast, many of *Dream*'s major performers (with the exception of Allan Mitchell's Theseus) had their passports revoked and were constructed as colonials: an American Bottom, an Asian Hippolyta (Lolita Chakrabarti), an African Oberon (Jeffrey Kissoon). Given these moves, it seems curious that no reviewer noted that pairing Sally Dexter's Titania, a white Englishwoman, with Kissoon's African Oberon threatened to replicate the fear of miscegenation that traces through *Othello*, or that the Athenian court, presided over by an English Theseus and an Asian Hippolyta, reversed the gender and racial differences so obvious among the fairies. Lepage's own rationale for his cross-cultural casting, he claimed, had nothing to do with race or with tokenism, 'get[ting] across the idea that black and white should work together'. Rather, he found it interesting 'to have a black Oberon who brings all of his blackness because he's the night ... and also when you see this man walk across the stage he carries all of Africa or West India with him ... ; [with Oberon and Titania], you see this part of the world meeting another ... and suddenly the colour of your skin or your accent are poetic icons.'[36] Lepage's transcultural poetics, however, faded into unreadability; instead, his 'poetic icons' foregrounded the symbolic centrality of colonised others within Britain, so that traces of interracial and intercultural tensions surfaced, displaced, in reviewers' comments on who could or could not speak blank verse or on unsuitable and bizarre performance styles.

But if what seemed either harsh or unfamiliar, including the 'oriental scratch and jangle' of the Javanese gamelan, might be associated with the colonial other, those images reminiscent of 'Peter Brook's Third World aesthetic visions' – such as Levine's black upstage dream screen rising to reveal 'a pink African dawn', the 'aboriginal chanting that turned Theseus' encomium to his hunting dogs into a tribal set piece', and the four golden showers that cleansed the muddy lovers[37] – were tinged with enough post-imperial nostalgia to be worth collecting. It would be no exaggeration to say that when critics – Richard Eyre, the National Theatre's artistic director, among them – objected that Lepage's *Dream* collapsed forest and court into the muddy space of the other, what was clearly at stake was a contamination of the social space described by John of Gaunt as 'This other Eden, demi-paradise, / This fortress built by Nature for herself, ... / This precious stone set in the silver sea' (*Richard II*, II.i.42–3; 46). Certainly in terms of the theatrical space itself, on press night the reviewers' grumbling body language could be read as a sign of the extent to which they saw themselves on the margins, while Lepage, masquerading as Caliban, took over the stage to refigure a *Dream* peopled with representatives of Empire. And if Theseus, the blind (British) rationalist, seems the perfect onstage figure for such reviewer-colonisers, the cover for the production's souvenir programme provides an even more tellingly contradictory image. Juxtaposing male body fragments that seem tied to different historical periods, it detaches the act of dream-vision from the sleeping self and redirects it onto the spectator. Not only, then, does the dreamer's body become the object of the spectator's gaze, but right at its centre, Angela Laurier's Puck gazes through a large hole in his back – the Empire turning the othering look back on itself.

Lepage himself might or might not entertain such a reading. Beyond mentioning how 'polluted the whole system built around Shakespeare is ... polluted with all these zillions of little cultural references that are wrong', he certainly did not, in his interviews with either Christie Carson or Richard Eyre, figure himself as an imperial iconoclast. In neither, however, are his ideas on theatre, interculturalism, and interpretation seriously challenged. Not only can he avoid or deflect questions because he is at the centre, but he is permitted to express himself in a rather graceful and liberal exchange which tends to position him as a postmodern high-culture artist, closer to the kind of figure to whom Linda Hutcheon's writing gives value than to, say, the more complex, intensely problematic position Kwame Appiah describes for a postcolonial, postmodern subject.[38]

If, as Appiah argues, the 'post' in both those terms is a space-clearing gesture that opens up a position from which to construct one's self[39] – and to fashion one's dream of a canonical text – then Lepage and his production can stake a claim to being both postcolonial and postmodern. Certainly his *Dream*, which yokes divergent cultural materials and identities into pastiche, collage, and bricolage, is oppositional to the grand literary and theatrical narratives that would draw national and cultural boundaries around 'Shakespeare' and manage 'his' meanings. As such, his practice can be aligned with Fredric Jameson's notion of the postmodern as a cultural dominant.[40] But insofar as Lepage's own claims for his free-floating play of imagistic borrowings threaten to dismantle politics as a transformative social practice, his production falls within what Teresa Ebert calls ludic postmodernism, a sphere she identifies as 'postpolitical' and describes as a textual practice that seeks open access to the free play of signification in order to disassemble the dominant cultural policy which tries to restrict and stabilise meaning.[41] In the case of Lepage's *Dream*, however, the ludic swerves away from the postpolitical to appear as the theatrical equivalent of T. S. Eliot's 'Waste Land' – a modernist otherness-machine for essentialising cultures. Such a move, of course, also recalls Brook's idealised notions of mediation, exchange and intercultural transfer, a 'culture of links between man and society, between one race and another, between micro- and macrocosm, between humanity and machinery, between the visible and invisible, between categories, languages, genres'.[42] For just as Brook claimed to have found, for *The Mahabharata*, a 'new' universal theatre language based on Indian ritual, myth, and anthropology, Lepage sought in Indonesian culture a philosophy and spirituality which matched his interpretation of the play as based on a hierarchy of good and bad spirits that meet in the human being, who is animated by the conflict within. Was he aware that the Indonesian national motto is 'Unity in Diversity'? Or that in Indonesia, resistance to unity is especially strong, distinguished as it is by over three hundred distinct ethnic groups spread among thirteen thousand islands stretching from the tip of Southeast Asia to the west coast of Australia? Did he recall the moment of Indonesian genocide in East Timor, for which the United States provided military and diplomatic support? To provide such a context is to trouble Lepage's 'Orientalism' (if it can be called that), to expose the contradictions in his desire to adopt a culture's mythology but without its attendant historical materiality, turning it into an abstraction which can be evoked in the name of transcultural unification or universal harmony.

If Brook's utopian vision of a theatrical practice that can erase barriers between cultures to express a shared truth has evolved considerably since his *Dream*, that production also marks a particularly contradictory nexus of intercultural exchanges. Among its repertory of signifying surfaces were a number of 'Eastern' borrowings: orientalist performance techniques, costumes based on those worn by Chinese acrobats, Indian raga, and Asian incantations. Yet those reviewers who did remark such signs tended to fold them into 'circus', an appropriately comfortable space of childlike delight where the thrill of performance itself could be celebrated. What made such a move acceptable? For one thing, since the circus had already received a high-culture gloss from Beckett's clowns (borrowed, in turn, from silent film), reviewers (Nightingale excepted) found it easy to appropriate 'low' culture in a hegemonic or ideological way to prove their own cultural supremacy. A similar functional transformation of signs applied to Brook's actors. Always already expected to speak beautifully, they might now be credited with exhibiting acrobatic physical dexterity: the cultivated, reserved British body could, after all, move between high and popular culture. But figuring Brook's *Dream* as a circus also suppressed another strand of discourse. In aligning the production's Oriental simplicity with a verbal as well as visual stylistic purity that contributed to restoring 'Shakespeare', several reviewers recalled Brook's uncomfortably confrontational *US*, his Artaudian protest against the Vietnam War. But they did so primarily to contrast *Dream*'s triumphant alliance between actors and audience, not to remember, for instance, the 1970 bombings in Cambodia. Here, Styan's title, *The Shakespeare Revolution*, functions as the perfect trope for such acts of remembering and forgetting, in which China's Cultural Revolution – which stopped all artistic reproduction for a decade – reappears as a Westernised ghost, attached to the name of Brook as well as that of Shakespeare.

In pointing to these dreamlike transformations of knowledge-making, I do not mean to diminish the undoubted significance for *theatrical history* of Brook's *Dream*: to do so would be to betray a fixed polestar of pleasure in my own Shakespearean dream-memory. Instead, I wish to problematise what is at stake in writing a history of theatrical aesthetics with 'Shakespeare' at the centre and to gesture toward another. Not only would I argue that Lepage takes *Dream* in a direction Brook had mapped out, but that its performance strategies emerge from a present-day moment when the Orient appears not, as Edward Said writes, 'as a theatrical stage affixed to Europe',[43] but *on* European stages, where its pure performative disciplines and supposed 'simplicity' have repeatedly, as productions by Brook and Ariane Mnouchkine bear witness, served to revitalise impoverished Western theatrical traditions of realism and naturalism. But if the Orient has become a haven, it has also produced a Zen-like form of theatrical practice that, risking a kind of ahistorical nirvana, can lead to theorising productions as archives or museum displays without legends, empires of plundered signs masquerading as installation art. As Patrice Pavis argues, 'our era and our western guilty conscience encourage both an alliance with foreign cultures and a functional transformation of all signs into a postmodern "supracultural" product that is icily but fatally beautiful.'[44] As icy and beautiful as Brook's *Dream*, perhaps. But hardly Lepage's, which seems more an instance of what Pavis calls the 'culture of sensuality', nourishing itself by importing Indonesian cultural styles like tea, as when Lepage incorporates the Catchak, a Balinese monkey chant, to greet Theseus and Hippolyta in the hunting scene. Yet when asked by Richard Eyre whether there is a danger in being a cultural tourist, Lepage replied, 'It depends how you borrow from other cultures and what your interest is in borrowing from that culture. ... I'm in search of what I am. ... I'm not trying to take good ideas from other people or other people's culture, I'm trying to see how that relates profoundly or universally to what I want to say or want to do.'[45] Mythologising his own subjectivity, Lepage goes to Shakespeare to test himself and in the process produces a *Dream*-text which legitimates his own intercultural artistry. On the one hand, insofar as Lepage's 'borrowings' not only serve as raw material for his own experiments in intercultural connections but contribute to fashioning himself as an individual sociotheatrical subject, he seems entirely complicit with the colonial practices he would deny. On the other, it seems possible that, faced with doing Shakespeare at a royally sanctioned London venue, Lepage's reliance on Indonesian psychic and symbolic forms was a move toward finding a space outside of either the British or the French Empire – an Archimedean point from which to explore and critique the insularity of British 'Shakespeare-culture'.

Cultures, of course, are like dreams: collections of signs, a traffic in images that can be potentially estranging, both for those practitioners who work in the space between cultures and for spectators of intercultural performances. Certainly, codes and conventions that are easily read by those within a particular culture may be opaque to outsiders who, in decoding them, turn them toward their own, more familiar 'shaping fantasies'. Where Lepage imagined constructing a metaphysical universe – one operating not horizontally, as in film, but vertically – in a theatrically pure, utopian 'empty space', what the reviewers wrote over his performers' bodies and his stunning oneiric images was a sociohistorical discourse. Voicing his suspicion of theorists like Victor Turner who believe that in performance some transcultural communitas may be achieved, Blau writes, 'Performance is a testament to what separates'; if indeed anything in it can cross cultures, it is the universal sense of a primordial breach suggested by the performer who, 'in a primordial substitution or displacement, is born on the site of the Other'.[46] Despite his avowedly universalist intentions, Lepage inadvertently erected a dream-screen to which his own sense of the unconscious as a Jungian catchall for a world-soul or a transcultural humanity seemed oblivious. There is, in other words, a Jamesonian political unconscious that threads through his *Dream* which, in seeking to mystify and naturalise culture, Lepage completely ignores.[47] The reviewers' vocabulary of oppositions gives that thread a pattern of interpretation, one mobilised by a historical moment of cultural anxiety in which a rising number of colonised 'immigrants' and the promise of a united Euroculture threaten to erase the idea of Britain. Operating according to James Clifford's 'salvage' paradigm,[48] their discourse voices a desire almost antithetical to the merging of worlds Lepage's *Dream* proposes: the desire not only to rescue something 'authentic' out of an encounter with performed Shakespeare, but to keep intact the boundaries of national – and theatrical – cultures. This desire, it could be argued, remains 'true' enough to Shakespeare's *Dream*, with its closural reassertions of class and gender hierarchies, that it can be drawn into view as the 'right' sort of dream to have – a move that, for most of its reviewers, situates Lepage's production in the nightmare space of the monstrous.

There is always, of course, the desire for some authentic field of dreams that will remain constant throughout the years. As a symbolic map of 'Englishness', the discourse encircling Lepage's *Dream* marks that space and that time – part of a past reminiscent of all that once was good and could be again. But given Shakespeare's recent adventures within contemporary cultural production, that nostalgic *Dream* has become a folk-cultural activity – an organic, mystical ritual recapturable for present-day Britons, if at all, only in the near-annual productions in Regent's Park. Nearly twenty-five years after the so-called Revolution, what 'Shakespeare', and especially performed Shakespeare, is now caught up in is an attempt to incorporate the global array that forms the imaginative landscape of contemporary cultural life and includes crossings, graftings, and modes of articulation between high- and low-culture media as well as among nations. That dream-field has already produced, and will continue to produce, theatrical performances which, to evoke the

Derridean turn of *Wayne's World*, might be called 'Shakespeare ... NOT!' or, more appropriate to this case, the other's dream. In seeking to negotiate further that distinctly multicultured as well as intercultural terrain, future studies need to take place not at the locus of examining director-auteurs and the ideotexts of their *mise-en-scènes* or the theatrical apparatus itself, but at the point of historical reception, where 'theatre' collides with spectators who may transform it into 'a strange, eventful history'. For it is there, at the site of knowledge-making and its attendant power, that questions similar to those Gayatri Spivak poses, though in a slightly different context, seem precisely the ones to ask.[49] Curiously and coincidentally, they are questions that Bottom, Shakespeare's intercultural dreamer, his own subjectivity called into question by a ravishing Other, might well find familiar: Who is this other dreamer? How is he – or she – named? Does he – or she – name me?

From Barbara Hodgdon, *The Shakespeare Trade: Performances and Appropriations* (Philadelphia, 1998), pp. 171–90.

NOTES

[Like Alan Sinfield, Barbara Hodgdon examines contemporary Shakespearean performance, but whereas the former deals with a range of work over two decades in relation to cultural history and company ideology, Hodgdon focuses upon one controversial production – Robert Lepage's Royal National Theatre *A Midsummer Night's Dream* in 1992 – as a means of investigating the covert ideological agendas of theatre criticism. Reading Lepage's *Dream*, and the generally scandalised critical response to it, in terms of their relation to Peter Brook's celebrated Royal Shakespeare Company production of the play, Hodgdon draws upon psychoanalysis as well as theories of the relations between postcoloniality and postmodernism to demonstrate the ways in which responses to the production were shaped by underlying anxieties about race, gender and nationality. Quotations are from *William Shakespeare: The Complete Works*, ed. Stanley Wells and Gary Taylor (Oxford, 1986). Ed.]

1. Herbert Blau, *To All Appearances: Ideology and Performance* (London and New York, 1992), p. 37.
2. Janet Staiger, *Interpreting Films: Studies in the Historical Reception of American Cinema* (Princeton, NJ, 1992), p. 81.
3. Peter Stallybrass and Allon White, *The Politics and Poetics of Transgression* (London, 1986), pp. 1–6.

4. Nicholas de Jongh, *Evening Standard*, 10 July 1992. This and other reviews of Lepage's *Dream* are reprinted in *Theatre Record*, 12 (July 1992).

5. Angela Carter, 'Overture and Incidental Music for *A Midsummer Night's Dream*', in *Burning Your Boats: The Collected Short Stories* (New York, 1995), pp. 276–7.

6. Peter Brook, *The Empty Space* (Harmondsworth, 1972), pp. 108–9.

7. J. C. Trewin, *Illustrated London News*, 12 September 1970; Sheila Bannock, *Stratford-upon-Avon Herald*, 4 September 1970; *The Times*, 29 August 1970. All reviews of Brook's *Dream* are from press cuttings in The Shakespeare Centre Library, Stratford-upon-Avon.

8. See Louis Montrose, '"Shaping Fantasies": Figurations of Gender and Power in Elizabethan Culture', in *Representing the English Renaissance*, ed. Stephen Greenblatt (Berkeley, CA, 1988).

9. Irving Wardle, *Independent on Sunday*, 12 July 1992; Lyn Gardner, *City Limits*, 3 February 1989.

10. Micheline Cambron, 'Autour du "Songe d'une nuit d'été": Les escaliers de la mémoire', *Cahiers de Théâtre Jeu* (*Échos Shakespeariens*) (1988), 45–8. Intriguingly, given Canada's postcolonial status, no critic mentioned the English map.

11. Clare Bayley, *What's On*, 15 July 1992; Michael Billington, *Guardian*, 11 July 1992; Wardle, *Independent on Sunday*, 12 July 1992; Benedict Nightingale, *The Times*, 11 July 1992; Charles Spencer, *Daily Telegraph*, 13 July 1992; Jane Edwardes, *Time Out*, 24 June 1992; Ian Shuttleworth, *City Limits*, 16 July 1992.

12. Nightingale, *The Times*, 11 July 1992.

13. Benedict Nightingale, 'Dream 2001 AD', *New Statesman*, 4 September 1970.

14. See Montrose, 'Shaping Fantasies', pp. 32–5.

15. Stallybrass and White, *Politics and Poetics of Transgression*, p. 4.

16. Dennis Kennedy, 'Introduction: Shakespeare Without His Language', in *Foreign Shakespeare: Contemporary Performance* (Cambridge, 1993), p. 6.

17. Lepage's previous and current work is grounded in the materiality of actors' bodies, especially in *Vinci* (1985–6), *Polygraphe* (1987), *Echo* (1989) and *Needles and Opium* (1991–4).

18. The trope of fragmenting and reuniting cultures runs through Lepage's work, in particular *The Dragons Trilogy* (1988–91), *Tectonic Plates* (1990–1) and *Needles and Opium*.

19. 'Robert Lepage in Discussion with Richard Eyre', *Platform Papers* no. 3, pp. 33, 35.

20. I borrow 'physical capital' from Mark Seltzer, *Bodies and Machines* (London, 1992), p. 45.

21. Quoted by Matt Wolf, 'Robert Lepage: Multicultural and Multifaceted', *New York Times*, 6 December 1992.

22. Nicholas de Jongh, *Evening Standard*, 10 July 1992; Malcolm Rutherford, *Financial Times*, 11 July 1992.

23. Gavin Millar, *The Listener*, 3 September 1970; J. C. Trewin, *Illustrated London News*, 12 September 1970.

24. Nightingale, *The Times*, 11 July 1992; Steve Grant, *Time Out*, 15 July 1992; Michael Coveney, *Observer*, 12 July 1992.

25. Martin Hoyle, *Plays and Players*, August 1992; Clare Bayley, *What's On*, 15 July 1992.

26. *Platform Papers*, p. 24. The chairs 'motif' also appears in Lepage's *Tectonic Plates*. For the mention of Gabriel, see Christie Carson, 'Lepage Interview, May 30, 1992', Author's Transcript, p. 15. My thanks to Carson for sharing the full transcript of her interview, sections of which appear in 'Collaboration, Translation, Interpretation', *New Theatre Quarterly*, 6 (1993), 31–6.

27. Pierre Bourdieau, *Distinction: A Social Critique of the Judgement of Taste* (Cambridge, MA, 1984), p. 66.

28. John Elsom and Nicholas Tomalin, *The History of the National Theatre* (London, 1978), p. 85.

29. Quoted in Loren Kruger, *The National Stage: Theatre and Cultural Legitimation in England, France, and America* (Chicago, 1992), p. 128.

30. Wardle, *Independent on Sunday*; Jack Tinker, *Daily Mail*, 10 July 1992; Grant, *Time Out*; Hoyle, *Plays and Players*; Kenneth Hurren, *Mail on Sunday*, 12 July 1992; Paul Taylor, *Independent*, 11 July 1992.

31. Grant, *Time Out*; Coveney, *Observer*; Wardle, *Independent on Sunday*; Tony Dunn, *Tribune*, 17 July 1992; Nightingale, *The Times*; Billington, *Guardian*.

32. Nightingale, *Times*; Rutherford, *Financial Times*; Maureen Patton, *Daily Express*, 10 July 1992; David Nathan, *Jewish Chronicle*, 17 July 1992; Grant, *Time Out*; Dunn, *Tribune*.

33. Sigmund Freud, *The Interpretation of Dreams*, in Standard Edition, vol. 5 (London, 1953–74), p. 514.

34. Billington, *Guardian*.

35. Nicholas de Jongh, *Standard*; Wardle, *Independent on Sunday*; Hoyle, *Plays and Players*.

36. Carson, 'Lepage Interview', p. 4. Lepage also speaks of deliberately casting Scots mechanicals 'because they're red-haired and white-faced and it might be a clownier ambience if we had good Scots who are ... naturally alive and funny. But some people said, "Oh, you want to show the different class, the Scots are the workmen and the Brits are the Court?" Well, if that comes out, then that is a comment that I am not responsible for.'

37. Coveney, *Observer*; de Jongh, *Standard*; Hoyle, *Plays and Players*.

38. See Linda Hutcheon, *The Politics of Postmodernism* (London, 1989). I find Hutcheon's formulations problematic because, unlike other theorists of the postmodern, she excludes popular culture. See Kwame Anthony Appiah, 'The Postcolonial and the Postmodern', in *My Father's House: Africa in the Philosophy of Culture* (New York, 1992), pp. 137–57.

39. Appiah, 'The Postcolonial and Postmodern', pp. 145–50.

40. Fredric Jameson, *Postmodernism, or The Cultural Logic of Late Capitalism* (Durham, NC, 1991).

41. Teresa Ebert, 'The "Difference" of Postmodern Feminism', *Col1ege English*, 53 (1991), 886–903.

42. Peter Brook, *The Shifting Point* (New York, 1987), p. 239.

43. Edward Said, *Orientalism* (New York, 1979), p. 63.

44. Patrice Pavis, *Theatre at the Crossroads of Culture*, trans. Loren Kruger (London, 1992), p. 211.

45. *Platform Papers*, p. 38.

46. Herbert Blau, 'Universals of Performance; or, Amortizing Play', *Substance*, 37/38 (1983), p. 157; quoted and paraphrased by Marvin Carlson, *Theories of the Theatre* (Ithaca, NY, 1984), p. 514. For Turner and others, see Richard Schechner and Willa Appel (eds), *By Means of Performance: Intercultural Studies of Theatre and Ritual* (Cambridge, 1990).

47. See Fredric Jameson, *The Political Unconscious: Narrative as a Socially Symbolic Act* (Ithaca, NY, 1981).

48. James Clifford, 'The Others: Beyond the "Salvage" Paradigm', *Third Text*, 6 (1989), 73–8.

49. Gayatri Chakravorty Spivak, 'French Feminism in an International Frame', in *In Other Words: Essays in Cultural Politics* (New York, 1987), p. 150.

10

Acting against Bardom: Some Utopian Thoughts on Workshops

SIMON SHEPHERD

DRAMAWORK: TWO INTRODUCTORY PROBLEMS

My aims in learning/teaching about Shackspare in drama workshops are: analysis of Shikespewer's work based on (a) knowledge of its production within a specific culture, and (b) knowledge of its reproduction within other specific culture/s; where each knowledge derives from a range of explorations which moves between a totalising description of a culture and analysis of verse patterns and editorial conjectures.

Before we carry out these aims we have to confront two problems which have bearing on student attitudes. The first is, roughly, institutional. Through its agents – teachers, administrators, examiners – the educational institution tends to tell students that drama is not a properly serious discipline (which can have some advantages, but I shall return to this at the end). Teacher support for the subject, as for any other, can be limited by other agents: theatre studies A level had problems with being 'new', problems with its 'acceptability' to universities, problems rebounding from the attack on university drama (which consisted of restricted budgeting and redeployment of departments). It stands alone in its examination modes: other cultural/literary A levels are book-centred and the pattern is repeated at degree level.

Administrations tend to indicate that drama causes timetabling problems, or that it has to happen in peculiar places because it requires strange and expensive facilities (which would change if its status as 'laboratory' work were recognised). So the decision to hold a drama workshop has to face a series of resistances, including that produced within the teacher (the 'effort' of doing drama).

The second problem emerges from the attitudes to dramatic text that students bring with them into a workshop. These attitudes originate in conceptions of dramatic characters as recognisably 'real' people, where (a) the text is aiming only for an imitation of 'reality', (b) that 'realism' is not defined within the specific cultures but is a transcendental quality the accuracy of which may be vouched for by students on their experience alone, (c) emphathetic engagement with characters is always the first basis for analysis of the text, and (d) characters are not an effect of text but autonomous entities who may sometimes function as mouthpieces for the author. Such attitudes are unsurprising in a society whose experience of drama is mainly derived from television performance. But that they are most stridently obvious in workshops on Sheikspure must connect with traditional assumptions about Shicksparean 'character'. These assumptions die hard, and, while Bradley-knocking may be currently fashionable, trendy Shagspur critics continue to reproduce unproblematised assumptions about dramatic persons. (In a recent intervention in *Shakespeare Survey* Peter Holland has shown some of the variety of things that Shapeskearean character might be;[1] and Bradley, to do him credit, at least thought that character was a problematic concept.) The continued marginalisation of performance analysis within Shaquespiere studies helps to preserve intact some of the student attitudes that cause problems.

DEALING WITH THE FIRST PROBLEMS

The institutional problem cannot be solved inside the workshop. One can only hope that the workshop produces sufficient pleasure, emotional as well as intellectual, to enable students and teachers to resist the variety of pressures which construct drama work as eccentric or unserious.

To tackle the problem deriving from expectations about 'character', teachers will employ a set of their own preferred exercises. These may:

(a) Construct modes of analysis that disprivilege character: e.g. divide the written text into units (which may be much smaller than scenic divisions); examine the unit as a sequence of actions, making a small tableau for every place where the action changes; present the unit as a set of tableaux; reduce these to three 'essential' tableaux; make a tableau of the whole unit, showing the structural relations of characters to each other, within hierarchies based on class, power, race, gender. In the opening of *A Midsummer Night's Dream* we might explore pictures of women and men, speakers and watchers, fullness/emptiness of the stage, repetitions and mirroring: an imaging of a gendered power structure. Actions and stage pictures become the key to the text's organisation of its dramatic meaning.

(b) Privilege character in order to problematise it: e.g. students work in small groups on a section of written text, with two group members providing a narrative of one character's thoughts throughout the section; perform the section according to these narratives, with one person speaking the thought-narrative while another 'acts' in accordance with that narrative: repeat the section, this time with the actors adding in the speeches printed in the Schäkspier text. It must be stressed that this exercise is *not* aiming to discover 'sub-text'. In attending to what the written text apparently gives, and that alone, it produces frustrations as the 'actor' cannot show all of the 'thought-narrative', or two different narratives find no way of relating to each other: the presentation of Hippolyta's narrative which coexists with Theseus's authority, the narratives of Helena and Hermia which link silence and rhyming couplets. Thus we may highlight how characterisation is organised through the selection/suppression of speech, through different categories of information, through interaction/autonomy, through relations between physical and spoken, and so on. Even if the exercise ends in confusion, 'character' is revealed as a set of specific and shifting effects of textual organisation.

FINDING WHAT'S THERE: DIFFICULT SPEECHES

A cultural materialist project attends to the *specific* modes of organisation and operation of a text. That's a banal point, but I make it for three reasons (outlined in this and the next sections).

Students and teachers rightly find Shuckspirean language difficult (it is indeed often more abstract and tortuous than that of his contemporaries). Drama work often seeks to dissolve that difficulty through techniques that improvise an analogous (often modern) situation (*Romeo and Juliet* as gang warfare, *Merchant* as racial harassment); or speeches may be chopped up, rearranged. spoken as unison choral work, split between various performers. All such techniques are (of course) modes of rewriting the Shagspärean text, often to satisfy the aims of a modernist or post-structuralist project: whether it be to produce new awareness through estranging an apparently sanctified and fixed text or to question assumptions about identity by unsettling an apparently coherent character.

But the rewriting can never remove the presence of what is always already there in the 'book', namely that difficult text. My suggestion is that we face this difficult text and present it, for itself, as a specific effect and as a potential source of pleasure. (This pleasure may derive from the 'force' of the language or from using performance to show up and critique a chunk of bardic self-advertisement.) Pedagogic strategies will vary, but I have tried to use the following:

(a) Break the speech into small sections of meaning/feeling, and (i) put the body into the text by finding a set of physical attitudes that correlate with (but do *not* necessarily illustrate) each section: gestures that have meaning in a contemporary world make space for themselves in the 'old' verbal text;[2] (ii) put the voice, as an instrument, into the text by selecting a mode of speaking for each section (*without* trying to establish an overall coherence governing these various voices).

Here I wish to digress to draw in an 'authority' on Sheeakespeaire delivery: for all his attention to poetry, Barton fudges the issue by claiming Szhachspir was 'the unconscious inventor both of characterisation in depth and of naturalistic speech', and that to the real actor (i.e. one of Barton's gang) the speech will be 'natural': Sheila Hancock: 'if I let it flow ... it seemed the most natural thing in the world'; Ian MeKellen: 'So rather than painting the line, I should think about it and let the voice do what it will?' Barton agrees with these apparently unscripted observations: 'we must trust our instincts and our experience'. Those who don't have the instincts which find the verse natural will discover themselves to be outside this privileged group. 'Poetry cannot be taught, though perhaps it can be released.'[3] Shickspooer as elite laxative.

Back to the exercises: it may be tempting to allocate the speech sections to individual members of a group and construct a group delivery. But this alters (or spoils) the pleasure derived from seeing and hearing one performer's body shifting through a set of attitudes and sounds. Group delivery could possibly be placed alongside solo delivery, and the different pleasure in each explored. My conjecture is that, for example, while the words may be unfamiliar, the potency of the performer's body may be recognised and understood. That potency affirms but goes further than the abilities in the watchers, and hence produces pleasure: a desire to be like that oneself, but also the comfort of not taking the risk oneself. This sort of exercise can lead into analysis of some of the characteristic pleasures of the renaissance stage: the audience relationship with a central individual who is both victim/deviant of the narrative and star within the acting company; the interplay of empathy, political emblematising and spectacular plenitude in that viewing relationship.

(b) Decide that the long or difficult speech need have no narrative or explanatory function, but that it is a piece of display (in a positive or negative sense); work on it by producing in the student's words the speech's simplest statement, discovering what is omitted and needs to be said, experiencing the need for image or metaphor, discovering that 'ornament' is specific content. The student works in her own words, but can pick usable phrases from the Shaikspoor text, if needed. Each new element has the aim of strengthening what is already there, so that the language proceeds in its connections as a necessary, because desired, elaboration. This is very different from the 'through-line' sought by professional actors, where the speech is mellifluously commandered into 'coherence'. Where the performer demonstrates her desires and pleasures in the elaboration, the difficult speech has the presence (and meaning) of acrobatics, display, spectacle, where these are bound up with and necessary to a character's or author's project, and a *performer's* project. The script which sets down what a performer might do is very different from the moment of doing, the actual performance. The performer's display is in tension with, adding to and limited by, the project of the role. The display highlights the real presence of the actor which itself is a point of identification, yet separation; the narrative of characters offers the promises of fulfilment and resolution. The relationship between these pleasures is very different from the dead, commodified verse-speaking of the pro.

MISSING THRILLS

One quality of the dramatic text which almost always disappears, in exercises or commentary, is the excitement generated by speed, suspense, thrills. With its various concentrations – New Criticism's parcels of imagery, poststructuralism's syntactic splitting of the subject, New Historicism's intertextual parallels – Sharpsquare criticism traditionally operates to slow up the text, to consider its significant moments rather than its diegetic dynamics. I suggest we explore the thrills of a scene's narrative by doing them, as thrillingly as possible. (This can produce complexities: the excitement of Jessica's escape comprises not just the suspense and naughtiness but her appearance as a boy in front of men who enjoy her thus; her thrilling focus is the escape from the house, theirs is her escaping; and against this, the written text denies the thrills which nineteenth-century actor-managers inserted, namely the moment Shylock discovers the escape: why?) Then we find the points of empathetic entry offered by the scene. Then we look at its jokes and its political excitements (for example the moment when the oppressed person answers back). Once the full range of its various pleasures is encountered, some discussion could follow: about the relationship between these pleasures, the correlation between pleasure and meaning, the particular issues/actions selected not just as sources of pleasure but as particular, and differing, sorts of pleasure.

REPRESENTING CHARACTERS

Like many other renaissance texts, the Sheepscare plays emerged from and within a highly productive tension between older (medieval) allegorical signification and newer (renaissance) representational fiction. This cues us to search scenes for the interplay of allegorical stage image and 'realistic' representation of character. This might involve exercises like those with which I began, but now brought into explicit tension: Miranda's thought-narrative, as victim of attempted rape, when confronting Caliban working against the emblem of a white virgin abusing a Black man while watched by an older white male colonist; the moral tableau of Katherina's submission to Petruchio working against the narrative of her character's desires and satisfaction. Different sorts of writing /staging raise problems about the reality presented by the stage.

For example, it may refer outwards, to the world in which the audience situates itself politically (in various ways) or it may produce the fiction of a world of its own, with its own rules, structure, and so on. Brecht suggested that at Coriolanus's first entry he is accompanied by armed soldiers, which causes the crowd to fall silent (though no stage direction specifies soldiers).[4] Brecht's image invites us to recognise a world where leaders are guarded, where their charisma is predicated upon the weaponry which makes space for it, where the state acts with violence against its citizens. This is a very different reality from that which presupposes a hero whose force of personality produces in 'ordinary' people a desire to be silent, where the logic of the crowd's quietness derives from the fact that Coriolanus is more interesting (and psychologically 'rich') as a dramatic character (partly because he is differentiated), and where the fictional heroism is in a mutually supporting relationship with star actor status. Without a discussion of 'false consciousness', ideological controls and so on, may I assert that each reality here is an equally tenable version of the power relations that are narrated. Workshop activity can insist that realism is not only not an end-point but is itself always to be thought of as a set of rhetorical structures and reality effects, that it is indeed always realisms.

My insistence on the banal points in this and the preceding two sections is intended to offer an escape from the all too constricting opposition between illusion and non-illusion (Shagzpére's plays show human nature as it really is. Oh no they don't. Oh yes they do. Oh know they don't. Oh yes they ...). 'Traditional' Shitspear criticism apparently focuses on 'realistic' characters in the plays and transcendent categories such as human nature. By way of challenge to this, leftist teachers insist on the non-illusionist, estranging devices and structures of the plays, which in turn can lead to a demolition of the transcendent categories (it doesn't always lead to this). Much anti-illusionism has a tendency to base its arguments on a version of the theories of poor old Brecht where his dramatic practice is presumed (in a blurring of empathy and emotion) to have no interest in generating audience emotion, or in connecting emotion with thought. (Brecht initially separated empathy and emotion, but in later works such as *Galileo* allowed that empathy could be a good thing; the Latin American theorist, Augusto Boal, distinguishes good and bad empathy.)[5] Anti-illusionism can thus end up not only killing off two interesting dramatists (Brecht being perhaps the sadder loss) but also dooming those of us on the left to a theatre without thrills. And I'm not having that.

HISTORICAL DIFFERENCE

In the activities described above, learners become involved in the process by which texts negotiate their meanings. Form is hence not divisible from content, but is seen to *be* content – in the sense that, for example, meaning is made through the specific structuring of a scene (try it, by restructuring the scene) or through the specific length and elaboration of a speech (try it, by cutting/shifting the speech). My sentence repeats the idea of specificity because the text is this and not that, because it could be no more than what its producers conceived as possible for it to be, originating at a finite cultural moment. If a text has a specific form, so also an audience has specific watching conventions: those of our time are different, inevitably, from those of Shakesbeer's. (A workshop can, just, problematise the activity of watching by designing a scene according to two different sets of perceived conventions, though the Elizabethan one will have to be highly conjectural.[6]) Again, players expect to adopt specific conventions of acting (which the workshop, albeit conjecturally for Elizabethan ones, can also explore). Players are organised in specific institutional relationships: the Elizabethan playhouse did not recognise author as a separate or privileged category; plays were produced to suit the company or theatre's reputation; they were worked on by the company within an economic structure which privileged shareholders and created the phenomenon of the star performer. (Workshops can, just, explore the differences between collective and hierarchised modes of production and performance, although everybody has to agree to a game whereby, for a fixed period, certain rules are observed and personalities privileged within the peer group. A group could select its own clown(s), finding a modern funny man appropriate to a Shikespehr role: use, say, 'Jimmy Tarbuck' to play Touchstone, then find other roles the same persona could play, perhaps Feste, and could not play, perhaps Malvolio or Antonio; the clown persona is taken by a performer who has a specific body and competence, as a performer; the competences interact with and foreground the existence of scripting for special effects. A similar exercise may involve people in the group taking the (inevitably) pastiche personae of tragic stars.)

These reflections on cultural specificity lead into a new area of investigation, that of historical difference. Everybody will acknowledge that Shapesneer's areas of political/social concern have to be different from the various groups of us (ourselves differing) who study his work in Britain in the 1990s (and our concerns will not be those of other social groupings): even if you make the areas of concern very abstract – for example the merits of social order versus disorder – the options are very different. Even for that notion so regularly invoked to link Sheikspeyre's world with ours, namely human nature, some of the previous exercises will have revealed differences between renaissance and modern conceptions of the person. Lastly, Elizabethans used a language that was semantically and syntactically different. A workshop can explore and foreground these historical differences. The option is, carefully, not to do an 'authentic' Elizabethan Shookspar performance *nor* a 'relevant' modern performance (*Romeo and Juliet* with leather jackets and motorbikes), but to show the points of conflict and divergence alongside one another, and within, perhaps, the same scene. This last might produce a properly relevant performance, one that stages the historicised text.

We need to see that the action of a play text is neither natural nor inevitable. Hence we might select a scene involving a dilemma or choice, play it to a certain point, then freeze the action and invite viewers to solve the problem by stepping into the scene and inventing/improvising a new text (have someone step in as Cordelia and invent a response to her dad, explore Benedick's answers to Beatrice's request that he kill Claudio). Additionally watchers can be invited to stop the scene at an earlier point if they feel it can be solved earlier. (These suggestions are a crude, but I hope not too trivialising, adaptation of the Forum technique of Augusto Boal's Theatre of the Oppressed, developed as a theatrical means of empowering dominated people to analyse and perhaps change their situation.) Obviously we end up *not* playing Shapesquire, but the exercise can reveal some of the precise limits of the thinking in the text: Skatesheer's text cannot envisage some of the solutions we can invent. By contrast, our solutions have to be restricted by the rules and information we are already given. The realisation of historical/cultural difference works in two directions: placing Sheepskewer's thinking and setting limits to modern interpretation, revealing the points beyond which we cannot go.

RACE, GENDER, CLASS DIFFERENCE

In a similar way, if less excitingly, we can play 'what if ... ', 'if only ...' games with the text: to encounter the selections/suppressions that have produced the precise shape of a scene or narrative. 'What if Gertrude and Ophelia had a scene together? What would they talk about? If they talked about the men in the play, what would they say?' One method of exerting pressure on the playing of a scene is to foreground those people playing Black, female, or lower-class figures. Tell them to ask at the start of every scene whether their character can enter into the scene; and for those who are in the scene to tell them why not. Why should Caliban not watch Prospero telling history to Miranda? Why are Stephano and Trinculo not seen serving their masters on the ship? After rehearsing/discussing a series of 'what if ... s', the group can produce a staging of a scene that shows all those moments when one decision is taken and not another, when one group of characters is present and not another; it may work through a structure of hesitations, looks for missing people, lines that change their focus.

In raising the question of what Black, female, or lower-class characters might do, I marked another area in which difference is noticeable: relations between the marginalised and the dominant. This area is worthy of separate study because it forces us to attend to the effects of Shitscare's status within our own culture, in that production of his plays continuously restates the inferiority of women, Blacks, and lower-class people.

Another digression to draw in 'authorities': my anonymous, undated copy of *How to Read and Enjoy Shakespeare* tells me that performers long to 'portray the finer characters of Shakespeare's plays ... the actress looks at the time when she may play the part of Portia, and put the Jew in his place'.[7] Barton tells us that 'Unlike many political playrights he usually articulates impartially the arguments on either side of a question'; 'I always wonder what a "politically committed" production is trying to prove and to whom'; Barton's own political views are 'Shakespearean in the sense that I am always acutely aware of the appalling mixture of right and wrong on both sides in most political situations': and political productions of Shaikspaire are usually motivated by designers and directors rather than actors.[8] Actors are – of course – expressive rather than dogmatic, interested in common humanity: as we'd expect, the political position of Barton's book leaves socially oppressed groups just where they are, his actors worry about getting too much sympathy for Shylock, Barton speaks of maintaining the 'right balance of sympathy in the play',[9] and tells us (so innocent of his racist language) that Shriekspare's characters are neither all black nor all white. Bogdanov's attempt to show on Channel 4 (and where else?) that 'Shakespeare Lives' was instead self-professedly political, using modern analogies in a way that denied historical specificity. More importantly, his political interpretation was very much assimilated to his own star status as a white male theatre director: the audience discussion that followed his workshop on a 'feminist' *Shrew* had him and his actors putting down/shutting up women in the audience: he and his actors seemed untroubled by the question of race in *The Tempest*. With authorities such as this, Shapesneer does his cultural damage unabated.

Back to the exercise: a workshop can create the conditions in which women, Black, lower-class students may be empowered to question the representation of characters in these groupings. The questioning will not look only at the general attitude of a scene (pro- or anti- the marginalised), but also at points for identification offered to the spectator, jokes, allocation of lines and actions. Women or Black students may suggest that women and Blacks do not behave as they are represented, but from here these students then have to try to locate *their own* experiences; as members of a group studying Shakes-peer, for example, they may be hardly typical of a whole community. At the same time their experience-based remarks are not invalidated. Our critique should interrogate Shaigspare's representation and the student's experience, so that the critique problematises and situates both the Shagspewer text and commentary. In addition here we have to stress that Shakesp-ear's texts are not realist, that we are not measuring the success of the realism with which he portrays Blacks. What we are doing is to identify how the texts are clearly worried about race and gender (more so than about lower-class people) and how this worry produces unstable representations (we once did *Merchant* with the Shylock actor slipping him into and out of various stereotypes). Women and Blacks are often part of the nightmare of a text; women and Black students can try playing, though it will be uncomfortable, the woman or Black as fantasy nightmare, as caricature and as realism, and try playing all these together.

We can play a scene so that the differences between performer and role become apparent. The woman performer plays a men's version of woman, the Black performer plays a white version of Blacks. Problems will immediately occur: for example, the early dialogue between Goneril and Regan is so conceived that any display of sisterhood between actresses only adds to the conspiratorial nastiness of the characters; any display of sceptical resignation to role can either augment the 'evil' cynicism of the characters or make them appear simply dull. The text has a specificity that restrains interpretive possibilities, at least within a realist staging (this point is elaborated by McLuskie[10]); a non-realist staging could perform what the written text cannot show.

A clearer, though differently focused, method of exploring distinctions between performer and role is to cross-cast: Blacks play whites, women men, men women. Such methods foreground and estrange the narrative of differences in the play and at the same time can suggest links between othernesses of race and gender. Cheek by Jowl's *Tempest* had a Black actress playing Miranda, who is usually played by a white woman. Automatically the person of the performer was separated from the role, while being fused with it in the narrative. The separation derived from the incomplete fit produced by racial difference, which in turn activated awareness of attitudes to race in the text. But it also insisted on the fictional Miranda as a version of a woman, constructed within specific limits, and always, as a male fiction, dependent for its realisation on the body of a real woman (and in the original staging the real woman was herself displaced as a referent by the material presence of the body of the boy-actor). This method of working may be feasible for professional groups, but it can place a lot of pressure on one or two students in a workshop. The burden can, however, be extended across a group: compare versions of men playing women directed by men, men playing women directed by women, women playing women directed by men, women playing women directed by women. And the same with Blacks and whites. If there are out-lesbian/gay students in the group, that role and experience can be similarly mobilised.

Because of the way many students are placed and constituted in this society (and I only really know about mine, but I don't think they're untypical) and because of the way some dominant radical criticism operates, the exercise can produce two main responses. It hovers between essentialism on one hand (women know what 'Woman' is) and valueless pluralism on the other (all versions are tenable and simply versions). But these two can (and must) be worked against each other: the pluralist position can force essentialism to historicise itself and discover social/cultural construction; the essentialist position would want to insist on an urgently real agenda and priorities which make pluralism impossible. The procedure is dialectical, and doing it we learn something about modes of Shaickspearian representation, possibilities for alternative playing, cultural/social specifics of the workshop group. The work involves an intersection, rather than a denial, of all these elements.

LEARNERS AS ACTORS

None of these exercises facilitates the conditions that produce random plurality, the notion that we may say what we like about Shape-skewer (and that's what makes him so good, because he has something to say to everybody, blah blah). Workshop exercises can, instead, put much pressure on contemporary modes of analysis, especially those that have a fairly unproblematised popularity or right-on-ness. Negotiate a feminist reading of *The Tempest* or *Othello* that is not racist, a Black reading of *Othello* that is not homophobic, a feminist reading of *Troilus and Cressida* or *Coriolanus* that is not homophobic. Alongside the uncomfortable task of problematising, let's work at the project of producing new pleasures in a text by making an explicitly Black, gay, feminist, lesbian, or working-class reading of it (the Bogdanov workshops merely dangled the possibility of these pleasures before grabbing them back as the property of the right-on white male middle class). In making our reading we might privilege – and eroticise – the procedures of a politically aware critical practice.

The suggestion about empowering certain categories of student brings me to a final point in this section. Most workshop work should proceed by constructing students not just as actors of a pregiven text but as agents: who interpret, who make, and without whom nothing is made, no text performed. Actors in the fullest sense. Many commentaries on the Bard, even progressive ones, even ones in this volume, are Sharkspear text-centred. Their hidden agendas implement the project of getting the meaning out of the text the Barred wrote; such agendas are indicated by discussions of close reading, ideas about discovering meaning (rather than making it), assumptions about the passive role of spectator or learner in relation to 'text'. The spectator is not simply an analyst, even where she is given the power to 'dominate' text by flicking backwards and forwards along a videotape. The spectator is also a being of desires and fantasies. (I remember a short discussion with a school group who had watched our production of *Merchant*: one lad wanted, 'provocatively', to raise the question of the so-called homosexual relationship between Antonio and Bassanio; he wanted to obtain pleasure by fantasising a homosexual relationship, even if only in discussion. Same production, another audience: lots of loud boys' laughter until the moment when Portia speaks of disguising herself as a man, and the actress does a brutally accurate rendering of adolescent male swagger: sudden whoops of girls' laughter.)

Although we have lost the noble tradition of theatre riot, the spectator is always potentially an agent. If we are to rethink the student as agent, we have to abandon the discursive construction of a historical Shirkspur and a modern interpretation, where one is fixed and 'for all time' and the other is an always unstable, provisional 'reading'. The past Shagsqueer depends on the present practices, as well as being separate from them. We could perhaps rethink the model and define 'Shak/espe/are' as a set of renaissance negotiations of meaning and a set of modern negotiations of meaning: there is always a connection between the two – the text available for restaging; there is always a distinction between the two – the text whose every moment of production is irrecoverable.

COMING DOWN FROM UTOPIA

But the workshop's agenda is set not only by what can be achieved within it but by what goes on outside it. Anathematised in government plans for universities, only recently recognised as an A-level subject, absent from the core curriculum, drama has an insecure status in the academy. I remember my late head of department supposedly quoting Arthur Pollard, that drama was the last refuge of the Marxists. That's a utopian formula if ever I heard one, and it's also an excuse for marginalising drama. Most writing about the Beard does little serious thinking about performance theory and practice; most Bored specialists would define themselves as playgoers rather than playmakers. Most exams privilege the book and the written word. In so far as drama work is used in teaching it is often relegated to an illustrative function, to back up and exemplify analysis of the 'book' but not to replace it. These observations, I should say, are based on university experience, where there is a connection between anti-dramatic prejudice and the unimaginative or reactionary teaching methods; in schools the situation is often very different. But from universities (which also help to train schoolteachers) there emanates a feeling that drama is not a proper subject.

For students drama work involves several sorts of physical or psychological risk-taking. To their families and numbers of peer groups, drama appears odd. Its strangeness can come from its general cultural status, where it is connected with 'entertainment' and arty-fartiness rather than proper work and with scandals about star lifestyles. It is also strange in its refusal of the social arrangements of much teaching and entertainment, where passive spectators/learners direct their attention to the activity of a performer/teacher. Within the workshop students are invited to make themselves vulnerable and to take risks that either unsettle their own repressed desires or conflict with their consciously perceived cultural/social identities. (I recall two students overheard contemplating the imminent practical part of their renaissance drama course: 'I don't think I'm going to do that bit. I've heard you have to hug each other.') For many students the risk-taking is also jubilant and empowering: the workshop liberates an energy which gives a positive charge to the 'specialness' of drama study. The pleasure and strength gained from workshops enable students to resist institutional pressures against their 'artiness'.

The workshop makes demands on all its participants. It can and should problematise the relationship of learner/teacher which is often so central to education's reproduction of repression. The 'liberalism' of the workshop may entail the teacher raking risks with her structural place, rather than that structure underpinning (and setting limits to) the liberalism. From students it requires not only a rehearing of a familiar text, but also a recommitting of urgency to making meaning from the text. The place from which the student speaks is itself on the analytic agenda. The workshop presents a new set of evaluative criteria. We no longer ask 'how successful' is this version/scene in 'bringing out the text', 'showing what's written'; but we can (and perhaps should) ask how successfully it realises some of the objectives I have spoken of earlier. We are now in a position to ask about the relationship of determination and agency: how does the text set limits to our work on it, how may our work change the text, how far does work on the text enable a new understanding of ourselves, our culture, our history, the text's production, and how far is that understanding limited by the work of the text?

These questions alert us to the role of the workshop as a model in miniature of the processes of educational reproduction and contestation. On one hand, the workshop is only part of an educational project (the exam course), it takes its originating moment from a pre-given text, it is facilitated by a teacher organising students. It's a liberal version of the potentially repressive structure. On the other hand, its methods involve contesting the truths of the pre-given text and of the students' role in reproducing these. These methods, working well, empower the student as learner: not only is the student's own experience made articulate within analysis but the strength of personal agency and the pleasure of group-work may be refound.

Within this model, the workshop group may, and often needs to, discuss their experiences of containment by course and institution, or text and analysis. The group is invited to become conscious of the social relations that the educational institution proposes and foregrounds, the extent to which these social relations need to be changed in order to fulfil the project of the workshop, and the limits on the possibility of that change. The status of the workshop is contradictory: in so far as playing is 'not-work', then its activities are relegated to the trivial, the merely illustrative, the luxuried and eventually unserious; in so far as playing is the opposite to work, its activities involve a new empowering that produces a critique of the structures and assumptions of 'work' constructed within oppressive relations. The contradictions inhabit the word 'acting': we act out the roles and assumptions of a pre-written text we set against the roles and assumptions of a pre-written text. We are shaped, but we shape. [...]

Teaching Ssssh-akespeare is only an act.

From *Shakespeare in the Changing Curriculum*, ed. Lesley Aers and Nigel Wheale (London, 1991), pp. 90–107.

NOTES

[Simon Shepherd's playful manipulation of Shakespearean nomenclature, which alludes to its varied inscriptions in the author's own lifetime and subsequently, highlights the elements of instability and difference within the texts that can be explored in the context of the drama practical. Answering the materialist challenge to the traditional protocols of Shakespearean performance, Shepherd gives specific examples of a flexible, theoretically informed and, above all, pleasurable workshop praxis that interrogates not only the realist, character-centred methodologies of the dominant forms of Shakespearean theatre practice but also the ideological and institutional imperatives implicit within the teaching situation itself. Ed.]

1. Peter Holland, 'The resources of characterization in *Othello*', *Shakespeare Survey*, 41 (1988), 119–32.
2. Eugenio Barba, 'The fiction of duality', *New Theatre Quarterly*, 5 (1989), 311–14.
3. John Barton, *Playing Shakespeare* (London, 1984), pp. 13, 15, 12, 23, 193.
4. Bertolt Brecht, *Coriolanus*, trans. Ralph Manheim, in *Collected Plays*, vol. 9 (New York, 1972).
5. Augusto Boal, *Documents on the Theatre of the Oppressed* (London, no date).
6. See Michael Hattaway, *Elizabethan Popular Theatre* (London, 1982); Peter Thomson, *Shakespeare's Theatre* (London, 1983); Andrew Gurr, *Playgoing in Shakespeare's London* (Cambridge, 1987).
7. *How to Read and Enjoy Shakespeare* (London, no date), p. 25.
8. Barton, *Playing Shakespeare*, pp. 188–90.
9. Ibid., p. 179.
10. Kathleen McLuskie, 'The patriarchal Bard: feminist criticism and Shakespeare: *King Lear* and *Measure for Measure*', in Jonathan Dollimore and Alan Sinfield (eds), *Political Shakespeare: New Essays in Cultural Materialism* (Manchester, 1985).

Further Reading

This is a selective list of works published in the past two decades which engage both with contemporary theory and feature performance as a significant component. Stage histories of individual plays are offered by the ongoing Shakespeare in Performance series published by Manchester University Press, and in Cambridge University Press's Shakespeare in Production series. Useful bibliographies of earlier criticism can be found in Jonathan Bate and Russell Jackson (eds), *Shakespeare: An Illustrated Stage History* (Oxford: OUP, 1996); and Stanley Wells (ed.), *Shakespeare: A Bibliographical Guide* (Oxford: Clarendon Press, 1990) and *Shakespeare in the Theatre: An Anthology of Criticism* (Oxford: OUP, 1997). Andrew Gurr's *The Shakespearean Stage 1574–1642*, third edition (Cambridge: CUP, 1992), is essential reading for any student of Renaissance theatre. Modern Shakespearean production, for the most part in Britain and the United States, has been comprehensively documented in the journals *Shakespeare Survey* (since 1948), *Shakespeare Quarterly* (since 1950) and *Shakespeare Bulletin* (since 1982); *Theatre Record* (previously *London Theatre Record*) reprints all national newspaper reviews of productions in Britain from 1980 onwards.

THE ELIZABETHAN AND JACOBEAN STAGE

Francis Barker, *The Tremulous Private Body: Essays on Subjection* (London: Methuen, 1985).

Leeds Barroll, *Politics, Plague, and Shakespeare's Theatre: The Stuart Years* (Ithaca and London: Cornell University Press, 1991).

Catherine Belsey, *The Subject of Tragedy: Identity and Difference in Renaissance Drama* (London: Methuen, 1985).

Michael D. Bristol, *Carnival and Theater: Plebeian Culture and the Structure of Authority in Renaissance England* (London and New York: Routledge, 1985).

——, *Big-Time Shakespeare* (London and New York: Routledge, 1996).

Douglas Bruster, *Drama and the Market in the Age of Shakespeare* (Cambridge: CUP, 1992).

Walter Cohen, *Drama of a Nation: Public Theater in Renaissance England and Spain* (Ithaca and London: Cornell University Press, 1985).

Anthony B. Dawson, '*Measure for Measure*, New Historicism, and Theatrical Power', *Shakespeare Quarterly*, 39 (1988), 328–41.

Janette Dillon, *Language and the Stage in Medieval and Renaissance England* (Cambridge: CUP, 1998).

John Drakakis, '"Fashion it thus": *Julius Caesar* and the Politics of Theatrical Representation', *Shakespeare Survey*, 44 (1992), 65–73.

Terence Hawkes (ed.), *Alternative Shakespeares 2* (London and New York: Routledge, 1996).

Jean E. Howard, *The Stage and Social Struggle in Early Modern England* (London and New York: Routledge, 1994).

David Scott Kastan and Peter Stallybrass (eds), *Staging the Renaissance: Reinterpretations of Elizabethan and Jacobean drama* (London and New York: Routledge, 1991).

Kathleen McLuskie, *Renaissance Dramatists* (Hemel Hempstead: Harvester Wheatsheaf, 1989).

Louis Montrose, *The Purpose of Playing: Shakespeare and the Cultural Politics of the Elizabethan Theatre* (Chicago and London: University of Chicago Press, 1996).

Stephen Mullaney, *The Place of the Stage: License, Play, and Power in Renaissance England* (Chicago: University of Chicago Press, 1988).

Stephen Orgel, *Impersonations: The Performance of Gender in Shakespeare's England* (Cambridge: CUP, 1996).

Annabel Patterson, *Shakespeare and the Popular Voice* (Oxford: Basil Blackwell, 1989).

Michael Shapiro, *Gender in Play on the Shakespearean Stage: Boy Heroines and Female Pages* (Ann Arbor: University of Michigan Press, 1994).

Meredith Anne Skura, *Shakespeare the Actor and the Purposes of Playing* (Chicago and London: University of Chicago Press, 1993).

Peter Thomson, *Shakespeare's Theatre*, second edn (London: Routledge, 1992).

Robert Weimann, *Shakespeare and the Popular Tradition in the Theater*, trans. Robert Schwartz (Baltimore: Johns Hopkins University Press, 1978).

——, *Authority and Representation in Early Modern Discourse* (Baltimore: Johns Hopkins University Press, 1996).

Martin White, *Renaissance Drama in Action* (London: Routledge, 1998).

Richard Wilson, '"Is This a Holiday?": Shakespeare's Roman Carnival', *English Literary History*, 54 (1987), 31–44.

Paul Yachnin, 'The Politics of Theatrical Mirth: *A Midsummer Night's Dream*, *A Mad World, My Masters*, and *Measure for Measure*', *Shakespeare Quarterly*, 43 (1992), 51–66.

Susan Zimmerman (ed.), *Erotic Politics: Desire on the Renaissance Stage* (London and New York: Routledge, 1992).

SHAKESPEARE IN PERFORMANCE, 1660 TO THE PRESENT

Jonathan Bate, *Shakespearean Constitutions: Politics, Theatre, Criticism, 1730–1830* (Oxford: Clarendon Press, 1989).

Susan Bennett, *Performing Nostalgia: Shifting Shakespeare and the Contemporary Past* (London: Routledge, 1996).
James C. Bulman (ed.), *Shakespeare, Theory and Performance* (London and New York: Routledge, 1996).
Carol Chillington Rutter, 'Fiona Shaw's *Richard II*: The Girl as Player-King as Comic', *Shakespeare Quarterly*, 48 (1997), 314–24.
Anthony B. Dawson, 'The Impasse over the Stage', *English Literary Renaissance*, 21 (1991), 309–25.
Michael Dobson, *The Making of the National Poet: Shakespeare, Adaptation and Authorship, 1660–1769* (Oxford: Claredon Press, 1992).
Jonathan Dollimore and Alan Sinfield (eds), *Political Shakespeare: Essays in Cultural Materialism*, second edn (Manchester: MUP, 1995).
Penny Gay, *As She Likes It: Shakespeare's Unruly Women* (London Routledge, 1994).
Michael Hattaway, Boika Sokolova and Derek Roper (eds), *Shakespeare in the New Europe* (Sheffield: Sheffield Academic Press, 1994).
Barbara Hodgdon, *The End Crowns All: Closure and Contradiction in Shakespeare's History* (Princeton, NJ: Princeton University Press, 1991).
——, *The Shakespeare Trade: Performance and Appropriations* (Philadelphia: University of Pennsylvania Press, 1998).
Graham Holderness, *Shakespeare's History* (Dublin: Gill and Macmillan, 1985).
——, '*Romeo and Juliet*: Empathy and Alienation', *Shakespeare Jahrbuch*, 124 (1987), 118–29.
——, 'Shakespeare in Production', *Gulliver (Deutsche-Englische Jahrbucher)*, 24 (1988), 120–35.
——, 'Production, Reproduction, Performance: marxism, history and theatre', in *Uses of History: Marxism, Postmodernism and the Renaissance*, ed. Francis Barker, Peter Hulme and Margaret Iverson (Manchester: MUP, 1991).
——, 'Shakespeare and heritage', *Textual Practice*, 6 (1992), 247–63.
——, (ed.), *The Shakespeare Myth* (Manchester: MUP, 1988).
Peter Holland, 'The Resources of Characterization in *Othello*', *Shakespeare Survey*, 41 (1988), 119–32.
——, *English Shakespeares: Shakespeare on the English Stage in the 1990s* (Cambridge: CUP, 1997).
Jean E. Howard and Marion F. O'Connor (eds), *Shakespeare Reproduced: The Text in Ideology and History* (London: Methuen, 1987).
John J. Joughlin (ed.), *Shakespeare and National Culture* (Manchester: MUP, 1997).
Dennis Kennedy, *Looking at Shakespeare: A Visual History of Twentieth-Century Performance* (Cambridge: CUP, 1993).
——, 'Shakespeare Played Small: Three Speculations about the Body', *Shakespeare Survey*, 47 (1994), 1–13.
——, 'Shakespeare and the Global Spectator', *Shakespeare Jahrbuch*, 131 (1995), 50–64.
——, (ed.), *Foreign Shakespeare: Contemporary Performance* (Cambridge: CUP, 1994).

Richard Paul Knowles, 'Shakespeare, 1993, and the Discourses of the Stratford Festival, Ontario', *Shakespeare Quarterly*, 45 (1994), 211–25.
——, '"The Real of It Would Be Awful": Representing the Real Ophelia in Canada', *Theatre Survey*, 39 (1998), 21–40.
Ania Loomba and Martin Orkin (eds), *Post-Colonial Shakespeares* (London: Routledge, 1998).
Joyce Green Macdonald, 'Acting Black: *Othello*, Othello Burlesques, and the Performance of Blackness', *Theatre Journal*, 46 (1994), 233–46.
Jean I. Marsden (ed.), *The Appropriation of Shakespeare: Post-Renaissance Reconstructions of the Works and Myth* (Hemel Hempstead: Harvester Wheatsheaf, 1991).
Stephen Orgel, 'The Authentic Shakespeare', *Representations*, 21 (1988), 5–25.
Peggy Phelan, 'Playing Dead in Stone, Or, When is a Rose not a Rose?', in *Performance and Cultural Politics*, ed. Elin Diamond (London and New York: Routledge, 1996).
Denis Salter, 'Between Wor(l)ds: Lepage's Shakespeare Cycle', *Theater*, 24 (1993), 61–70.
Elizabeth Schafer, *MsDirecting Shakespeare: Women Direct Shakespeare* (London: The Women's Press, 1998).
Robert Shaughnessy, *Representing Shakespeare: England, History and the RSC* (Hemel Hempstead: Harvester Wheatsheaf, 1994).
——, 'The Last Post: *Henry V*, War Culture and the Postmodern Shakespeare', *Theatre Survey*, 39 (1998), 41–62.
Alan Sinfield, '*King Lear* versus *Lear* at Stratford', *Critical Quarterly*, 24 (1982), 5–14.
——, *Faultlines: Cultural Materialism and the Politics of Dissident Reading* (Oxford: Clarendon, 1982).
Peter J. Smith, *Social Shakespeare: Aspects of Renaissance Dramaturgy and Contemporary Society* (Basingstoke: Macmillan, 1995).
Alden T. Vaughan and Virginia Mason Vaughan, *Shakespeare's Caliban: A Cultural History* (Cambridge: CUP, 1991).
Gary Jay Williams, *Our Moonlight Revels: 'A Midsummer Night's Dream' in the Theatre* (Iowa: University of Iowa Press, 1997).
W. B. Worthen, *Shakespeare and the Authority of Performance* (Cambridge: CUP, 1997).

GENERAL PERFORMANCE THEORY

Herbert Blau, *To All Appearances: Ideology and Performance* (London and New York: Routledge, 1992).
Patrick Campbell (ed.), *Analysing Performance: A Critical Reader* (Manchester: MUP, 1996).
Marvin Carlson, *Performance: A Critical Introduction* (London: Routledge, 1996).
Keir Elam, *The Semiotics of Theatre and Drama* (London: Methuen, 1980).
Patrice Pavis, *Theatre at the Crossroads of Culture*, trans. Loren Kruger (London: Routledge, 1992).

Thomas Postlewait and Bruce A. McConachie (eds), *Interpreting the Theatrical Past: Essays in the Historiography of Performance* (Iowa: University of Iowa Press, 1989).
Janelle G. Reinelt and Joseph R. Roach (eds), *Critical Theory and Performance* (Ann Arbor: University of Michigan Press, 1992).

Notes on Contributors

Michael D. Bristol is Professor of English at McGill University. He is the author of *Carnival and Theater* (London and New York, 1985), *Shakespeare's America/America's Shakespeare* (London, 1990) and *Big-time Shakespeare* (London and New York, 1996).

Alan C. Dessen is Peter G. Phialas Professor of English at the University of North Carolina, Chapel Hill. His publications include *Elizabethan Drama and the Viewer's Eye* (Chapel Hill, 1977), *Elizabethan Stage Conventions and Modern Interpreters* (Cambridge, 1984), *Titus Andronicus* for the Shakespeare in Performance series (Manchester, 1989) and *Recovering Shakespeare's Theatrical Vocabulary* (Cambridge, 1995). He is co-author, with Leslie Thomson, of *A Dictionary of Stage Directions in English Drama, 1580–1642* (Cambridge, 1999), and has been editor of the 'Shakespeare Performed' section of *Shakespeare Quarterly* since 1994.

Barbara Hodgdon is Ellis and Nelle Levitt Distinguished Professor of English at Drake University. She is the author of *The End Crowns All: Closure and Contradiction in Shakespeare's Histories* (Princeton, NJ, 1991), *Henry IV, Part Two* in the Shakespeare in Performance series (Manchester, 1996), and *The Shakespeare Trade: Performances and Appropriations* (Pennsylvania, 1998). She is the editor of *The First Part of King Henry the Fourth: Texts and Contexts* (New York, 1997) and of the Arden 3 *Taming of the Shrew*, and is an Associate Editor of the *Arden Shakespeare third series electronic partwork and complete performance edition* (1999).

Graham Holderness is Professor of English, Dean of Humanities, Language and Education, and Director of Research at the University of Hertfordshire. His books include *Shakespeare's History* (Dublin, 1985), *The Taming of the Shrew* in the Shakespeare in Performance series (Manchester, 1989) and, as co-author, *Shakespeare: The Play of History* (Basingstoke, 1988) and *Shakespeare: Out of Court* (Basingstoke, 1990). He is the editor of *The Shakespeare Myth* (Manchester, 1988) and *The*

Politics of Theatre and Drama (Basingstoke, 1992). He is one of the general editors of the Shakespeare Originals series, for which he has edited *King Lear* (Hemel Hempstead, 1995), and co-edited *Hamlet* (1992) and *Henry the fift* (1993).

Kathleen McLuskie is Professor of English at Southampton University. She has published widely on Shakespeare and Renaissance drama, and is the author of *Reniassance Dramatists* (Hemel Hempstead, 1989) and, in the English Dramatists series, *Dekker and Heywood* (Basingstoke, 1994). She has co-edited (with Jennifer Uglow) *The Duchess of Malfi* in the Plays in Performance series (Bristol, 1989) and is co-editing the Arden 3 *Macbeth*.

Simon Shepherd is Professor of Drama at Goldsmiths College, University of London. His publications include *Amazons and Warriors Women: varieties of feminism in seventeenth-century drama* (Brighton, 1981), *Marlowe and the Politics of Elizabethan Theatre* (Brighton, 1986), *Spenser* in the Harvester New Readings series (Hemel Hempstead, 1989), with Peter Womack, *English Drama: A Cultural History* (Oxford, 1996) and, with Mick Wallis, *Studying Plays* (London, 1998).

Alan Sinfield is Professor of English at the University of Sussex. His publications include *Literature in Protestant England 1560–1660* (London, 1983), *Alfred Tennyson* (Oxford, 1986), *Literature, Politics and Culture in Postwar Britain* (Oxford, 1989), *Faultlines: Cultural Materialism and the Politics of Dissident Reading* (Oxford, 1992), *Cultural Politics – Queer Reading* (London, 1994) and *The Wilde Century* (London, 1994). He is editor of *Society and Literature 1945–1970* (London, 1983) and co-editor, with Jonathan Dollimore, of *Political Shakespeare* (Manchester, 1985).

J. L. Styan is Franklyn Bliss Snyder Professor of English Literature and Professor of Theatre Emeritus at Northwestern University. His books include *The Elements of Drama* (Cambridge, 1960), *Shakespeare's Stagecraft* (Cambridge, 1967), *The Shakespeare Revolution* (Cambridge, 1977), *Modern Drama in Theory and Practice* (Cambridge, 1981), *All's Well that Ends Well* in the Shakespeare in Performance series (Manchester, 1984), *Restoration Comedy in Performance* (Cambridge, 1986), and *The English Stage* (Cambridge, 1996). In 1995 he received the Robert Lewis medal for Lifetime Achievement in Theatre Research.

Robert Weimann is Professor of Drama at the University of California at Irvine. His books include *Shakespeare and the Popular Tradition in the Theater* (Berlin, 1967 and Baltimore, 1978), *Authority and Representation in Early Modern Discourse* (Baltimore, 1996) and *Author's Pen and Actor's Voice: Performance, Authority and Space in Shakespeare's Theater* (forthcoming).

W. B. Worthen is Professor of Dramatic Art at the University of California, Berkeley. He is the author of *The Idea of the Actor* (Princeton, 1984), *Modern Drama and the Rhetoric of Theater* (Berkeley, 1992) and *Shakespeare and the Authority of Performance* (Cambridge, 1997). He is editor of *The Harcourt Brace Anthology of Drama* (New York, 1996) and *Modern Drama: Plays, Criticism, Theory* (New York, 1994), and a past editor of *Theatre Journal*.

Index

All's Well that Ends Well, 26, 31
An Apology for Actors, 52, 106–7
Antonio and Mellida, 107
Antonio and Cleopatra, 26, 37, 48, 54, 57, 182
Appiah, Kwame, 209
Artaud, Antoinin, 7, 10, 166, 176, 211
Arts Council, 171–2, 180
As You Like It, 27, 104
Auerbach, Eric, 94

Bakhtin, Mikhail, 11, 16, 144–5, 151, 156
Bartholomew Fair, 110
Barton, John, 7, 67–9, 70, 139, 173–4, 182–3, 187, 221, 227–8
Bayley, Clare, 204
Beaumont, Francis, 124
Beckerman, Bernard, 42, 50, 62
Beckett, Samuel, 7, 176, 186, 211
Bennett, Tony, 196
Berry, Ralph, 188
Bethell, S. L., 6
Betterton, Thomas, 159
Billington, Michael, 190, 206
Blau, Herbert, 195, 213
Boal, Augusto, 18, 224, 226
Bogdanov, Michael, 182, 185, 190, 228
'The Boke of Mayd Emlyn', 109
Bourdieu, Pierre, 205
Bradbrook, M. C., 4, 62
Bradley, A. C., 44, 219
Braunmuller, A. R., 72
The Brazen Age, 56–8
Brecht, Bertolt, 7, 10, 13, 18, 172, 177, 190, 224
Bristol, Michael D., 11, 16
Brook, Peter, 8–9, 17–19, 25, 176–7, 182–3, 186, 198–203, 208, 210–12
Brooke, Rupert, 207
Brooks, Cleanth, 63
Brown, John Russell, 62, 65–7
Bruster, Douglas, 11
Burke, Kenneth, 74

Calderwood, James L., 7
Cambron, Micheline, 199–200
Canadian National Arts Centre, 196
Captain Thomas Stukeley, 53
The Captives, 56
Carson, Christie, 209
Carter, Angela, 198
Catherine and Petruchio, 124, 132
Cavell, Stanley, 154, 164–5
Chambers, E. K., 4
Cheek by Jowl, 229
Clark, Stuart, 111
Clifford, James, 213
Cohen, Walter S., 82
Coleman, Ronald, 163
Coleridge, Samuel Taylor, 25, 159–61
Colie, Rosalie, 166–7
Collier, John Payne, 4
Coriolanus, 182, 190, 224, 230
Coveney, Michael, 204

Crosland, Anthony, 178
Cukor, George, 163
Cymbeline, 150, 183

David, Richard, 64–5
Davis, Natalie, 146
Day, John, 54, 118
de Jongh, Nicholas, 198
de Witt, Johannes, 4
Derrida, Jacques, 214
Dessen, Alan, 14
Dexter, Sally, 206, 208
Doctor Faustus, 46, 123
Dollimore, Jonathan, 10–11
A Double Life, 163
Dragons Trilogy, 202, 204
Dryden, John, 5, 42–3
Dunbar, William, 109
Durkheim, Emile, 16, 142–3, 145

Eagleton, Terry, 70
Ebert, Teresa, 210
Edmond Ironside, 53
Edwards, Philip, 128
Eliot, T. S., 6, 210
Elsom, John, 187
English Stage Company, 179
Etchells, Tim, 19
Every Man in His Humour, 32
Eyre, Richard, 6, 208–9, 212

The Fair Maid of the West, 53
Fitzgeffrey, Henry, 112
Fletcher, John, 54, 57
Foakes, R. A., 102
Folger Shakespeare Library, 4
Forcier, André, 164
Forman, Simon, 201
Fortune by Land and Sea, 55
Foucault, Michel, 10, 186, 204
The Four Prentices of London, 56
Freud, Sigmund, 44, 194, 207
Furness, Horace Howard, 158
Furnivall, F. J., 4

Gardner, Lyn, 199
Garrick, David, 66, 124, 132, 159
Genet, Jean, 10
Gibbons, Brian, 45
Gilbert, Miriam, 70
Grant, Steve, 203
Granville Barker, Harley, 6, 62
Gray, Terence, 3
Greenblatt, Stephen, 10, 11, 78, 143, 152, 154
Greene, Robert, 79–80, 123
Greg, W. W., 4
Griffith, D. W., 163
Guinness, Alec, 28
Guneikeon, 117–18
Gurr, Andrew, 1, 3
Guthrie, Tyrone, 40

Haec Vir, 113
Hall, Peter, 7, 17, 172–86, 187, 204
Halliwell-Phillipps, J. O., 4
Hamlet, 26, 28, 68–9, 87, 95, 135, 149–50, 181
Hands, Terry, 184, 186–7
Harbage, Aflred, 5, 53
Harvey, Martin, 124
Heilman, Robert, 63
1 Henry IV, 173
2 Henry IV, 49, 94, 173
Henry V, 1, 2, 4, 26, 52–3, 57, 81, 88–96, 131, 184–5, 186–7
1 Henry VI, 54, 173
2 Henry VI, 57, 96, 173, 174
3 Henry VI, 48, 173, 174
Henry VIII, 1
Henslowe, Philip, 4, 102
Heywood, Thomas, 52, 53, 55–8, 101, 106–7, 117–18
Hic Mulier, 113
Hodgdon, Barbara, 17
Holderness, Graham, 15
Holland, Peter, 219
'Homilie Against Excess of Apparell', 112
Howard, Jean E., 11
Hoyle, Martin, 204
Hurstfield, Joel, 83

Ibsen, Henrik, 5, 44
Irving, Henry, 66
The Island Princess, 54–5
The Isle of Gulls, 118–19

James I, 119
James IV, 123
Jameson, Fredric, 209–10, 213
Jardine, Lisa, 101
Jensen, E. J., 100
Jones, Eldred, 11
Jonson, Ben, 32, 52–3, 62, 80, 110
Julius Caesar, 182

Kavanagh, James, 64
Kean, Edmund, 62, 159
Kemble, John Philip, 159
Kemp, William, 81
Kemps Nine Daies Wonder, 81
Kennedy, Dennis, 202
King John, 182
King Lear, 7, 31, 32–4, 42, 44, 48, 95–7, 176, 183, 186
Knight, G. Wilson, 6, 61–2, 66
The Knight of the Burning Pestle, 124
Komisarjevsky, Theodore, 124
Kott, Jan, 174–7, 183, 185, 198, 201–2, 206
Kyd, Thomas, 123
Kyle, Barry, 183

Lamb, Charles, 62, 159
Lambarde, William, 83–4
Laurier, Angela, 200, 205–6, 208
Lear, 190
Lepage, Robert, 17, 194–217
Leviathan, 80
Levine, Michael, 200, 208
A Looking Glass for London and England, 123
Lord Burghley, 79
Lyttelton, Oliver, 205

Macbeth, 30, 34–5, 43, 45, 46–8, 88
McKerrow, R. B., 4
McLuskie, Kathleen, 15, 229
Madden, Donald, 28
The Mahabharata, 210
The Maid's Metamorphosis, 115–17
Malone, Edmond, 3, 4
Marlowe, Christopher, 123
Marowitz, Charles, 176, 190
Measure for Measure, 26, 95, 182
The Merchant of Venice, 161, 188–9, 221, 228, 231
A Midsummer Night's Dream, 7, 17, 26–7, 102–3, 177, 194–217, 220
Millar, Gavin, 203
Miller, Jonathan, 188–9
Mitchell, Allan, 204–5, 208
Mnouchkine, Ariane, 211
Monck, Nugent, 3
Montrose, Louis, 199, 201
Moodie, Susanna, 157–8
Much Ado about Nothing, 35–6, 110, 150
Mullaney, Steven, 11, 12, 79
Murray, Timothy, 80

Nightingale, Benedict, 188–9, 200–2, 211
Noble, Adrian, 183
Nunn, Trevor, 172–3, 181–2

Old Vic, 205
Olivier, Laurence, 4, 28, 66, 206–7
Oregon Shakespeare Festival, 44
Osborne, Francis, 119
Othello, 16, 38–40, 50, 129, 142–70, 208, 230

Panasonic Globe Theatre, 4
Parkin, Frank, 178–9
Pavis, Patrice, 212
Pennington, Michael, 68–9
Pericles, 50, 54
Poel, William, 3, 6, 124
Pollard, Arthur, 231
Pollard, A. W., 4

Ragland, Fanny, 160
Rhodes, Ernest L., 50
Richard II, 173, 209
Richard III, 28, 173, 175–6, 185
Righter, Ann, 7
The Roaring Girl, 105

Romeo and Juliet, 28–30, 45–6, 48, 221, 226
Romeo and Juliette, 202
Royal Court Theatre, 172
Royal National Theatre, 6, 17, 171–93
Rylance, Mark, 2
Rymer, Thomas, 159

Said, Edward, 211
Schlegel, Johan, 3, 160
Seville, David, 118
Shakespeare in Love, 4
Shakespeare's Globe, 1–3, 9, 12, 13
Shakespeare Memorial Theatre, 205
Shakespeare Quarterly, 9, 65
Shepherd, Simon, 12, 13, 18
Sher, Antony, 28
Sidney, Philip, 52–4, 134
Siemon, James R., 74
Sinden, Donald, 70
Sinfield, Alan, 12, 17
Sonnet 20, 114–15
Spall, Timothy, 205–7
The Spanish Tragedy, 123
Spivak, Gayatri, 214
Staiger, Janet, 196–7
Stallybrass, Peter, 197, 201
Stanislavsky, Constantin, 73
Stendahl, 161–3
Stoppard, Tom, 190
Stubbes, Philip, 111–12
Styan, J. L., 5, 7, 13–14, 62, 198, 211
Suchet, David, 68
Swan Theatre, 3, 4
Swander, Homer, 65–6

The Taming of a Shrew, 15, 123–34
The Taming of the Shrew, 15, 107–9, 123–41, 182, 185, 190, 228
Tarlton, Richard, 81
Tate, Nahum, 42
Taylor, Gary, 12
The Tempest, 55–6, 181, 188–9, 203, 228, 230
Théâtre du Nouveau Monde, 199
Theatre Workshop, 172
Thom, William Taylor, 160
Thompson, Ann, 125
The Thracian Wonder, 56
Thurber, James, 43
Tieck, Ludwig, 3
Tilley, Morris Palmer, 50
Tillyard, E. M. W., 5–6, 173–5, 185
Titus Andronicus, 46, 57, 182
The Travels of Three English Brothers, 54
Trewin, J. C., 180, 203
Troilus and Cressida, 36–7, 43, 81, 95, 186, 230
Twa Merrit Wemen and the Wedo, 109
Twelfth Night, 30–1, 70, 117, 119
The Two Gentlemen of Verona, 104–6
The Tyde taryeth no Man, 84

Viscount Esher, 205
Volpone, 50

Wanamaker, Sam, 1
Wardle, Irving, 199
Warner, David, 180–1
The Wars of the Roses, 7, 173–6, 185
Watson, Douglass, 28
Weimann, Robert, 14–15, 17
Wells, Stanley, 12
Wesker, Arnold, 190
White, Allon, 197, 201
Williams, Emlyn, 28
Williams, Raymond, 14, 50–1, 179
Wilson, Harold, 180
Wilson, John Dover, 4
The Winter's Tale, 31–2, 37–8, 51, 54
Wolfit, Donald, 28
Womack, Peter, 12
Woods, Ron, 44
Wooster Group, 19
Worthen, W. B., 14, 19